YESTERDAY'S
RAILWAYS

YESTERDAY'S RAILWAYS

PETER HERRING

David & Charles

A DAVID & CHARLES BOOK

First published in the UK in 2002

Copyright © Peter Herring 2002

Distributed in North America
by F&W Publications, Inc.
4700 E. Galbraith Rd.
Cincinnati, OH 45236
1,800,289,0963

A catalogue record for this book is available from the
British Library.

ISBN 0 7153 1387 8

Commissioning Editor: Jane Trollope
Executive Art Editor: Ali Myer
Desk Editor: T F McCann
Designer: Lisa Forrester
Picture Research: Prue Waller
Production Controller: Jennifer Campbell

Printed in Italy by Rotolito Lombarda
for David & Charles
Brunel House Newton Abbot Devon

CONTENTS

INTRODUCTION

In telling the story of yesterday's railways, two key dates stand out. One is 1900, and not solely because it ushered in the new century. The year roughly coincided with some new and remarkable changes on Britain's railways – changes in locomotive engineering and carriage design, in travelling conditions and train speeds, and in the nature of the near-monopoly on transport enjoyed by the railways.

The other key date simply has to be 1968. It was the last summer of steam, at least as far as scheduled services were concerned. British Railways disposed of the remains of its standard-gauge steam fleet and placed its faith, and its future, in diesel and electric traction.

Inevitably, the story ventures outside those dates. Events and developments before 1900 influenced what followed. Moreover, the story of British steam failed to follow the official script and end, as was intended, in 1968.

During the seven decades between 1900 and 1968, the make-up of Britain's railways altered dramatically. Some of these changes occurred gradually, mainly because of wider social and economic developments. Often, it took far too long for their impact to be acknowledged. Other shifts were precipitated by events: two world wars, the railway company amalgamations of 1923, their nationalisation in 1948 and then the modernisation plans of the 1950s and the drastic rationalisations of the 1960s. In less than seventy years, railways exchanged dominance for decline. There were high points, of course, the times when – unlike today – railways made the headlines for the right reasons. Unfortunately, expectation often turned to disappointment. Great opportunities were missed, usually at a political level. But not all of the railways' problems have been self-inflicted and, equally, not all can be directly attributed to the internal combustion engine.

Throughout the upheavals, Britain's railways continued serving both their passenger and freight customers and, all things considered, serve them well, which is chiefly a tribute to an often unfairly maligned workforce.

These, then, are recollections of all that went to make up yesterday's railways, from the significant events to the legendary locomotives, and the roles those railways played in everyone's lives.

Peter Herring
Surrey, 2002

7

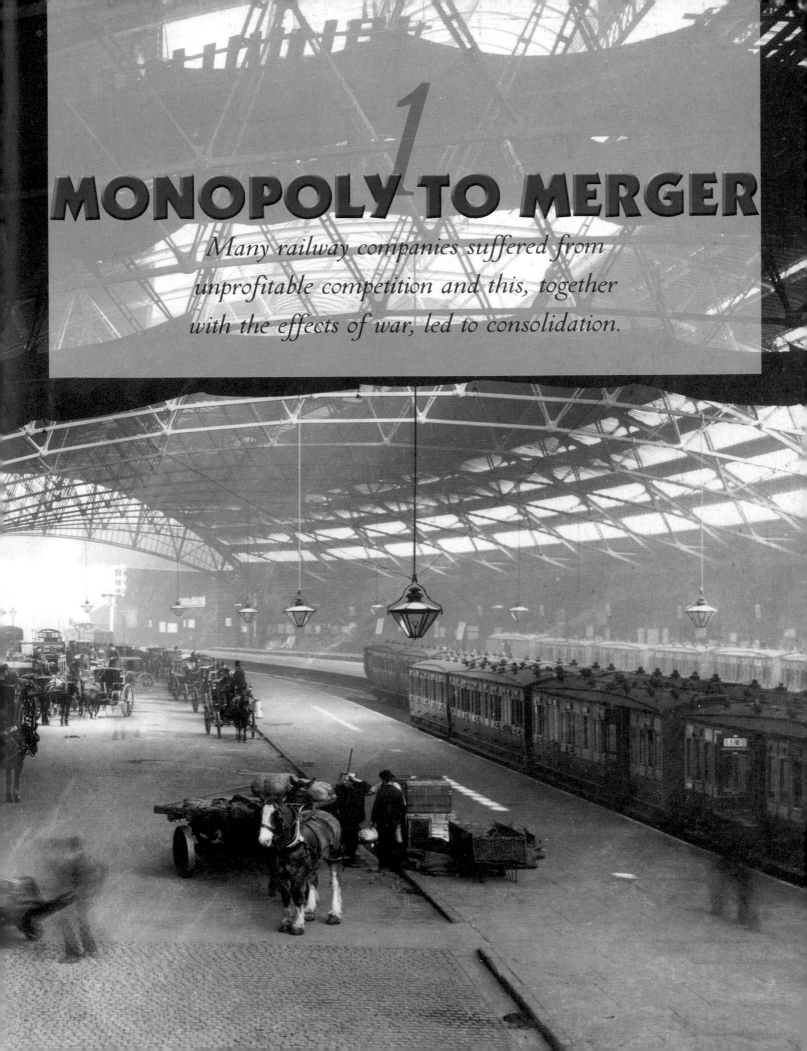

1 MONOPOLY TO MERGER

Many railway companies suffered from unprofitable competition and this, together with the effects of war, led to consolidation.

A GLORIOUS CHANCE

In national importance and public esteem, the railways of Britain reached their zenith between 1900 and 1914. Sadly, the pride of the nation did not always act in the interests of the nation.

Britain in 1900 remained confident of its status in the world, and that confidence was reflected in its railways. Although overhauled economically by the United States and rivalled by Germany, the country's overseas trade had reached unprecedented levels. The vital role played by railways in the nation's prosperity was plain to see (not that everyone shared in that prosperity, with over 30 per cent of the population still trapped in poverty). Railways' pre-eminence, at least in long-distance passenger and goods transport, was unchallenged.

Trains were carrying increasing numbers of people and volumes of freight. In parallel, engineers had refined the skills and resources required to build more powerful locomotives to cope with these extra loads. The standard of passenger travel was improving, too, with some services belonging in the luxury category.

Crucially, railway companies, both large and small, inspired fierce loyalty among their staffs. What was true then – that the quality of a railway service is only as good as the people providing it – is equally applicable today. Responsibility for the passengers and goods entrusted to their care was taken very seriously. There was pride in doing the job well, and that pride was nowhere more apparent than in the trains and the locomotives that hauled them. Usually, even the most humble goods engines gleamed.

However, pride and loyalty can bring mixed blessings. Even the biggest railway companies could be very parochial in outlook and for every visionary, such as the Great Central's Edward

By 1900, the 4-4-0 was the predominant express passenger engine type in Britain. Two of the North Eastern Railway's stock of 4-4-0s, M1 class No1629 and an unidentified Q class locomotive leave from York with an east coast express in 1900. Heavier carriages, introduced on the NER from 1893, led to such double-heading at peak holiday times. No1621 lives on in the National Railway Museum, York.

Watkin, there were managers who placed company interests above the wider good of the industry. Those who cared to look further could see the beginnings of a drift away from the railways, especially in areas where lines had been built more for the convenience of the railway company than the passenger or freight customer.

It remains a period remembered for a host of outstanding engineers: Churchward of the Great Western; Drummond of the London & South Western; Wainwright of the South Eastern & Chatham; McIntosh of the Caledonian; Hughes of the Lancashire & Yorkshire; Ivatt of the Great Northern; Worsdell of the North Eastern; and Robinson of the Great Central. The locomotives they designed combined beauty of line with a level of engineering excellence in a way that would never be repeated.

This was also a time before railways were subject to the whim of politicians and governments. Quite the opposite: the companies themselves formed a key component of the industrial and political establishment. They enjoyed considerable influence in parliamentary circles, many MPs having close ties with railway concerns. In one all-important respect, however, this power and influence were squandered. With railway building all but complete, here at last was the opportunity to organise the companies into an integrated network that served the nation's needs without sacrificing the benefits of competition. It was a glorious chance, and it was missed.

Above: Edwardian elegance evident in the elaborate livery of the preserved SE&CR D class 4-4-0 No737. Below: Equally well turned-out, a LNWR guard at Euston, 1907.

ALL PART OF THE JOB

At the turn of the century, 90 per cent of signalmen and crossing keepers worked 12 hours a day, rarely had a day off, and had only two or three days' holiday a year. Drivers and firemen did not enjoy much leisure time either, working anything from ten to 15 hours on an average day. It was common for them to spend up to 18 hours on the footplate, with only the occasional Sunday off. Theoretically, platelayers and gangers did better, working a mere ten-hour day with Sundays off, 'except for emergencies'. Unfortunately, there was almost always some emergency maintenance work to be done.

To become an inspector was a worthwhile ambition, with shifts lasting only ten hours and few Sunday rosters. There was a very real incentive to work up through the ranks of fireman and driver. A driver might receive £1 a week (roughly the national average wage), whereas a porter was paid just 15 shillings. By 1911, 49 per cent of railway employees earned less than £1 5s 0d a week.

Despite the working hours, railways were viewed as comparatively good employers; working on the railway was seen as a 'safe' job. The companies were also hughly regarded for the education and training programmes offered to all grades of employees.

A RIOT OF INDIVIDUALITY

With over 120 different companies, there was no shortage of individuality, or competition, among Britain's railways in the first decades of the 20th century.

In 1917, a Parliamentary Enquiry coined a colourful phrase to sum up Britain's railways. It described them as 'a riot of individuality', and this at a time when the network was nominally under wartime government control. There were over 120 companies ranging in size from the London & North Western – then the largest public joint stock company in the world – to the minnows such as the Southwold Railway in Suffolk and Devon's Lynton & Barnstaple.

Joining the London and North Western Railway at the top table were the Great Western, the Midland and the North Eastern, closely followed by the Great Northern, Caledonian, North British, Lancashire and Yorkshire, and London and South Western Railways. A further group embraced the smaller railways of Scotland, Wales, southern and eastern England. These ranged from the rural Cambrian and Highland to the London Brighton and South Coast Railway, with its intensive – and expanding – commuter traffic.

There was considerable rivalry between the companies, much of it beneficial to the passenger. Travellers from London to Manchester were

Among the most celebrated of Caledonian Railway designs were the 'Dunalastair' class 4-4-0s. No733 passes Etterley Junction with a down train.

offered ample services by the L&NWR, Midland and Great Central; the Midland and Great Northern competed for the London/Leeds traffic. Holidaymakers could choose between the Great Western's and London & South Western Railway's trains to the West Country. However, rivalry had its downside. There were many examples where railways' reluctance to co-operate only served to

In 1864, a number of Welsh lines became part of the Cambrian Railways system. Its trains operated over 300 route miles, extending to coastal resorts such as Barmouth, which is where Cambrian '28' class 2-4-0 No28 Mazeppa was heading with a six-coach train one day in 1900.

Right: Two elegantly attired female passengers stride along the platform at Euston before boarding a London & North Western Railway boat train for Liverpool, 1918. Standing by the train doors, the porters are equally smartly dressed.

inconvenience passengers. A prime example was poor connecting services. Competition was also expensive for the railways so Services, lines and stations were duplicated and resources diluted. Companies tended to measure success by the scale of their networks and operations, rather than returns on capital investment. So long as profit levels remained acceptable, glaring inefficiencies were tolerated.

Railway building continued up to 1914, although the Great Central's 'London Extension' was the last 'new' main line. As the GCR learned, construction now represented a huge capital investment. Other projects tended to be 'route shortening' lines, such as the Great Western's 'cut-off' which reduced the journey time from Paddington to the south-west by avoiding Bristol.

By 1912, the national route mileage stood at 23,441. On the freight side, competition from canals had been all but eliminated, not least because many of the canal companies were now railway-owned. Additionally, several railway companies diversified into shipping services. With revenue increasing, the future appeared secure (although costs were growing at a faster rate). Annually railways carried 16 tons of goods per person and, on average, that person made 35 train journeys each year. However, the competition for his or her fare was intensifying, especially in major cities. By 1914, there were 2,500 miles of urban electric tramway and, more ominously, over 400,000 motor vehicles of various kinds in service. Significantly, the private car was no longer confined to the wealthy but was within the range of many middle-class families. The outbreak of war that August, however, forestalled any coordinated response the railways might have delivered to this challenge.

ON THE RIGHT PATH

Time was when the volume of freight traffic on Britain's railways threatened to bring some lines to a standstill, the Midland Railway's 'coal route' through South Yorkshire, Derbyshire and Nottinghamshire to London being a prime example. With passenger trains given priority, non-perishable freight – especially coal – was held in yards, colliery sidings and loops for hours on end. An engine crew might spend its entire shift without turning a wheel. It was hopelessly inefficient but, so long as sufficient coal was delivered to keep the fires burning, no one was overly concerned.

Proper organisation was eventually imposed, along with greater use of modern communications such as telephone reporting. The regulation of train running was improved and more effective use made of line capacity.

The Midland led the way in centralised telephone control. It was subsequently adopted by the Great Western, which also handled a large volume of coal traffic, the North British and ultimately by all railways.

One outcome of better organisation was the principle of pathing. This began with a sheet of graph paper on which was plotted the maximum number of trains that could be despatched through any one section of line over a given time period. All possible 'paths' were mapped out, regardless of whether the timetable asked for that density of working or not. The thought behind the 'train path' is that, at a particular time of day, there is, or should be, a clear run available through a section for a certain class of train. The 'path' is fixed on the timetable graph, to be allotted to a regular service or held in reserve for a relief train or a special working. Since train speeds varied widely, there were paths for every type of traffic.

The early years of the 20th century saw the first exercises in main-line electrification. Even for a coal-rich country such as Britain, in certain situations the case for electrification was overwhelming. For a given weight of locomotive or railcar, electrification can deliver greater power and smarter acceleration. It offers excellent reliability and on routes with dense traffic flows, electrification lowers operating costs. For example, with multiple unit trains, the turn-round time is the time it takes the driver to walk to his cab. Electric locomotives can be expected to complete two round trips in a day where steam might only manage one. The drawback is that electrification is an immensely complex and costly process. Very few major electrification projects have not been underwritten by governments, or similar organisations.

Nevertheless, the first electric railway in Britain was a privately funded affair. Built by Magnus Volk and opened on 4 August 1883, it ran along the seafront at Brighton, in Sussex. The North Eastern Railway and the Lancashire & Yorkshire Railway were the first main-line companies to experiment with electrification. The NER inaugurated electric services in the Newcastle area in 1904, the same year that the L&YR electrified its line from Liverpool to Southport. These early schemes adopted direct current (dc), at a voltage of around 600-650, and fed through conductor rails laid alongside the running track. The Midland Railway, though, opted for alternating current (ac) on the line between Lancaster, Morecambe and Heysham. Electrified in 1908-09, the 6,600 volt supply was conveyed along overhead contact wires suspended from lineside masts. In the motor coaches of the trains, transformers reduced the supply to a lower voltage suitable for the traction motors.

On 1 December 1909, the London, Brighton & South Coast Railway inaugurated a similar scheme on its cross-capital line between Victoria and London Bridge. This was the beginning of an electrification programme that would eventually extend throughout southern England, although the method adopted would not be the LB&SCR's overhead ac format, but the third rail dc system introduced in July 1915 by the London & South Western Railway on its lines out of Waterloo.

North of the River Thames, in 1914, the L&NWR electrified its line between Willesden and Earls Court, the first stage in the electrification of the inner-suburban routes between Euston and Watford and Broad Street and Richmond. Again, third rail dc was the chosen power source but, in 1915, the NER experimented with a 1,500dc overhead system for its coal-carrying line between Newport, on Teesside, and Shildon, in County Durham. Trains were hauled by double-bogie locomotives with traction motors mounted in their axles. Encouraged by the success of this project, the NER then proposed electrifying the York-Newcastle main line and even got as far as building a prototype locomotive specifically for this purpose. However, financial constraints and consequences of the 1923 grouping left the idea stillborn. Remarkably, it would not be until after World War II that any main-line electrification would be completed outside of Southern Railway territory.

LAST BUT NOT LEAST

The building of England's last main line — the Great Central's London Extension — was all about one man's vision.

The Manchester, Sheffield & Lincolnshire Railway began operations on 1 January 1847 and, through a series of amalgamations and take-overs, became one of the major components of the trans-Pennine railway network. Principally a freight railway, it shifted vast tonnages from the South Yorkshire and Nottinghamshire coalfields. Its operations extended from Liverpool on the west coast to Immingham on the east. Many a railway company chairman would have been content with such an empire, but not Edward Watkin.

Watkin became General Manager of the MS&L in 1854 and assumed the role of Chairman ten years later. He had an ambition that would see the company going far beyond merely competing for traffic in the north of England. For Edward Watkin, the ultimate goal was Paris and the rest of Continental Europe. To achieve this he planned to build a new railway between Annesley in Nottinghamshire and London, which became known as the London Extension, and acquired interests in railways in south-east England, including the Metropolitan (which served London) and the South Eastern (which gave access to Channel ports). Additionally, he had also taken a stake in the Submarine Continental Railway (SCR) that was backing the construction of a tunnel under the English Channel.

Since Watkin saw his railway becoming part of an international railway system, he insisted it be built to the more generous Continental loading gauge. In the event, Watkin's route to Paris never got beyond London because of problems in gaining links to the Channel ports and the abandonment of SCR's planned tunnel between England and France. The London Extension, however, did become a reality in 1899, allowing through services between Manchester and a new London terminus at Marylebone to be commenced by MS&L — by then renamed the Great Central Railway. The route took in Sheffield, Nottingham, Leicester and Rugby and continued to Verney Junction, north of Aylesbury. Incongruously, this remote rural junction (it stood in fields far from any village) was the northern outpost of one of Watkin's other enterprises, the Metropolitan.

Agreement had been reached for Great Central trains to share the Metropolitan's lines into London, but the arrangement only worked as long as Edward Watkin held the reins of both companies. Since, he was now in his seventies and decided to relinquish his chairmanships, a bout of bickering between the GCR and the Metropolitan quickly ensued. The latter refused the GCR access to its connection with the District (Inner Circle) line at Baker Street – a vital link in the GCR's proposed north-south route that would have taken its trains through the Thames Tunnel and on to the tracks of the South Eastern Railway. As its relationship with the Metropolitan became more precarious, the GCR gained an alternative route into London by building a short line between its own station at Woodford and Banbury, a station on the Great Western Railway's Birmingham line.

In the quality of its engineering, the 'London Extension' was on a par with Brunel's Great Western, or Robert Stephenson's London & Birmingham. It not only ran first-rate passenger expresses, but also handled quite a considerable quantity of freight. Despite this, the route was a commercial failure. It may have fared better had Edward Watkin's European link been realised; instead, the last main line to be built became the first to be axed. When the last stopping services were withdrawn in March 1963, the line, its locomotives and rolling stock had been permitted

POWERFUL OPPONENTS

The proposed Bill for the Great Central's London Extension met fierce opposition When presented to Parliament in 1891. Some of its opponents – rival railway companies such as the Great Northern and Midland – were predictable, others less so. The GCR's original plan to build its London terminus in Boscobel Gardens, St John's Wood, incurred the wrath of the local artistic community. The poets and painters were only placated when the location was switched to Marylebone Road. However, the GCR then had to take on the outraged ranks of the Marylebone Cricket Club who objected to a tunnel beneath one corner of Lord's cricket ground. Together with undertaking to return the hallowed turf to pristine condition, the GCR agreed to reclaim some adjacent wasteland, which it donated to the MCC. This 'sweetener' cost the GCR some £40,000. Royal Assent for the London Extension Bill was delayed by such disputes until the end of 1893.

to descend unchecked into a lamentably run-down condition. A once-great railway had been systematically destroyed. It said it all when, on the last day of through services, 4 September 1966, a Stanier Class 5MT 4-6-0 managed to fail at the head of the 8.15am Nottingham-Marylebone service.

SITTING COMFORTABLY?

Prior to the 1870s, few passengers sat comfortably on a train journey.
Forty years on, though, more than the rich and the royal travelled in style.

Railways may have presented everyone with the opportunity to travel, but any egalitarian notion that it might become a communal experience was premature. On board a train, just as in society as a whole, class mattered; first, second and third were simply substituted for upper, middle and lower. It could still be a rough ride in the four-wheel coaches of the Victorian era but at least the first class accommodation was reasonably well appointed. Second class was considerably more spartan, but the best you could hope for in third class was to stay dry and hope there were no delays to prolong the ordeal. The job of the third class carriage was to cram as many people as possible into the space available. Naturally, standards varied and on some long distance trains, particularly those of the Great Western, London & North Western and Midland Railways, travelling third class was a much more civilised experience.

However, until the 1870s, no passengers had access to the more basic amenities. It was only at this time that the L&NWR began equipping some of its sleeping cars with lavatories. The first dining car did not enter service in Britain until 1 November 1879. Named *Prince of Wales*, it operated on the Great Northern Railway between Kings Cross and Leeds and, to guarantee its exclusivity, the coach was closed off from the rest of the train. Patrons could spend the entire journey wining and dining.

It was the Midland Railway that finally forced a change of attitude towards the third class passenger, but the reforms it initiated in 1872 caused consternation among rivals. First, it announced that third class passengers would be allowed on board all its train services. Moreover, it abolished second class altogether, with third class becoming second in all but name. As soon as replacements were built, the old, grim third class carriages were broken up. The Midland also took the bold step of reducing its first class fares and was soon able to counter its critics by pointing to a rise in passenger receipts. Before long, other companies came round to the Midland's way of thinking. Now the competition was in providing passenger amenities, not restricting them.

In 1891, the Great Western was the first British railway to introduce a corridor train, on its Paddington to Birkenhead service. Two years later, the L&NWR demonstrated how much passenger travel had improved when it inaugurated an all-corridor afternoon express from Euston to Glasgow and Edinburgh. Known to all simply as 'The Corridor', this was a sumptuously-appointed train with no less than four dining cars. Yet anyone could ride it for just one penny a mile.

By 1900, the rivalry in passenger travel was intense. Most companies had adopted electric lighting and steam heating as standard. First class carriages now ran on smooth-riding bogies and were being built – lavishly upholstered and splendidly decorated – to the limits of the loading gauge. Some railways went further and added an extra touch of luxury. The Lancashire & Yorkshire, for example, introduced 'club' cars on certain residential express trains between Manchester, Blackpool and Southport. Each member of the 'club' had his armchair.

Unfortunately, better carriages were also heavier carriages and many of the crack expresses of the 1900s were loading to over 400 tons. These called for more powerful locomotives that consumed more coal, at a time when coal prices were rising. Churchward of the Great Western was one who sought a two-way solution. He built bigger (and more efficient) engines but also found ways to successfully lighten coach construction without compromising on the quality of the accommodation or reducing the numbers carried.

With the exception of the streamlined fliers of the 1930s, express trains were never more elegant than in the period leading up to World War I and the railways flourished as a result. It had taken time to make the transformation, but now just about everybody was sitting comfortably.

Photographed around 1905, passengers enjoy a meal in one of the LNWR's well-appointed dining cars. Note the electric lighting, by then becoming commonplace.

THE SWINDON STANDARD

George Jackson Churchward's blueprint for the Great Western was novel for its time and far-reaching in its impact.

It is generally accepted that George Jackson Churchward was responsible for the most significant transition in British steam locomotive design. It is tempting to invest some symbolism in the fact that his appointment in 1902 as Locomotive Superintendent of the GWR more-or-less corresponded with the end of the Victorian era. That was simply coincidence but, unquestionably, Churchward became the most influential British locomotive engineer since Robert Stephenson. Along with equipping the Great Western with a fleet of modern, reliable engines, Churchward established a blueprint for his successors to follow. Charles Collett and Frederick Hawksworth needed to do little more than refine and develop the principles their predecessor laid down.

Importantly, and unlike the London & North Western's Francis Webb for example, Churchward was not an absolute dictator. If, at a design meeting, there was a question about axle-loadings, then the views of the Civil Engineer would be sought. If an aspect of boiler construction was under discussion, then the head boilersmith would attend. Such receptiveness to advice helped Churchward avoid mistakes born out of dogmatic inflexibility or a misguided zeal for experiment. Noticeably absent from the list of Churchward's locomotive designs are the 'duds' that marred the careers of, say, Webb and Dugald

Light work for one of Churchward's 'Star' class 4-cylinder 4-6-0s, No4049 Princess Maud, pictured near Box on a two-coach train for Bristol on 22 June 1936. It was withdrawn in July 1953. Both the 'Castles' of 1923 and the 'Kings' of 1927 evolved from the 'Star' class.

A REVOLUTIONARY IN TWEEDS

G. J. Churchward came from a Devon family. He was born at Stoke Gabriel, a village on the River Dart south-east of Totnes, in 1857 and was educated at Totnes Grammar School. An evident interest in engineering led to him serving an apprenticeship on the South Devon Railway. When the SDR was absorbed by the Great Western, Churchward was transferred to the GW works at Swindon. Over a period of 20 years from 1877 to 1897, he rose from the post of draughtsman, by way of Carriage Works Manager, to become Chief Assistant Locomotive, Carriage and Wagon Superintendent.

Fortunately for Churchward, his superior, William Dean, was approaching retirement and playing an increasingly marginal role in the day-to-day running of the locomotive department. Consequently, for fully five years, he faced little interference as he pursued his (and others') novel ideas on locomotive construction.

These ideas were tried, to far-reaching effect, on a number of experimental designs. Crucially, Churchward shifted away from the dogged independence that characterised the Great Western to consider ideas from further afield, notably the United States, France and Germany. It was from the first that he adopted the 4-cylinder configuration first used on the 'Star' class 4-6-0s, and subsequently on the 'Castles' and 'Kings'. A 2-cylinder 'Saint' 4-6-0 was the recipient of the revolutionary Schmidt superheater from Germany.

Churchward succeeded Dean as Locomotive Superintendent in the summer of 1902, by which time he had developed a passion for public service. He became chairman of the New Swindon Urban District Council, and then mayor of the town. His other work included the chairmanship of the Technical Education Committee, which encouraged the training of apprentices.

G. J. Churchward cut an impressive figure, his tweed suits and trilby hat giving him the look of a country squire. However, he was far from aloof and saw himself very much as part of a team (although indisputably its leader). During World War I, Churchward was heavily involved in converting his Swindon workshops to meet Government demands for munitions and weapons, while ensuring the continuing provision of locomotives and rolling stock for the war effort. It earned him a CBE in the 1918 Birthday Honours. Later, in 1920, Churchward was made the first honorary freeman of the Borough of Swindon.

When only 63 years old, Churchward retired as Chief Mechanical Engineer of the GWR in December 1921. During his 19 years in the post he had supervised the construction of a fleet of 888 engines. In the ensuing decades, a further 1,250 would be built to his basic designs. Churchward's work on boilers, superheating, cylinders and the fundamentals of standardisation would have far-reaching effect. Nigel Gresley of the LNER, as well as Richard Maunsell of the Southern Railway acknowledged his influence, while William Stanier took his ideas with him to the LMSR.

Tragically, Churchward's retirement lasted only 12 years. His house gave access to the Bristol main line and he was in the habit of taking a stroll alongside it. On the morning of 19 December 1933, he was hit by 'Castle' class locomotive No4085 *Berkeley Castle* at the head of a down Fishguard express and died instantly. Churchward suffered from slight deafness and had experienced bouts of vertigo brought on by eye trouble. It may have been that these contributed to the accident. The verdict of the coroner's court jury was accidental death and this visionary among locomotive engineers was buried in a corner of Swindon's parish church.

Drummond. His one true flop was the solitary Pacific of 1907, No111 *The Great Bear*, and that had as much to do with misjudgements elsewhere.

There was no 'magic formula' behind Churchward's success. He simply adhered to principles that are as relevant today as they were in 1902: identify the need, make the product to meet it, and apply economies of scale wherever possible. The family likeness shared by every Great Western locomotive built between 1902 and 1950 signifies more than a desire for uniformity of appearance.

Churchward replaced William Dean at a time of dramatic change in the demands placed on motive power. Trains were becoming longer and rolling stock heavier as carriage designs became less spartan. Railway administrators were seeking faster schedules, especially where there was competition for traffic. Churchward recognised that it was pointless striving to squeeze another ounce of performance from the outdated 19th century classes. Even his famed 'City' class 4-4-0 was an interim measure.

For Churchward, the key to building better engines was to design more efficient boilers. The most visible common feature of his range of 'Swindon Standard' boilers was their taper. This ensured that the greater part of the water content was concentrated at the firebox end where the heat was at its greatest. Moreover, the depth of water there would remain largely unaffected by 'surging' within the boiler as the locomotive was being worked on a down gradient.

In 1901, he drew up a scheme for just six basic locomotive types to meet the GWR's main-line operating requirements (this at a time when such

Churchward's 4700 class 2-8-0 of 1919, his last design for the GWR, was a superb locomotive but its usefulness was compromised by its weight and long coupled wheelbase. One of only nine to be built, No4705 leaves Westbury, in Wiltshire, with the 2.00pm goods from Acton in London to Hackney yard, Newton Abbot, on 15 June 1963.

standardisation was practically unheard of). There were two 4-6-0s, one for mixed traffic work, the other for express passenger duties. Secondary passenger services would be catered for by a 4-4-0, while suburban and branch lines would employ 2-6-2 and 4-4-2 tank engines. For heavy freight, Churchward settled on a type new to Britain, the 2-8-0.

Significantly, these designs shared more than the 'Standard' boilers. Other components such as bogies, cylinders and motion parts were also interchangeable, with the benefit of cutting down design and construction time. Such 'mass' pro-duction cut costs and ensured a stock of spare

parts was always available, so cutting the time locomotives spent idle at the workshops awaiting replacement parts.

Consolidating Churchward's reputation, many of his ideas were adopted by other main-line railway companies. This was the case even with the British Railways Standard locomotive classes introduced some 20 years after his tragic death in 1933. Churchward's tenets were not superseded by any radical advances in steam technology, only by the coming of diesel and electric traction. At the enforced demise of Western Region steam in 1965, his ideas were no more life-expired than his engines.

When it appeared in January 1908, No111 The Great Bear was the first British 4-6-2, or Pacific. Churchward had warned that the engine would be of limited use, but the GWR's directors enjoyed the kudos of having 'Britain's biggest locomotive'.

JOINING THE FIGHT

During World War I, Britain's railways supplied more than transport. Their workshops made munitions, their engines were requisitioned, and large numbers of railwaymen were called to the colours. For many, there was no return ticket.

Government departments had prepared for the possibility of war with Germany. As early as 1912, the Board of Trade had created a body that would assume overall charge of Britain's railways and, at the outbreak of war in August 1914, this Railway Executive Committee took control of all main line railway companies and most minor ones. The companies continued to manage day-to-day running, but the government now had the power to augment, divert or even cancel services in order to meet military needs.

This new partnership had no time to bed in. In the first 16 days, railways had to carry the thousands of men, horses and guns of the British Expeditionary Force to Southampton for embarkation to France. It was an exercise that would be repeated time-after-time over the

Standing beside their belt-driven machines, women workers briefly halt the production of artillery shells to pose for the camera in the Lancashire & Yorkshire Railway's works at Horwich, near Bolton in Lancashire.

ensuing four years as the railways assumed responsibility for the movement of vast numbers of troops and supplies. Not all the traffic was through the Channel ports. Trains conveyed men and fuel to the north-eastern tip of Scotland for the sea passage to Scapa Flow, base of the Royal Navy's Grand Fleet. Speed restrictions meant that the nightly naval specials between London Euston and Thurso took over 21 hours to cover the 717 miles. (Train speeds had been cut to reduce wear and tear on the track.) From 1917, American forces were transported from Liverpool, where their transatlantic ships docked, to the Channel ports.

The government not only employed the railways in the war effort, it made significant use of railway equipment and personnel. Between 1914 and 1918, 184,475 – or 49 per cent – of railway staff of military age joined the armed forces. It left many railways severely depleted in key positions, especially as there was no policy of 'reserved occupations' – jobs regarded as too important for their occupants to be lost to the armed forces (something that changed with World War II).

There was also a request for locomotives and several railways supplied them, over 600 in total. The London & North Western, Midland, Great Western and North Eastern made substantial contributions, the last loaning 50 0-8-0s. The greatest demand was for the engines that were also most needed at home: medium-powered and heavy freight engines. As a result, government authority was given to build new engines for war service, the design chosen being the Great Central Railway's 8K class 2-8-0 of 1911. Over 500 were built for use by the Railway Operating Division (ROD).

Efforts were made to discourage civilian travel but to little effect. In 1917, draconian measures were adopted, with the abolition of cheap fares and a big increase in ordinary fares. Many of the pleasures of rail travel, such as restaurant cars, were lost to the war. In contrast, an extraordinary number of special trains were run. Even the

ENGINE OF WAR

Midland Railway 0-6-0 goods engine No2717 was one of 81 members of its class lent to the Railway Operating Division during World War I. All but three were despatched to France or Flanders. No2717, however, experienced rather more front-line action than most. On 30 November 1917, while on the Line between Peronne and Cambrai, it was 'captured' by the Germans. Along with more normal duties, the locomotive was pressed into action as an improvised machine gun post. The Germans even gave it a new number – 01251. It was frequently strafed by rifle and machine gun fire, with the steam dome suffering many hits.

Recovered by the British after the Armistice, in November 1918, No2717 was returned to the Midland's workshops at Derby. For a time, it became something of a museum piece. Eventually, however, it returned to normal traffic, as did all but one of the Midland's 80 other 'war engines'.

South Eastern Railway, not one of the bigger concerns, ran an astonishing 101,872 specials between 5 August 1914 and 31 December 1918, an average of over 60 trains a day.

The government also called upon the facilities of railway workshops. The opening exchanges of the conflict established that government

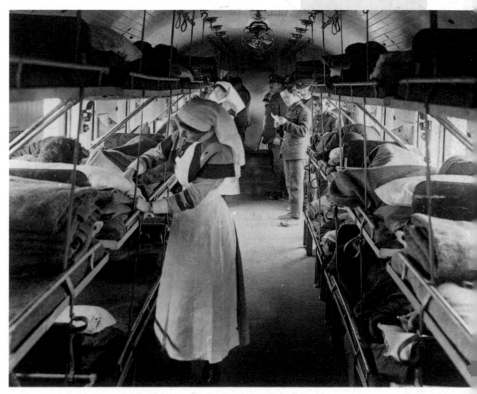

Officers check, while nurses attend the wounded on board a British ambulance train on 27 April 1918. Twelve such trains had been formed within the first month of war.

MILITARY SERVICE

Along with using the national network, all three branches of the armed services built railways. Among the more notable military systems were those serving the Royal Navy dockyards at Chatham in Kent, and Faslane in western Scotland, and the Royal Arsenal at Woolwich in south-east London. There were extensive systems around in Dumfriesshire, Scotland, and Catterick in North Yorkshire. The Army also set up railway training centres at Longmoor, in Hampshire, and in Derbyshire, where a Midland Railway branch line metamorphosed into the Melbourne Military Railway. To the dismay of railway enthusiasts who enjoyed its open days, the Longmoor system closed in 1969. However, one of the most extensive army railways, the 48-mile system serving depots in and around Bicester, Oxfordshire, still operates today.

Narrow gauge railways were laid between supply points and the battlefront. Near the Belgian city of Ypres, British troops head for the front line with loads that include shuttering to shore up trench walls.

ordnance factories alone were incapable of meeting the demand for munitions. They also confirmed plans to convert rolling stock into ambulance trains were to be implemented. By the end of August 1914, 12 such trains were ready.

The Midland Railway's works at Derby was one that played an important role in munitions production. One shop, staffed by women, was responsible for the renovation and refilling of brass cartridge cases. Records indicate that one 18-pounder case passed through no less than five times. Weekly output was 130,000 and, in all, over 7 million cases were processed. Other work undertaken at Derby included the manufacture

of howitzer cradles, carriages and limbers, axle-trees, flanged plates for guns, breech bolts, bomb cases, and fuse parts. The workshops produced stampings and castings of all kinds, along with lamps, loading derricks and machinery for the Railway Transport Expeditionary Force.

Towards the end of the war some work was done at Derby for the infant Royal Air Force, including the forging of flywheels and the machining of aluminium high compression pistons for aircraft engines. The original test beds for the Rolls Royce plant at Derby were also machined in the railway workshops.

Compared to World War II, railways were little damaged by enemy action, but they emerged very much the worse for wear. The heavy wartime traffic had been handled by a reduced staff and locomotives had to run higher mileages between general repairs. Consequently, the maintenance of locomotives, rolling stock and track was badly in arrears.

The companies were also in financial difficulty. The government had not allowed railway rates and charges to rise in line with wages and prices and, by the period 1919 to 1920, the network was running at a loss of £45 million a year.

The Railway Executive Committee maintained its hold on the network until 15 August 1921, at which point a decision had to be taken about its future. The choice was straightforward: amalgamation or nationalisation. There was little doubt about which was the more politically palatable and an amalgamation of the numerous private railways saw the emergence of the 'big four' regional railways running alongside some smaller private groupings.

DISASTER AT QUINTINSHILL

The worst accident in the history of Britain's railways occurred during World War I and, although it involved a troop train, its causes had little to do with wartime conditions. The location was Quintinshill, north of Carlisle and some 1.5 miles into Scotland. Here there was a signal box and two passing loops (long sidings alongside the north- and southbound main lines that could accommodate slow trains in order for faster services to overtake them).

On the morning of 22 May 1915, the midnight express from Euston to Glasgow was running late. At 6.13am, Carlisle despatched a northbound local train ahead of the express. At Quintinshill, it should have been placed in the 'down', or northbound, loop to allow the express to pass but that was already occupied by a goods train. The 'up', or southbound loop was also about to be filled by a coal train. The local train was therefore switched to stand on the 'up' (southbound) main line.

There was nothing irregular or inherently dangerous about this, so long as the required precautions were observed. The signalman in the next signalbox to the north, at Kirkpatrick, should have been advised that the line was blocked, and, at Quintinshill box, a 'collar' should have been placed over the relevant signal levers to prevent them being inadvertently pulled. Neither of these actions was taken. The signalmen were distracted by the presence of the goods train guards in the signalbox; one was apparently reading out items of war news from a newspaper.

Kirkpatrick box then offered Quintinshill a southbound troop special, running from Larbert to Liverpool. Utterly forgetting the presence of the local on the southbound main line, the Quintinshill signalman accepted it. The signals were also cleared for the Glasgow express.

The troop train smashed into the stationary local at around 70mph. The train was reduced from 15 coaches and a length of 213 yards to 67 yards of wreckage. Before preventive action could be taken, the double-headed express ploughed into the debris. The wooden bodied carriages, which were lit by gaslight caught fire and burnt for the best part of 24 hours.

It is estimated that 227 lost their lives, and that 246 were injured, but the exact number of fatalities could not be established as regimental records had been destroyed in the inferno. Both the Quintinshill signalmen were convicted of manslaughter and given life sentences.

The bitter irony of the Quintinshill disaster was that the soldiers involved were destined for the Gallipoli campaign, an ill-conceived and ill-fated battle where probably many would have lost their lives.

2
THE GOLDEN AGE

Luxury trains, lightning speeds, legendary locomotives — did this represent a golden age, or just so much surface gloss?

FLYING SCOTSMAN

Nº 2795

A COMING TOGETHER

The biggest shake-up of Britain's railways took place in 1923, when, not always willingly or seamlessly, a multitude of competing companies merged to form the 'big four'.

As they recovered from their wartime exertions, railway managements pondered what would happen when they were freed from the last vestiges of government control. Some would have concluded that they were no longer in any financial condition to operate as independent concerns and contemplated amalgamation. Catching up on four years' neglected maintenance – of engines, rolling stock and track – was beyond them. Many, though, would have hoped for a return to something approaching the pre-war status quo. At government level, however, something much more far-reaching was envisaged. Under the newly established Ministry of Transport, schemes were formulated for a drastic reorganisation of the railway system. Purely on economic grounds, some degree of unification was inevitable, but that it would also broadly benefit the nation was inarguable. What was lost in competition would be more than made up for by co-operation and a consolidation of resources.

The 'grouping', as the amalgamations were termed, took effect from 1 January 1923. Overnight, some 120 railway companies – along with their crests, their liveries and their loyalties – disappeared into four large concerns. Inevitably, there were monumental clashes of policy, opinion and personality, most notably on the London Midland & Scottish Railway where the top brass of the erstwhile London & North Western and Midland Railways tussled for supremacy. One wit had a description for this vast, sprawling network – all 7,790 route miles of it – that now stretched from London to the limit of Britain's railway system in the north of Scotland. It was, he opined, one 'ell of a mess'.

The second largest group, the London & North Eastern, came together a little more amicably,

AN UNWANTED INHERITANCE

The 'big four' railway companies inherited problems as well as assets in 1923. The Southern had a particular headache in Kent and Sussex. There had been no nationally agreed loading gauge when the South Eastern Railway completed its line between Tunbridge Wells in Kent and Hastings, on the Sussex coast, in 1852. That the tunnels were narrower and lower than those being dug elsewhere mattered little while the SER alone supplied the locomotives and rolling stock. By the 1920s, however, this anomaly was causing severe operational problems. Hastings was a popular seaside destination and the towns and villages in nearby Kent and Sussex were becoming part of the London commuter belt. The small engines that fitted the tunnels could not haul the heavier trains.

First the Southern Railway and later British Railways, both of whom adhered to a more generous loading gauge, had to make special provisions for the line, both with rolling stock and locomotives. Ideas were put forward to widen the tunnels, or even by-pass them, but were dismissed on grounds of cost and the time the line would have to be closed.

Richard Maunsell's 'Schools' 4-4-0 was the most famous solution to the 'Hastings problem', closely followed by the 6-car 'Hastings' diesel multiple units of 1957. The line's future came under threat when the latter became due for replacement in the early 1980s. There was no justification for building a new series of units specifically for the Hastings service. A solution was found by taking up the double track in the tunnels and relaying a single track down the middle. Standard gauge coaches could all now pass through and the line was subsequently electrified. Over the decades, the instruction 'Not to work between Tonbridge and Hastings' was carried on an amazing variety of rolling stock. The interchange of goods vehicles across Britain and on the Continent meant the warning could be seen anywhere from Scotland to Switzerland.

while the Great Western merely absorbed every standard-gauge concern west of Shrewsbury and the Severn Estuary. The Southern, though, was under-prepared. It had failed to integrate its constituent companies during the lead-up to the grouping. During the first six months of 1923, the vital post of general manager changed hands three times as representatives of the LB&SCR, L&SWR and SE&CR took turns at the helm. Only at the end of the year was the L&SWR's Sir Herbert Walker appointed permanently. Luckily for the Southern, Walker's appointment proved to be the right choice.

Many, of course, disliked this new centralised control. Railway customers, accustomed to personal service from local representatives, were unhappy dealing at long-distance with the big companies. Employees of smaller railways, such as the Highland, were saddened to see their beloved engines lose their individuality. Once they had cared for them, but now they went south for repairs and returned with their stirring Gaelic names repainted in small, barely legible letters. To add insult to injury, these cherished names were often misspelled.

THE NEW ORDER

The so-called 'big four' companies were made up of over 120 companies. Of the old names, only the Great Western survived the transition. The composition of the new companies after the grouping in 1923 was as follows:

Great Western Railway
Constituent companies: Alexandra (Newport & South Wales) Docks & Railway Company; Barry Railway; Cambrian Railway; Cardiff Railway; Great Western Railway; Rhymney Railway; Taff Vale Railway (plus 26 subsidiary companies).

Southern Railway
Constituent companies: London, Brighton & South Coast Railway; London & South Western Railway; London, Chatham & Dover Railway; South Eastern Railway (these last two nominally independent but administered under the South Eastern & Chatham Railway Managing Committee); (plus 14 subsidiary companies).

London, Midland & Scottish Railway
Constituent companies: Caledonian Railway; Furness Railway; Glasgow & South Western Railway; Highland Railway; Lancashire & Yorkshire Railway; London & North Western Railway; Midland Railway; North Staffordshire Railway (plus 27 subsidiary companies).

London & North Eastern Railway
Constituent companies: Great Central Railway; Great Eastern Railway; Great Northern Railway; Great North of Scotland Railway; Hull & Barnsley Railway; North British Railway; North Eastern Railway (plus 26 subsidiary companies).

One of the Southern's more welcome inheritances was a series of 22 superheated 4-4-0s built for the South Eastern & Chatham Railway in 1914, the L class. Twelve were built by Beyer Peacock but, more interestingly, 10 were ordered from the German builder, Borsig of Berlin, including No1776, seen here passing Shortlands, Kent, with a southbound train.

WHEN SPEED WAS THE ESSENCE

They were the names — Flying Scotsman, Tregenna Castle, Papyrus, Princess Elizabeth, Silver Link and, of course, Mallard — forever associated with the quest for speed on Britain's railways during the 1930s.

Profile of power — 'Princess Coronation' class Pacific No46240 City of Coventry in its British Railways guise, at the head of a west coast express. Introduced in 1937, the 'Coronations' matched fast running with the power required to take heavy trains over the stiff climbs of the Lancaster-Carlisle-Glasgow route.

Before World War I, surprisingly few scheduled services averaged more than 50mph. At the grouping in 1923, although most main lines offered their quota of expresses, only two trains in Britain exceeded the 'mile-a-minute' average of 60mph. Even the famous 'Flying Scotsman' could only average 47.75mph between London and Edinburgh. The focus of the ensuing fifteen years, however, was speed: average speeds, speeds maintained on non-stop runs and, of course, the ultimate accolade of 'the world's fastest locomotive'. Two factors sparked this quest for speed: the increasing power of locomotives, and increasing competition from other forms of transport.

It began on one date — 9 July 1923 — and with one train, a run-of-the-mill afternoon service from Cheltenham to Paddington. That day, the Great Western retimed the train to sprint from Swindon to Paddington (77.25 miles) in just 75 minutes, an average speed of 61.8mph with a nine coach load totalling 265 tons. This was now the fastest scheduled service in Britain and, on the inaugural run, the message was driven home when it arrived three minutes early after sustaining an average of 64.2mph. In 1929 the 'Cheltenham Flyer', as it was now called, was accelerated further to become the fastest train in the world. However, its 'Castle' class engines were capable of more and, in 1931, the GWR stipulated an average speed of 71.4mph, the world's first 70mph-plus schedule. The GWR's publicity neglected to mention that, when the train's more leisurely progress from Cheltenham to Swindon was taken into account, its average speed dropped to a more modest 52mph!

Not content with its world record, on 6 June 1932 the Great Western staged a special run behind No5006 *Tregenna Castle* that kept up a start-to-stop average of 81.6mph between

Swindon and Paddington. However, the 'Flyer' remained one of just five 60mph averages in the public timetables.

By this time, the Great Western had some serious competition in the locomotive power stakes, principally from the Gresley-designed Pacifics of the LNER. These were engines that could maintain 80mph averages on reasonably level track and were to prove that they could regularly reach maximum speeds of around 100mph. On 30 November 1934, while on a test run from Leeds to Kings Cross, A1 Pacific No4472 *Flying Scotsman* achieved the first authenticated 100mph on the 'racing ground' between Little Bytham and Essendine, which was located 12 miles south of Grantham, Lincolnshire.

Five months later, on 5 March 1935, A3 No2750 *Papyrus* was entrusted with a further test run, this time over 268.25 miles between Kings Cross and Newcastle. With a load of 217 tons, the Pacific averaged 70mph on the outward run, but the fireworks were saved for the return. Again on the Little Bytham-Essendine stretch, *Papyrus* averaged 105.4mph, with a maximum speed of 108mph. The speed record had been broken once again. Moreover, *Papyrus* had set another world record by maintaining 100mph for a distance of 12.75 miles. These runs were about more than record-breaking. The LNER was assessing the feasibility of introducing high-speed scheduled services to both Newcastle and Leeds. Impressed by the performance of the diesel powered 'Flying Hamburger' running between Berlin and Hamburg, the LNER had even considered hiring one for trials. Nigel Gresley, however, kept faith with steam, if not with tradition. His new Pacific design, classified A4, was striking in every respect, from its streamlined casing to its silver-grey livery. On a demonstration run for the press on 27 September 1935, the doyen of the class, No2509 *Silver Link* twice attained a speed of 112.5mph. And for the 21 miles between Stevenage and Offord, the speed did not once drop below 100mph.

On board, a few of the passengers became somewhat disconcerted by the swaying of the carriages, but on the footplate, the ride was astonishingly smooth. The first the crew knew of the passengers' anxiety was when Nigel Gresley emerged from the

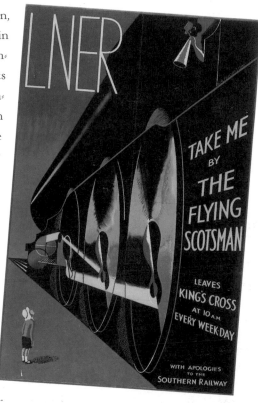

Mimicking a Southern Railway's poster (see page 84), the LNER promotes its high-speed east coast service.

THE DRIVER'S TALE

At the regulator of LNER A4 Pacific No2509 *Silver Link* on the never-to-be-forgotten trial run of the 'Silver Jubilee' on 27 September 1935 was driver Arthur Taylor of King's Cross depot, London. Taylor did more than set a new world speed record for steam traction of 112.5mph. For the first time a locomotive maintained a speed of 100mph or more for 25 consecutive miles.

Arthur Taylor joined the Great Northern Railway in February 1895, aged 18. As was usual for footplatemen, he began as an engine cleaner. By September 1898, he was undertaking firing turns and became a 'passed fireman' in March 1910. It took him 17 years, until July 1912, to reach the status of fully fledged driver.

Following the appearance of the Gresley Pacifics in 1922, Taylor's engine for several years was No4476 *Royal Lancer*. In due course, he graduated to the 'top link' of senior drivers at King's Cross and it says much for his reputation that he was given charge of the first A4 Pacific to be delivered from Doncaster. His achievements earned him an OBE and he retired in 1941. Arthur Taylor died in September 1959, aged 82.

corridor tender and said to driver Arthur Taylor, 'Steady on, old chap. Do you know you have just done 112 miles an hour?'

Three days later, Silver Link inaugurated the high-speed 'Silver Jubilee' service, Britain's first streamlined train. The four hour schedule for the 268.4 miles between Newcastle and Kings Cross made this the fastest scheduled service in the world over such a distance. On 27 August 1936, at the head of the northbound 'Silver Jubilee', A4 No2512 *Silver Fox* set another record: its 113mph at Essendine was the highest speed ever recorded for a steam-hauled train in Britain carrying fare-paying passengers.

By this point, however, the accolade of 'fastest locomotive' had passed to Germany (by now, the pursuit of the record had become a three-way affair between Britain, Germany and the United States). Engine No05.002, a 3-cylinder streamlined 4-6-4 of the Deutsche Reichsbahn, had taken the title by some margin with a speed of 124.5mph on 11 May 1936.

The 'Royal Scots' of 1927 represented the LMSR's first attempt to speed up its prestige services.

The locomotives that sparked the inter-company rivalry of the 1920s and 1930s were the Great Western's 'Castle' class 4-6-0s, among them No5020 Trematon Castle, seen passing Exeter St Thomas on a Wolverhampton-Kingswear service.

Over on the west coast, the London Midland & Scottish Railway, initially had little to compete with the Gresley Pacifics. Moreover, its management showed no inclination to become involved in a speed contest. Its priority was for engines that could undertake long, non-stop hauls, such as Euston-Glasgow, with heavy loads. By 1936, William Stanier's 'Princess Royal' Pacifics were doing precisely that.

However, late in 1936, a brief period of east coast-west coast rivalry was inaugurated. On 16 November, the second of the 'Princess Royals', No6201 *Princess Elizabeth*, worked a special from London to Glasgow (401 miles) at a record-breaking non-stop average speed of 68.2mph. This was increased to 70mph on the following day's return run. These runs were a prelude to the introduction of a new streamlined train to rival those of the LNER, the 'Coronation Scot'.

The motive power for the service was a refined, more powerful version of the existing Pacific design, the 'Princess Coronation'. Within weeks of emerging from Crewe, the first of the class, No6220 *Coronation*, was breaking records — and crockery. On 29 June 1937, on a trial run from Euston, it touched 114mph between Madeley and Crewe. Some of the 'timers' on board disputed the figure but what was indisputable was that on the approach to Crewe, with its 20mph speed limit, No6220 was doing 52mph. The brakes did their job, and the train stayed upright, but the contents of the restaurant car finished up in pieces on the floor!

The LMSR held the British speed record for just over a year. Then, on 3 July 1938, history was made when one of Gresley's A4s, No4468 *Mallard*, not only took the British crown, but the world's. The story of how Mallard attained its record of 126mph is told in 'The Famous Locomotives' chapter (p.104) but the event marked the end of the era of record-breaking, at least for steam locomotives. During 1939, Germany took the record for diesel, and Italy for electric traction. The former stood until 1972, the latter until 1954; *Mallard*'s steam record, however, looks set to stand for all time.

A speed of 100mph was first reliably attained by one of Nigel Gresley's LNER A1/A3 class Pacifics, an example of which — No2743 Felstead of 1928 — awaits departure from King's Cross. In the background stands one of Gresley's more humble designs, N2 class 0-6-2 suburban tank No4607.

THE GRESLEY ERA

For three stirring decades, the name of Nigel Gresley and the locomotives he built made headlines that reverberated far beyond railway circles.

Sir Nigel Gresley stands alongside A4 No4498 at Doncaster, the 100th Pacific-type locomotive built to his designs. Rightly, the LNER board voted to name the engine after the great locomotive designer.

Sir Nigel Gresley will always be associated primarily with the exploits of his Pacific classes and the crack expresses they hauled. However, the sum of his achievement was more far-reaching. He equipped the London & North Eastern Railway with a complete range of advanced locomotive types, from shunting tanks to fast freight engines. For this reason, many connoisseurs of locomotive design do not judge the highpoint of Gresley's career to be the record-breaking 126 mph run of his A4 Pacific, *Mallard*, which still stands today.

Instead, they point to the V2 2-6-2, arguably the finest heavy mixed traffic class built for any British railway. That said, the days of steam offered few more awe-inspiring sights than a line-up of Pacifics at the Kings Cross bufferstops, all bearing illustrious, evocative train headboards.

In his early years as Locomotive Superintendent of the Great Northern Railway, Gresley
was content to build on the work of Henry Ivatt,
his predecessor. He introduced an eight-coupled
mineral locomotive, a doughty shunting engine
(the so-called 'Ardsley tank') and a general purpose 2-6-0, or Mogul. This was superseded by two
beefier Mogul designs, the second of which was
the first British locomotive to carry a boiler six
feet in diameter.

This 3-cylinder 2-6-0 of 1920 (GNR H4 class,
LNER K3) was additionally noteworthy as the
first application of the refined version of Gresley's
conjugated valve gear. Developed in conjunction
with Harold Holcroft, this – along with the
3-cylinder layout – became the standard for
almost all Gresley's later locomotives. An exception was one of Gresley's final designs for the
Great Northern, a strong, nippy 2-cylinder 0-6-2
tank. The N2 became the mainstay of suburban
services out of Kings Cross for over 30 years.

The key event of the last days of the Great
Northern, however, was the appearance of the
first two Gresley Pacifics. The third, built under
LNER auspices, was No1472 (later 4472) *Flying
Scotsman*, which registered the first authenticated
100mph run and gained lasting fame.

Following his appointment as Chief
Mechanical Engineer of the LNER in 1923,
Gresley had charge of the locomotive affairs of all
its constituent companies. His approach was only
to impose his ideas where they were needed.
Where the previous regimes evidently had the
right motive power, as was the case with the Great
Central and Great Eastern, he did not interfere.
The B17 'Sandringham' 4-6-0 was his one contribution to passenger services on these routes, just
as the D49 4-4-0 – the last of its type built for the
LNER – was introduced on to secondary services
in Yorkshire, the North East and Scotland.

It was, though, his Pacific designs, particularly
the streamlined A4 of 1935 that set the seal on
the Gresley legend in the minds of the general
public. Of his other locomotives, the V2 2-6-2
proved its worth as a freight hauler during World
War II, while the K4 2-6-0 became the star
performer on the West Highland line between
Glasgow and Mallaig. The V1 and V3 classes
were first-rate passenger tanks and the most
numerous of the Gresley designs, the K3 Moguls
and J39 0-6-0s, were all strong, hard-working,
durable machines.

Gresley often broke new ground with his
designs and not all enjoyed success. The most

The A4 Pacific was the most celebrated of Gresley locomotives, but many observers consider his finest design to be the mixed traffic V2 2-6-2 of 1936. Altogether 184 of these superbly-proportioned 3-cylinder engines were built, including No4874 (at Darlington, in March 1940). As BR No60903 of King's Cross shed, it passes Harringay with a fast freight for the north.

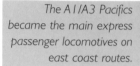

The A1/A3 Pacifics became the main express passenger locomotives on east coast routes.

spectacular failure was the revolutionary 4-cylinder compound built in 1929/30 and alternately known as the 'Hush Hush' or, less flatteringly, the 'Galloping Sausage'. This huge machine sported a high-pressure (a remarkable 450 pounds per square inch) water-tube boiler of a type normally used in ships. It was fabricated by Yarrow & Company of Glasgow and installed on a 4-6-4 chassis constructed at Darlington Works. The expectation was that No10000 would yield worthwhile fuel economies. The reality was the complete opposite, and the flaws went beyond mere teething troubles. In 1937, after a long spell in storage, No10000 was discreetly withdrawn and rebuilt along the lines of a streamlined A4.

Amazingly, even this maverick survived into the British Railways era, as No60700. Of the 1,500 or so steam locomotives built to Gresley's designs, only four were withdrawn before 1948 and one of those was an A4 Pacific destroyed during an air raid. Regrettably, only 11 Gresley engines live on in preservation.

Not all of Gresley's innovations were successful. Much was expected of the high-pressure 4-cylinder compound 4-6-4 No10000, seen here crossing the Forth Bridge, after it entered service in 1930. It employed a marine-type water tube boiler. Teething problems meant that of its 1,888 days on the LNER's books, 1,105 were spent in Darlington Works.

A GLITTERING CAREER

Son of a Derbyshire rector, ninth of the Gresley baronets, Herbert Nigel Gresley was born in Edinburgh on 19 June 1876. He enjoyed only modest academic success before leaving Marlborough College for a railway career. His first employer was the London & North Western Railway. For five years from 1893, he was a pupil of Francis Webb at Crewe. His apprenticeship completed, Gresley moved to the Lancashire & Yorkshire Railway, gaining valuable drawing office experience under the innovative John Aspinall. Then, as foreman of the L&YR's running shed at Blackpool, he learned the harsh practicalities of operating steam locomotives. By 1901, Gresley was the Assistant Works Manager of the L&YR's carriage works at Newton Heath, Manchester and, aged only 28, became Assistant Superintendent of the Carriage and Wagon Department.

With little prospect of advancement on the L&YR, in 1905 Gresley joined the carriage and wagon department of the Great Northern Railway. Six years later, and still only 35, he succeeded Henry Ivatt as the company's Locomotive Superintendent.

Gresley's career reached its zenith during the 1920s and 1930s, with some of the finest and most famous locomotive designs ever built. They, and the east coast expresses they hauled, excited attention everywhere and, in 1936, his achievements were recognised with a knighthood. In his honour, the LNER decided that the 100th Gresley Pacific, A4 No4498, would be named after its designer. Although after 1938 his health declined, Gresley continued to work with enthusiasm. He was taken ill shortly after the debut of his last locomotive design, the V4 2-6-2 of 1941, and died of a heart attack on 5 April that year.

Gresley had the confidence and vision to pursue an independent path, yet was open to ideas from outside. He acknowledged his debt to the pioneering work of Churchward on the Great Western and sought discussions with engineers from overseas, notably France's André Chapelon. Gresley's personal assistant on the LNER, Oliver Bulleid (who went on to become Chief Mechanical Engineer of the Southern Railway), described his chief in these words:

'He was incapable of ill-temper, but what I appreciated most was his wide-ranging interest in all engineering. He was always ready to adopt any suggestions, but only after consideration. It could be felt that if he agreed to try anything it would almost certainly be a success. He had a wonderful memory, was extremely observant and amongst other things could read a drawing in a way given to few.'

After two years in store, the experimental No10000 was rebuilt as a conventional 3-cylinder 4-6-4. In the process the external casing that had earned it the nickname 'Galloping Sausage' was replaced by A4-style streamlining. In this guise, the solitary member of the W1 class – seen thundering through Harringay on a northbound express – remained in service until June 1959.

AN ANXIOUS TIME

As the bringers of industry's raw materials and conveyers of its products, Britain's four main railway companies inevitably suffered the effects of the economic slump of the early 1930s.

In May 1926, the Trades Union Congress called a General Strike in support of miners resisting a pay cut. Railways were among the key industries affected and the government called a state of emergency. Troops and volunteers were brought in to maintain essential services, among them these naval ratings seen shunting wagons by hand at Nine Elms goods depot in south London.

The growing social unrest of the 1920s had already caused difficulties for the railways, most dramatically in the General Strike of 1926. Now, the 'Great Depression', triggered by the Wall Street Crash of 1929 brought mass unemployment and deprivation to many parts of Britain. As the slump began to bite, railways saw traffic decline sharply from the volumes carried before and during the war years. Simultaneously, competition from road transport grew stiffer. In 1930, pay cuts of two shillings in the pound were imposed on railway workers. Wage levels were not restored until 1937.

Britain's locomotive builders faced similar problems. Glasgow's North British Locomotive Company met with trade barriers even in traditional markets such as Australia. Additionally, the high value of the Pound against the Deutschmark gave German manufacturers such as Borsig and Maffei an advantage. Unable to compete on price, by 1927 NBL faced extinction. Its workforce dropped from 8,000 in 1920/21 to below 2,000 in 1932. Only the demands of World War II and the restocking of the world's railways after 1945 kept the company alive.

There were bright spots. Middle Class Southern England remained relatively prosperous and generated a boom in house/building across London's suburbs. Urban railways, such as the Metropolitan, profited handsomely from the growth in city/bound traffic, but by far the greatest number of commuters were carried by the Southern on its ever/widening network of electrified lines.

The rest of the 'big four' companies found alternative ways of boosting morale and – they hoped – profits. The high/speed luxury trains of the 1930s, and the chase for speed and haulage records, represented a defiant riposte to the prevailing mood of despondency and apprehension.

THE ART OF THE POSTER

Paradoxically, the troubled decades of the 1920s and 1930s were also the heyday of the unfailingly bright and optimistic railway poster. Regarded perhaps as a refreshing antidote to the gloomy pronouncements of newspaper billboards, posters were a key element in railways' publicity campaigns and in the competition for passengers. Each of the 'big four' companies refined its own distinctive style of poster advertising. Leading artists were commissioned and many of the results were striking and innovative. The subjects may well have been traditional – beaches, landscapes, picture-postcard towns and villages, historic cities, bathing belles – but the approaches were often highly original.

Railways also liked to remind passengers of the role they played in the nation's economic life and bucolic scenes would compete for space on platforms and in booking halls with powerful images of goods depots, factories, mines and steelworks. Posters played a key role in creating a good public image. This was nowhere better demonstrated than on London's Underground where, under the guidance of Frank Pick, posters were used to publicise services and encourage travel. Pick transformed the look and the public perception of the service, and such was the range of artists he employed, that the Underground became revered as an important art patron.

Nº 4 SEA BATHING

EAST COAST JOYS
travel by L·N·E·R
TO THE DRIER SIDE OF BRITAIN

PUBLISHED BY THE LONDON & NORTH EASTERN RAILWAY   HAYCOCK PRESS, LONDON

even popularised in song, although Sam did not endure in the nation's memory quite as long as the LNER's 'Jolly Fisherman' who found Skegness so bracing!

One member of the LNER's advertising department, Francis Goodricke, summed up the impact of posters during the interwar period:

'If for a moment it could be supposed that pictorial posters had no advertising value at all, their decorative value alone would still have justified their production.'

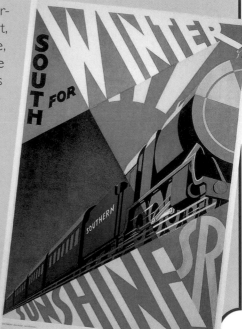

In 1927, the LNER elevated poster art further by mounting the first of series of poster exhibitions. Initially, the venue was the board room at King's Cross but the show subsequently moved to the New Burlington Galleries. Under John (later Sir John) Elliot, the Southern Railway made full use of posters to publicise its electrification programme and its services to the south coast. It created the character of 'Sunny South Sam', who was

1925
WEMBLEY

C. R. W. NEVINSON

MAKE UP A PARTY
AND OBTAIN FROM ANY
L·N·E·R STATION OR OFFICE
PARTICULARS OF
SPECIAL FACILITIES BY L·N·E·R

SOUTH for WINTER
SOUTHERN
SUNSHINE
SR

PLEASANT JOURNEYS

Once, carriage heating and electric lighting counted as luxury in train travel. Then a cabinetmaker from New York proved that passengers were happy to pay a premium to ensure a pleasant journey.

Since the 1860s, the name 'Pullman' has been synonymous with luxury train travel. Appalled by the accommodation provided on most services, George Mortimer Pullman, a cabinetmaker from Brocton, New York, set new standards for US railroads with his custom-built rolling stock. In 1873, his Pullman Car Company reached an agreement to supply vehicles to the Midland Railway, and Britain's first Pullmans entered service between London and Bradford in 1874. The cars were prefabricated at the Pullman works in Chicago and assembled at Derby. By the end of the year, 36 were in service, including 11 sleeping cars.

The layout of the coaches followed the American pattern, with the parlour cars consisting of a single open saloon. Unfortunately, this was not to the taste of many British passengers who preferred the comparative privacy of compartment coaches. The Midland introduced another Pullman service, this time from London to Manchester, in 1878 but the public reaction remained lukewarm.

Undeterred by the Midland experience, the London, Brighton & South Coast Railway inaugurated the first all-Pullman train in Britain in 1881. It also had the distinction of being the first British train to be electrically lit throughout. On 2 October 1898, the LB&SCR instituted a 60-minute 'Limited Pullman' service between Victoria and Brighton that evolved into the famous 'Brighton Belle' (see *right*). After this, Pullmans steadily appeared on more routes in the east and south of the country.

Britain's most glamorous trains, however, were those operated during the 1930s, particularly by the LNER. It set the standard with new stock for the Kings Cross-Edinburgh 'Flying Scotsman'. The facilities – regarded by some as gimmicks – included a hairdressing saloon, ladies' 'retiring room' and a cocktail bar. Restaurant cars were furnished in Louis XIV style with armchairs, concealed lighting and hand-painted decor.

However, the trains that truly captured the public imagination were three luxurious streamliners, all rostered to be hauled by Nigel Gresley's A4 Pacifics. The first, the 'Silver Jubilee' of 1935, marked the jubilee of King George V and ran between Kings Cross and Newcastle. It seated over 200 and the facilities included a bar offering a choice of no fewer than 46 cocktails. Four-course meals were served at your seat.

In the coronation year of King George VI and Queen Elizabeth, 1937, the LNER added two more streamliners: the 'Coronation' from London to Edinburgh, and the 'West Riding Limited' which journeyed from Kings Cross to Leeds. In summer months the 'Coronation' included an observation car at the rear. The decor of the whole train was described by one commentator as 'more like a boudoir than a railway carriage'. All three services proved both popular and, for the LNER, profitable.

Somewhat reluctantly, the LMSR responded to the LNER's success by introducing its streamliner, to be hauled by the new 'Princess Coronation'

New rolling stock was provided for the LNER's 'Flying Scotsman' service between London King's Cross and Edinburgh Waverley in 1928, the year non-stop running was introduced. First class restaurant cars were furnished Louis XIV style and diners sat in comfortable free-standing chairs. Ladies, it is noted, lunched in their hats!

Pacifics. However, the accommodation on board the Euston to Glasgow 'Coronation Scot' did not rival that of the LNER trains. In truth the 'Scot' was a more a face-saver for the LMSR, borne out by the fact that the rolling stock consisted largely of refurbished vehicles. New coaches were not constructed until 1939, when an entire 'Coronation Scot' train went on exhibition in the United States. The brief, but spectacular, era of the high-speed luxury streamliner ended the same year, on 31 August, four days before the outbreak of war. It had been an entertaining diversion from the railways' main business, but it showed the potential was there to offer improved services on a broader level – if they cared to put their minds to it.

BRIGHTON'S 'BELLE'

The London, Brighton & South Coast Railway began running its all-Pullman 'Southern Belle' between Victoria and Brighton in 1908, describing it as 'the most luxurious train in the world'. It was a service rather than a single train, with two trips (later increased to three) in each direction. It was set a 60-minute non-stop schedule and, at summer weekends, could be loaded to 11 or 12 vehicles, amounting to a load of 400 tons. The last steam-hauled 'Southern Belle' ran on 31 December 1932. Thereafter, the train was taken over by five-coach multiple units, the first electrically powered Pullmans anywhere. Three services were run daily in each direction, usually formed of two units to make a ten-car train. From 1934, the service was renamed the 'Brighton Belle'.

Some were sceptical about the value of a Pullman journey lasting only 51 miles, but the service proved very popular, not least with Brighton's artistic community. Commuters enjoyed a standard of service normally only available to long-distance travellers, with the London-bound morning service renowned for the kippers served at breakfast.

Apart from the war years, the 'Belle' ran uninterrupted until 1972, when British Railways' Southern Region considered the rolling stock 'worn out'. Its demise probably had more to do with having to provide 14 train attendants for what was a relatively modest number of passengers.

THE CAPACITY FOR CHANGE

From trailing the other 'big four' railway companies in terms of locomotive development, William Stanier's 'mighty restocking' put the LMSR out in front.

In its first eight years, the LMSR had built less than 400 locomotives that might be described as up-to-date. In a locomotive fleet of over 9,700, it was a pitifully poor effort. Its passenger services generally depended on either pre-1923 classes fast approaching retirement age or underpowered 4-4-0s. Freight fared little better, with the load shared between ageing 0-8-0s and hard-working, but limited 0-6-0s. Worryingly for the LMSR board, its Chief Mechanical Engineer, Sir Henry Fowler, appeared incapable of turning the situation around.

Early in 1931, Fowler was shepherded into the post of Assistant to the Vice-President and replaced as CME by Ernest Lemon. He was, though, only a stopgap. In truth, the LMSR had no one on its staff capable of lifting the company from its position, which was — in terms of locomotive development — as the least progressive and most inadequately equipped of the 'big four'. It needed someone untainted by the bitter

Unlike his counterpart on the LNER, Nigel Gresley, Stanier was not one for experimentation (which was just as well as the LMSR's motive power situation could not justify it). His one foray into the unknown was the so-called 'Turbomotive' of 1935. The Swedish-inspired Pacific design passes Hatch End, probably on its way to Liverpool.

rivalries that divided the engineering teams at Crewe and Derby. The new man would also be familiar with current thinking on locomotive design. For Sir Harold Hartley, the LMSR Vice-President in charge of engineering and research, the man to modernise the LMSR was William Arthur Stanier, and he was promised a free hand in undertaking it.

Stanier came from the Great Western, a railway that had instigated a similar modernisation programme a quarter-of-a-century earlier. He had been at the core of the Churchward revolution and appreciated its guiding principles. Unsurprisingly, since his expertise lay in application rather than innovation, Stanier imported those principles to the LMSR. Even if he had wanted to, he had little scope or time for experiment. Instead Stanier played to his strengths: a sound knowledge of contemporary workshop practice; the skill to get the best available performance from proven techniques; and the practical experience to tackle the problems of high maintenance and running costs.

Upon taking up his post with the LMSR in 1932, Stanier took stock of his inheritance. With its numerous and diverse classes of L&NWR, L&YR and Midland origin, plus those of the constituent Scottish companies, it was all far removed from the policy of standardisation prevailing on the GWR. For Stanier, only a similar policy would allow the LMSR's locomotive department to meet current and future demands, and counter increasing competition. It was to be a process of 'scrap and build', what one commentator called 'a mighty restocking' of the LMSR's motive power fleet. There were three prime requirements. The first was for an express

A TRUE PROFESSIONAL

What sort of individual did the LMSR succeed in prising away from Swindon? As an engineer, Stanier's credentials were impeccable and he had railways in the blood. Born in Swindon on 27 May 1876, he was the son of a chief clerk of the Great Western Railway. Educated at Wycliffe College, Stanier started his apprenticeship at Swindon in 1892. Upon its completion he joined the drawing office and became engaged in locomotive design work. Other positions followed, including a spell in charge of locomotive depots in the London area. This led to his return to Swindon as assistant to the locomotive works manager and other promotions followed until he became manager himself in 1920. When Charles Collett replaced G.J. Churchward as CME of the Great Western in 1922, Stanier soon became his principal assistant.

Collett was only five years older than Stanier, which meant that he had no immediate prospect of gaining the Chief Mechanical Engineer's post at Swindon. Despite his loyalty to the GWR, the offer that came from the LMSR in 1931 was irresistible. His move earned the blessing of the GWR Chairman, Viscount Churchill, and the good wishes of his colleagues at Swindon, where he was held in high esteem. William A. Stanier became CME of the LMSR on 1 January 1932.

Stanier had the capacity to recognise talent and make good use of it. He assembled a sound team from within the LMSR ranks, Robert Riddles and George Ivatt among them. They found Stanier to their liking. He was a man of few words, decisive but not doctrinaire.

Misjudgements were acknowledged then rectified. A very approachable individual, Stanier treated his engine crews and workshop staff as he would the company chairman.

A deep bond grew between Stanier and his team. His personality and diplomacy eventually united the warring factions within the LMSR, which allowed its locomotive department to forge ahead of its rivals. It was no coincidence that Stanier's key assistants came to dominate the locomotive side of the nationalised British Railways.

As an engineer, Stanier was held in high regard, not only by his colleagues on the LMSR, but throughout the railway community. In 1936, he went to India as part of a team reporting on railway operations for the British government. That year, he was also elected President of the Institution of Locomotive Engineers.

World War II saw Stanier increasingly involved at a national level, first with the Railway Executive (which had been set up to run the railways on behalf of the government). Posts followed with the Ministry of Production and the Aeronautical Research Council, as well as a directorship with Power Jets Ltd.

Stanier was knighted in 1943 and became a Fellow of the Royal Society the following year. In the USA, he was awarded an honorary Doctorate of Science. It was fitting recognition for a professional engineer who had served his employers, and his country, so well. In 1944, Stanier resigned as CME of the LMSR, although he had not been directly concerned with locomotive matters there for over two years. Sir William A. Stanier FRS died on 27 September 1965 aged 89.

---

passenger locomotive capable of taking 500-ton trains single-handed from London to Glasgow. Next, the LMSR urgently needed a versatile mixed-traffic engine, similar to the GWR 'Hall'. The final priority was for a modern heavy freight locomotive.

Though convinced of the rightness of Great Western practice, Stanier was honest enough to acknowledge its limitations. It soon became apparent that what worked with Swindon engines

did not necessarily transfer to the conditions prevailing on the LMSR. Such flexibility was prudent. A couple of miscalculations early on came close to jeopardising his position. There were those in the LMSR hierarchy who were keen to point out the failings of Stanier's designs.

The very first Stanier engine, a 2-cylinder Mogul, was one of them. It incorporated several tried-and-tested GWR features and performed well, if unspectacularly. The prototype was

outshopped from Crewe in October 1933 sporting a GW-style safety valve bonnet. If this gesture was intended to make Stanier feel at home, it failed. He swiftly ordered its removal.

Greater scrutiny was reserved for the next Stanier project, the much-vaunted Pacific design for the Euston-Glasgow run. The two prototypes of the 'Princess Royal' class appeared in 1933 and, by LMSR standards, were awesome machines. However, their massive boilers were insufficiently served by the Swindon-type superheater, and they steamed poorly. The problem was resolved, and the class went into limited production in 1935.

There were more intractable failings with the 3-cylinder 5XP 4-6-0 introduced in 1934 for secondary passenger work. The need for such locomotives was so pressing that the risk was taken of ordering a quantity straight off the drawing board with no prior evaluation of a prototype. Unfortunately, they proved poor steamers, and the class underwent several modifications before, in 1935, being named in honour of the Silver Jubilee of King George V and Queen Mary. The 'Jubilees', as they were known thereafter, finally proved up to the job and for three decades were the mainstay of LMSR/LMR cross-country workings and the masters of stopping services on the West Coast and Midland main lines.

THE SAD TALE OF THE 'TURBOMOTIVE'

Normally, William Stanier was averse to exotic experiments but the third of his Pacific-type locomotives used a new, and promising method of propulsion. In Sweden, the performance of a turbine-driven 2-8-0 had created great interest. Significant savings in fuel and maintenance costs were claimed for the Ljungstrom turbine. It had other attractions, too, including the elimination of hammerblow to the track.

Using turbines supplied by Metropolitan Vickers, the 'Turbomotive', as No6202 would soon become known, was built at Crewe in 1935. Measured up against some other British locomotive experiments, it was remarkably successful. Performance figures were excellent: 2,000 horsepower generated at over 70mph with a 500 ton load on a gradient of 1 in 300 for example. However, the predicted fuel savings did not fully materialise. Nevertheless, but for World War II, a quantity of turbine-driven engines may have been produced. Instead, No6202 suffered from the problems that afflict any 'one-off', chiefly long waits for spare parts. The engine's best year was 1936, when it ran 73,268 miles.

When, in 1950, its turbines needed replacing, BR decided to rebuild the locomotive as an almost conventional member of the 'Princess Royal' class, and named it Princess Anne. Sadly, only four months out of Crewe Works, No46202 Princess Anne was wrecked in the Harrow-and-Wealdstone rail disaster of October 1952.

Not all of Stanier's designs had to go through this prolonged gestation, involving the adaptation of Swindon niceties to the 'common denominator' of the LMSR. Four were successful from the outset: the 8F heavy freight 2-8-0; the 3-cylinder 2-6-4 tank; that quintessential Stanier engine, the Class 5 4-6-0 (the 'Black Five'); and Stanier's masterpiece, the 'Princess Coronation' Pacific.

Between 1933 and 1937, William Stanier and his design team produced a range of locomotives that went on to serve the LMSR and British Railways for over five decades. At the highpoint of production, between 1935 and 1939, Crewe Works was replacing around 220 engines each year. By the time he was seconded to the wartime Ministry of Production department in 1942, 1,280 Stanier-designed locomotives were in service. Hundreds more were built up to 1951 and, in 1968, Stanier engines closed the book on BR steam.

On 25 May 1937, the first of the streamlined 'Princess Coronation' Pacifics was rolled out of Crewe Works for inspection by, among other luminaries, its designer. Wearing a bowler, William Stanier stands in conversation by the front buffer.

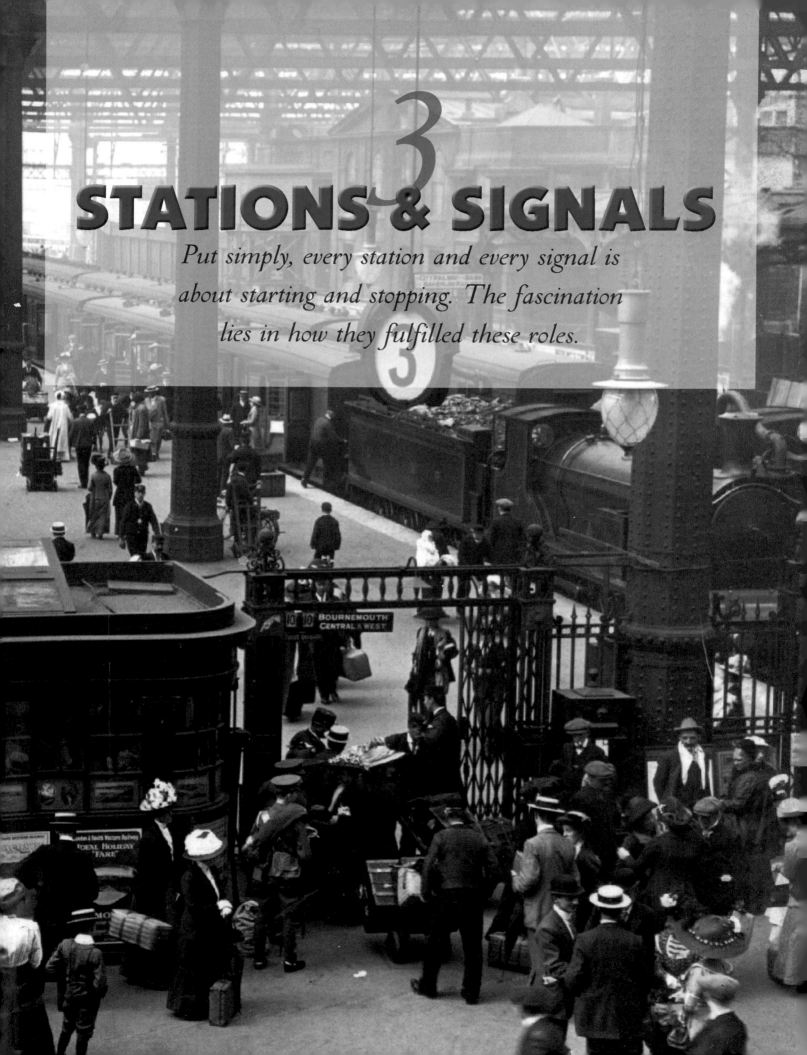

3
STATIONS & SIGNALS

Put simply, every station and every signal is about starting and stopping. The fascination lies in how they fulfilled these roles.

IMAGE BUILDINGS

It was where a railway welcomed its customers, but the impression left by a station was created by more than bricks and mortar, or concrete and glass.

For any self-respecting railway company, its stations were more than places where passengers boarded and alighted from trains. They were where it could take the first,

The great sweep of York's station roof, dating from 1877.

and perhaps most important, step in projecting its public image. The architecture of its major stations had to impress and inspire confidence. If the station looked a shambles, what did that say about the safety of the trains?

Naturally, beyond the spires, arches and porticos, the station also had to provide the necessary facilities: somewhere to book tickets, enquire about services, examine timetables and take shelter while waiting. The opportunities to refuel mind and body – refreshment rooms, bars and bookstalls – were later additions. However, as early as 1848, the London & North Western Railway, accepted an offer from W.H. Smith & Son to sell newspapers on its stations. It was the beginning of W.H. Smith's rise to become the largest retailer of books, newspapers and magazines on Britain's railway network.

As traffic expanded, so did station facilities. In came separate ladies' rooms, offices for the staff (particularly the stationmaster), parcels and left luggage offices, and the all-important lamp room where, before the introduction of mains electricity, the station's oil lamps were stored and refilled. Later, kiosks selling sweets and tobacco were erected and larger stations might also boast fruit and flower stalls, a shoe repairer's and a barber shop along with other retail outlets.

However, these were all peripheral pleasures. No one – except perhaps John Betjeman and Nikolaus Pevsner – consoled themselves with studying station architecture while their train was delayed. They wanted an explanation, an estimated time of arrival, and only people could provide those. From the stationmaster down, no station – no railway, for that matter – was better than the people who served it.

THE SOUL OF THE PLATFORM

The importance of the stationmaster, as the most high-profile among the visible representatives of his company, was not always fully appreciated. Depending on the size of his station and its mixture of traffic, he had surprisingly diverse responsibilities. It was to the stationmaster that the railway's customers would address their questions about the service offered, be it passenger, parcels or a pigeon special. People expected him to know the answers, whether it was a question of goods rates, train times, connecting services or the arcane rules and regulations enshrined in the 'Conditions of Carriage'. He was, of course, always at the receiving end of complaints when any service failed to live up to expectations.

At smaller stations, especially those with a high percentage of goods traffic, the stationmaster would be well acquainted with the peculiar demands of local businesses and traders. To most passengers, however, the stationmaster was a somewhat imposing figure, immaculate in his uniform and peaked cap (or, at important stations, even a top hat – for special occasions). At such stations, he might be in charge of a staff of over 150. While working within his area of responsibility, even locomotive crews were obliged to follow his instructions.

Two of the stationmaster's key responsibilities were safety in train working and the security of buildings, equipment, stores and money. After coming on duty, he would call on his supervisors to discuss any difficulties likely to arise during the day. He would examine traffic notices relating to special train workings or engineering operations, and in the telegraph office check the flow of messages. At a large station, the telephone system would have been in use all the time, passing instructions from one location to another. The stationmaster was also required to visit signal boxes within his domain and check the signalman's train register.

Three important aspects of working on which the stationmaster tried to keep a daily check were train punctuality, the cleanliness of trains, and staff performance. Events right across the system could affect train running; but every delay occurring at the station would be recorded and probably notified to the district office. Alongside such routine duties he would have to deal with the unexpected, anything from fare-dodgers to train failures.

Above: Off-peak at Liverpool Street's suburban platforms, 3 June 1920.

THE LONDON TERMINUS

With one exception — the rebuilt Euston — London remains served by a ring of thirteen main-line stations constructed between 1838 and 1899. None shares the same architecture, or the same atmosphere.

London's stations led double lives. At Waterloo, a traveller looking up at the destination indicator might have been about to board an ocean liner express for Southampton. Equally, he or she could have been checking the time of the next service to Surbiton. An intermingling of local and long-distance trains was a feature of all the capital's principal stations, resulting in some striking contrasts in passenger accommodation (and in the passengers themselves, for that matter).

With the opening of Marylebone Station in 1899, the 'ring' of main line stations around central London was completed, and remains intact for the most part today. The Great Central Railway had grand ambitions for its four-platform terminus, but Marylebone was never as busy as the Great Western's Paddington. Facing fierce competition from other companies and attracting only light commuter traffic, it is no wonder that Marylebone was described, with heavy irony, as 'an oasis of peace amidst London's noise and bustle'. This haven was chosen by British Railways as the location of their headquarters between 1949 and 1991.

London's first terminus, opened in 1836, was at London Bridge. It was followed in 1838 by Euston, the name coming from the family that owned the land on which it was built. Architect, Philip Hardwick, included an imposing Doric arch — a tangible interpretation of the station's role as a gateway to the north. Eleven years later a magnificent Great Hall and Shareholders' Room were added, but this was all so much window-dressing. Euston Station itself was a clutter of piecemeal, haphazard enlargements and

well deserving of the rebuilding plans put forward by the LMSR in the 1930s. These were halted by the outbreak of war but, in 1968, a new station was opened in conjunction with the electrification of the West Coast Main Line. The demolition of the Doric portico and Great Hall caused a furore, although it is difficult to see how they could have been fitted into the new structure. All that survives of the old Euston is the statue of Robert Stephenson that graced the Great Hall and the two entrance lodges that stand either side of the entrance on Euston Road.

Two other companies built stations on the Euston Road. In 1852, the Great Northern Railway opened King's Cross, an elegant Italianate-style building designed by Lewis Cubitt. Unlike Euston, the layout at King's Cross was very 'passenger-friendly', and remained so even after the construction of adjacent suburban platforms between 1875 and 1895. Operationally, however, the station presented problems: within fifty yards of the platform ends, all trains were funnelled into the picturesquely named 'Gas Works Tunnels', and faced a fierce climb on a gradient of 1 in 107. During World War II, long corridor trains often extended beyond the platforms and into the tunnels.

In 1868, King's Cross gained a grand neighbour on the opposite side of Pancras Road, simply called St Pancras. The Midland Railway's new station boasted the largest single-span arch in Britain. At 110 feet high and 243 feet wide, engineer W.H. Barlow's web of iron and glass is exceeded only by three other station arches in the world, all in the United States. Not content with this engineering grandeur, the Midland added its

Opposite: Sunshine and shadows on the eastern side of Victoria Station, originally home to the London, Chatham & Dover Railway and, for a time, the Great Western. It was from these platforms that the continental boat trains departed, although the carriages on the right have a more 'local' look.

Victorian Gothic hotel — the work of Giles Gilbert Scott — in 1876. Additionally, a large goods depot, known as Somers Town, was included on the western side of the development. Following its closure, the depot has become the site of the new British Library. St Pancras itself has also been threatened with demolition, yet has not only survived but been selected as the terminus for the Channel Tunnel Rail Link.

Brunel's Paddington rivals St Pancras for grandeur and spaciousness. The original plan was for Great Western trains to share the London & Birmingham (later London & North Western) terminus at Euston, a proposal that the GWR's directors wisely rejected. The first station in what, at the time, was the village of Paddington, opened in 1838 and remained in use until 1854, by which time Brunel's new three-span structure was complete. Among London's main-line stations, Paddington has been particularly fortunate insofar as subsequent alterations and extensions have been largely sympathetic to the original

conception. It survived the changeover from broad to standard gauge in 1892 and, in 1916, the incorporation of a fourth roof span and additional platforms (by 1931, Paddington was handling over 200 departures each day). Only the German Luftwaffe managed to disturb the architectural equilibrium, damaging the Great Western offices and boardroom during an air raid in 1941. These were only partially reconstructed.

The other major terminus serving the south-west is Waterloo, located on the south bank of the River Thames, and established by the London & South Western Railway. Like Euston, the station was something of a hotchpotch during the nineteenth century. Unlike Euston's proprietors, however, the L&SWR did something about it and, in 1900, set about building what would by 1921 become the largest and, arguably, the finest station in the kingdom. A vast ridge-and-furrow roof embraced 21 platforms and a spacious concourse, while the elegant curved frontage housed the L&SWR's offices. Waterloo's crowning glory was — and remains — its imposing entrance. Built of Portland stone and inscribed with the names of the company's war dead, the 'Victory Arch' stands at the head of a sweeping flight of steps.

On the north side of the Thames stands Victoria, the aptly titled 'Gateway to the Continent'. This was the terminus for the 'Golden Arrow', 'Night Ferry' and other boat train services. Until 1924, Victoria consisted of two separate stations, the first built by the London, Brighton & South Coast Railway and opened in 1862. Two years later, the London, Chatham & Dover Railway opened for business next door. Rebuilding of the Brighton station was undertaken between 1906 and 1909 but, with the LC&DR terminus to one side and Buckingham Palace Road to the other, there was no scope for sideways expansion. The LB&SCR therefore extended the platforms to accommodate two trains simultaneously. After the Grouping, the Southern Railway cut an arch in the wall between the stations and renumbered the platforms consecutively. The distinctions of 'Brighton side'

TERMINAL DECLINE

Although several London terminuses have undergone major changes in recent years, only two of them have disappeared entirely: Holborn Viaduct and Broad Street.

Opened in 1865, the latter was the city station of the North London Railway.

At one time, it was London's third busiest terminus, with over 700 services a day heading for Watford, Richmond and the northern suburbs. In 1900, 50,000 passengers each weekday used its trains, rivalling the Great Eastern's station at Liverpool Street, which had been built next door.

By the 1920s, five of its eight platform 'roads' had been electrified. The London & North Western, which had absorbed the North London, provided handsome and well-appointed trains for the new service. They were colloquially known as 'Oerlikon stock', after the Swiss manufacturers of the electrical equipment employed.

After World War II, however, Broad Street experienced a gradual decline. Passenger numbers dropped to 9,000 a day in 1969 and the place took on a melancholy air. Platforms were shut and the roof partially removed to reduce maintenance costs. The only reminder of Broad Street's existence lives on in the name of the development, Broadgate.

and 'Chatham side' remained, with the cross-Channel services concentrated in the latter.

Victoria is the most westerly of several termi-nuses that serve London's southern suburbs. Another is the station nearest the heart of the capital, Charing Cross. Opened in 1864 by the South Eastern Railway, its six platforms still han-dle a considerable volume of commuter traffic, as well as services to Sussex and the Kent coast. On leaving the station, trains cross the Thames on Hungerford Bridge. Charing Cross was one of several London stations to boast a hotel. Its inte-rior was particularly sumptuous; no less a figure than the poet, Sir John Betjeman, considered its dining room to be the finest in London.

Further along the Thames, the combined through station and terminus at Blackfriars opened in 1886. It had been preceded in 1877 by a six-platform terminus and hotel at Holborn Viaduct, built by the London, Chatham & Dover Railway to relieve congestion at its Ludgate Hill station. The latter was closed in 1929 but has been revived as part of the Thameslink network, which has brought trains back onto the old through lines to link up with London

Underground's Metropolitan Line at Farringdon. Though Blackfriars has been extensively rebuilt, the 54 stones that formed its entrance arch have been incorporated in the new concourse. They bear the names of destinations, at home and abroad, that were once accessible from Blackfriars. Cannon Street, along the river from Blackfriars, was built by the South Eastern Railway to cater for commuters working in the City of London. It was once notable for its splen-did, 190-feet span trainshed and Baroque towers. They framed many a memorable photograph from the age of Southern steam.

The most easterly of the Southern's terminuses was London Bridge. Originally the home of the London & Greenwich Railway, it came to be used by a number of companies. By the 1860s, the sta-tion needed enlargement but the then occupants, the South Eastern Railway and the London, Brighton & South Coast Railway, could not agree on a plan. In 1863, they opened two new adjacent stations and built a wall to divide them. The SER then constructed five high level through plat-forms that allowed trains to go on to its new city stations at Cannon Street and Charing Cross.

Built by the South Eastern Railway in 1866, Cannon Street conveyed City of London commuters to and from north Kent through Dartford and Sevenoaks. It also provided services to the coast, notably Hastings and Ramsgate. In this 1950s scene, a four-car electric unit shares the station with 'West Country' Pacific No34005 Barnstaple. The splendid arched roof was demolished in 1958.

With further enlargement, by 1902 there were 21 terminal and through platforms and the viaduct leading away from the station had to be widened to accommodate eleven tracks. Although the Southern Railway linked the two stations in 1928, finding your way around London Bridge has never been straightforward.

The handful of platforms at Fenchurch Street caused little confusion, especially as the number of destinations was limited. Built in 1841, and tucked away in a side street, it has always been one of London's quietest stations, only coming alive during the rush hours. Although owned by the Great Eastern and then by the LNER, most of the trains leaving and arriving at Fenchurch Street were operated by the Midland Railway and its successor, the LMSR. The London, Tilbury & Southend Railway, which served Southend-on-Sea and Shoeburyness, had been absorbed into the Midland in 1912. Serving Essex and the Thames Estuary remains Fenchurch Street's sole function, although the generations of express tank locomotives that once sprinted the seven miles to Barking have been replaced by less exhilarating electric multiple units.

When, in 1874-75, the Great Eastern replaced its Shoreditch terminus with a new station at Liverpool Street, there were those who predicted 'white elephant' status for the £2 million neo-Gothic structure. However, such was the growth in commuter traffic from north and east London, and from Essex that, by 1894, the GER had added eight more platforms on the Bishopsgate side of the station. The new section came to handle trains to Chelmsford, Colchester and the Essex coast, and was a beneficiary in 1949 of electrification using the overhead system. The original platforms served Enfield, Chingford, and the Lea Valley, while the longer central platforms

Above right: The entrance to the L&SWR's 'necropolis' station adjacent to the main terminus at Waterloo. Left: Inside the Great Central Railway's Marylebone station in summer 1921.

YOUR LAST TRAIN

What to do with London's dead was a question posed by the capital's population explosion during the late 19th century. The London Necropolis & National Mortuary Company believed it had the answer as the city's burial grounds ran out of space. It obtained permission to build a vast cemetery at Brookwood, west of Woking, some 30 miles from London. The key factor, however, was that the cemetery was situated beside the London & South Western railway line from Waterloo. At Waterloo itself, a dedicated 'necropolis station' was built next to the main terminus and one or two trains each day conveyed both the deceased and mourners to Brookwood. The service ceased in 1941.

accommodated express services to East Anglia. With a road dividing the station, getting around Liverpool Street was something of a trek until the rebuilding in 1991. The work, which retained the magnificent west-side trainshed with its cantilever roof, is sympathetically done and one of London's busiest stations is now one of its most agreeable.

DOWN TO THE STATION

Remarkably, in cities such as York, Chester and Bristol, railway stations were the largest buildings built since the medieval cathedrals. It was a link some railway companies liked to emphasise.

A Birmingham-Paignton train starts away from Bristol Temple Meads behind Stanier 5MT 4-6-0 No44805. The present station – a joint effort by the GW and Midland Railways – dates from 1878 and replaced Brunel's original terminus.

Victorian railway builders generally sought a high standard of station architecture. Many of the first stations of importance were drafted along classical lines, with John Dobson's design for Newcastle Central – built between 1846 and 1855 – one of the finest. Further south along the East Coast Main Line, York station remains equally impressive.

Designed by Thomas Prosser, its three arched roofs, laid out in a long, sweeping curve, represent railway architecture at its best. Built by the North Eastern Railway to replace an earlier structure, the station dates from 1877 yet still performs its modern role supremely well.

However, such structures proved too expensive for some companies, while others opted for

more exotic forms. The late Victorian fashion for Gothic grandeur is nowhere better expressed than in the Midland Railway's London terminus, St Pancras, or at Carlisle Citadel. Other architectural styles adapted for railway use included Norman castles or Tudor and Jacobean mansions. At Liverpool Street, and in north London, the Great Eastern Railway's stations took on an almost ecclesiastical feel.

Gradually, apart from their terminus buildings, railway companies evolved a 'company style' for station architecture. They aimed at a measure of standardisation, principally because considerable savings could be made by mass-producing items such as doors and window frames. The London & North Western used wooden construction extensively and was able to bring about standardisation

on a large scale. On the other hand, the North Eastern Railway's brick built suburban stations resembled the Victorian villas inhabited by the more prosperous of their regular passengers.

To economise on the building of its 'London Extension', the Great Central Railway built island stations with a single, broad platform serving both north- and southbound trains. The matter of access was solved by building a staircase down from a road overbridge. Examples survive on the preserved section of the GCR, at Loughborough, Quorn and Woodhouse, and Rothley. Some stations, such as the LNWR station at Rugby, comprised one long island platform, sufficiently wide to accommodate bay platforms at each end.

A particular feature of the British station was its platform canopy or awning. These varied from

By now privately preserved, LNER A3 Pacific No4472 Flying Scotsman leaves Edinburgh Waverley with an excursion to north-east England in June 1968. Waverley is a 'through' station, rather than a terminus, and was rebuilt to its present form during the 1890s. Its location, at Edinburgh's historic centre, has always been controversial.

flat, timber decks to the elegant glass and iron canopies favoured by the Midland. Much local station building, however, became utilitarian in the extreme, while many large stations grew piecemeal fashion. For anyone unfamiliar with the eccentricities of the layout, they could be very confusing places indeed. A good example was Edinburgh Waverley, which caused local outrage when built in the elegant heart of the city with lines cutting through the green space of Prince's Gardens.

Some companies were reluctant to embark on large-scale reconstruction until it was forced upon them. Even allowing that it spanned World War I, the rebuilding of Waterloo, in London, took 20 years. Some stations were rebuilt more than once – Birmingham Snow Hill, Crewe and Preston – for example. Glasgow Central was also constructed in two stages, first in 1879 and then 1901-06, but succeeded in becoming one of the most agreeable and conveniently laid-out terminals in the country.

A host of fine stations disappeared with the line closures of the 1960s, but many wayside buildings survive, either converted to new homes or business premises or simply lying derelict. They still allow the extraordinary diversity of railway architecture to be appreciated. So do many of the stations on preserved railways, from the charm of Horsted Keynes on the Bluebell Railway, to the clean, simple functionalism of Bolton Street, at Bury, on the East Lancashire Railway.

The problem for British Railways and its successors has been reconciling the need to care for its architectural inheritance, which includes many listed buildings, and supply the facilities expected by passengers and staff on a modern railway. For the most part this has been achieved. However, there have been notable disasters, of which the 1960s rebuilding of Birmingham New Street is arguably the worst. This station became a gloomy, unwelcoming basement laden with choking diesel fumes that can only be dispersed at the price of the station becoming a freezing, dusty wind tunnel.

STEAM ON SCREEN

Many film-makers have often seen great opportunities in railway stations, and railways themselves for that matter. The all-too-believable atmosphere and characters within the station add enormously to the appeal of David Lean's *Brief Encounter* (1945). It is, after all, a lump of ash from a passing locomotive that lands in Celia Johnson's eye and prompts the fateful encounter with Trevor Howard. (Although purporting to be set in the Home Counties, *Brief Encounter* was filmed at Carnforth, in Lancashire.)

Another great director, Alfred Hitchcock, used trains to great effect both in *The Lady Vanishes* (1938) and *The Thirty Nine Steps* (1935), with Robert Donat in the lead role. Less dramatically effective – indeed, it is all rather laboured – is *Train of Events* (1949) starring Jack Warner as an engine driver involved in a train crash. Enthusiasts love the film, though, as it features extensive footage shot around the Willesden locomotive depot in London!

Another London location, King's Cross, is at the heart of one of the finest of the Ealing comedies, *The Ladykillers* (1955), which has Alec Guinness at his most sinister and Peter Sellers at his funniest. The comic potential of the rural railway is exploited in two other British films, *Oh, Mr Porter* (1937), which has Will Hay on top form as an idle and incompetent station-master, and another of the Ealing comedies, *The Titfield Thunderbolt* (1952). And who can fail to have been touched by the first version of Edith Nesbit's *The Railway Children* (1971). Escaping steam can never have been used to better effect than in the reunion between father and daughter – except, perhaps, to draw attention to Marilyn Monroe's attributes in 1959's *Some Like It Hot!*

Above: Filming at Marylebone Station, London, August 1974. Here, preserved GW 4300 class 2-6-0 No5322 has a role in the espionage caper One Of Our Dinosaurs Is Missing.

In the hands of the railway companies royalty certainly fared better than some station buildings did. Almost from the start, the larger companies considered it their duty to provide special transport for the monarch. Some built entire trains of sumptuously appointed vehicles for the royal entourage. The locomotive(s) and coaches of royal trains were always immaculately turned out and a unique engine headcode was devised to clearly identify the regal service from all other rail traffic.

The first royal railway journey was made by Prince Albert and his brother, Ernest, from Slough to Paddington on 14 November 1839. Queen Adelaide, widow of King William IV, first travelled by train in 1840. She seemingly enjoyed the experience since the London & Birmingham Railway soon built a four-wheeled saloon for her personal use.

On 13 June 1842, Queen Victoria became the first reigning monarch to travel by train. Again the journey was from Slough to Paddington, the Queen having come from Windsor by coach. She pronounced herself 'quite charmed' by the experience and went on to use trains to travel to all parts of Britain, although never at speeds greater than 40 miles per hour. Anything above that would result in a reprimand.

Queen Victoria's journeys involved considerable planning. For her journey between Holyhead and Windsor on 27 July 1900, various instructions were issued including:

'A look-out man must be placed on the engine tender of the Royal Train and must keep his face towards the rear of the Train, so as to observe any signal that may be given.'

King Edward VII did not want to travel in the vehicles used by his mother. As a result, no fewer than three new royal trains entered service during his brief reign, including vehicles still regarded as masterpieces of the coachbulder's craft. However, it was an expensive way to travel, as bills sent to the royal household between 1904 and 1909 make clear. Charges were levied not only for passengers, but for the menagerie of royal dogs.

King George V and Queen Mary found the Edwardian saloons to their liking and no more royal carriages were built until 1941, by the LMSR. With war raging, it was recognised that the vehicles could be a target for air attack, so they were armour-plated. They were withdrawn from service in 1977.

The Royal Train is still used on occasions, with haulage entrusted to a brace of specially maintained Class 47 diesel-electrics, Nos47798 *Prince William* and 47799 *Prince Henry*.

A right royal reception at Newcastle-upon-Tyne in September 1906 for King Edward VII (in plumed helmet at lower left of picture) and Queen Alexandra.

THE LEVERS OF POWER

From the remotest country outpost to a huge installation controlling a major junction or city terminus, the role of signals – and signalmen – has always been the same: to safely regulate the passage of trains.

A fine array of semaphore signals frames rebuilt 'Patriot' class 4-6-0 No45514 Holyhead as it starts away from Shrewsbury with a local service to Crewe. As the locomotive was allocated to Camden depot (1B) in London, this was almost certainly a 'running-in' turn after an overhaul at Crewe Works.

There was much for a signalman to learn. First, he had to understand the principles that governed the entire signalling system. Second, he had to be familiar with every signal and set of points in the section of line controlled from his signal box. Third, he had to recognise his codes: bell codes that told him about the trains entering his section, and the codes formed by lamps (or discs) mounted on the front of locomotives to classify each train. Express passenger, stopping goods, light engine, even a royal train, all were indicated by different arrangements of lamps. As if that were not enough to assimilate, he had to be acquainted with any documents – special traffic notices, for example – of relevance to the signal box, or boxes, in which he worked.

The procedures that every signalman was required to follow, including the actions to be taken in emergencies, were enshrined in books of rules and regulations: the 'Signalman's General Instructions' and 'Block Regulations'. They would be examined on these, and on every other aspect of the job, before being 'passed out' and given responsibility for a signal box.

'Block Regulations' referred to the basic signalling system employed throughout Britain's railways. It was known as 'Block Working'. Every line was split into sections each controlled by a signal box. Trains were kept apart by maintaining an appropriate distance, or section, between them. Importantly, the 'section' was an interval of space, rather than time, between trains. This allowed the length of sections to vary with local conditions. On open stretches, where trains ran at high speed, the distance could be considerable. Approaching a busy station, where trains were moving relatively slowly, the sections might be only a few hundred yards long and trains could pass from section to section close behind each other. This was essential if rush-hour commuter services were to be efficient. Nevertheless, no train could enter a 'block section' until the train ahead had cleared by a safe margin.

It was the signalman's job to set up the 'road' for approaching trains. At major junctions this could be a complicated process. A diagram above the signal levers displayed the track layout with the points marked with numbers. These corresponded to the numbers on the levers. The signalman was helped in selecting a road by reference to a detailed working timetable. This listed all the engine and stock movements that did not appear in the public timetable, together with their precise times. The approaching train would also have been 'described' to him in advance by a bell code sent by the signal box controlling the previous section. Automatic locking devices ensured that, as far as was practicable, the signalman could not move points to set up conflicting train movements, or give 'proceed' signals that could lead to collisions. Having dealt with the train, the signalman was required to enter in a train register the times and circumstances of all signals received and sent. Apart from the discipline this instilled, if there was an incident, the register was indispensable evidence at any inquiry. At busy signal boxes, 'booking boys' were employed to keep the register.

Much of Britain's signalling was still mechanical at the time of nationalisation, with signal box levers changing the positions of semaphore signals by means of wires and rods. However, electrically-operated colour light signalling had been introduced on busy sections as far back as 1920, when the Liverpool Overhead Railway became the first overground line in Britain to use colour light signals. The system of signalling with lights was used even earlier in underground railway tunnels – with the first application being in 1898 on the Waterloo & City Railway in London. Lights could not be used on overground railways until lamps and lenses had been developed that generated a light powerful enough to be seen over distances during the daytime.

With the spread of electric power, it became clear that the best type of signalling to develop was a system that combined electrically powered signals and operation of points. Combining power

One of the H15 class 4-6-0s designed by Robert Urie for the London & South Western Railway, No30333 takes the West of England line at Clapham Junction on 5 August 1950. It is passing under the timber-built, 103-lever 'A' signal box.

working and electrical interlocking eliminated the need for levers as the signals could be operated by switches and buttons mounted on panels, While the points would be moved automatically by electric motors. This enabled a complex 'road' to be set up in a few seconds. First installed in the 1930s, these panels allowed much larger areas to be controlled from a single location. Electricity also made the monitoring of rail traffic easier as an electrical 'bridge' was formed across rails carrying low voltage 'track circuit' currents when a train entered the section. This made the circuit active, illuminating a light on the signalman's track diagram, enabling him to be aware of the position of every train.

The creation of large 'panel' boxes, one of the key components of the 1955 Modernisation Plan, meant the closure of many of the familiar lineside signal boxes. For signalmen, the physical side of the work – the pulling and releasing of levers – may have gone, but the role remained the same.

Inside the signal box at Dunbridge, on the Southampton-Romsey-Salisbury line, with the track diagram (top right) and the bell codes listed. Such vintage installations were becoming a rarity when this photo was taken in August 1974.

63

4
RURAL RAILWAYS

Picturesque branch lines; ribbons of steel
snaking across moors, valleys and rivers —
all serving the remote corners of the country.

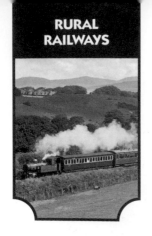
WE HAD BRANCHES EVERYWHERE

From Dornoch Firth to Malvern Wells, from Ballachulish to Hayling Island, at Three Cocks Junction and Tollesbury, once there were branches to just about everywhere in the country.

The 6.25-mile branch between Axminster and Lyme Regis opened in 1903 and from 1913 to 1960 was home to William Adams' famous 'Radial Tanks', one of which, No30583, is seen near Combpyne. The branch closed in 1965, but No30583 survives on the Bluebell Railway.

In his film guide, Leslie Halliwell summed up the 1952 Ealing Studios comedy *The Titfield Thunderbolt*, as 'Showing the England that is no more'. Made a decade before the axe began to fall on the majority of British Railways' branch lines, it tells how a motley group of locals resolve to save their picturesque railway by way from closure. Overcoming mishaps and sabotage by the rival bus company, they succeed in their endeavour. Much is owed to a quirk of the licensing laws relating to the serving of alcoholic beverages on moving trains!

The film conveys the charm of the country branch, if little of its harsh reality. Even in 1952, the viability of many of the rural branch lines in England, Scotland and Wales was questionable. Ten years on, it is unlikely that the villagers of Titfield would have saved their railway. Closure notices would have been posted and a progressive run-down of services, seemingly devised to discourage passengers, initiated. An inadequate replacement bus service would have been offered and, after a token public meeting or two, train services withdrawn. Soon after, the track would

have been lifted and the line's structures demolished. Nature would quickly reclaim the trackbed while the village wrestled with a growing parking problem. Residents would complain about traffic congestion blighting what had once been a pleasant and peaceful place to live.

It has to be admitted that many branch lines had outlived their usefulness. Some, built for a specific source of traffic, became redundant. Others had suffered progressive run-down since before World War II, something all-too-evident in the antiquated rolling stock and elderly engines they employed. For many, the appearance of suitable modern locomotives, such as the 2MT 2-6-2 tanks of the LMSR, came too late. The traditional caricature of a branch line engine, a wheezing, creaking museum piece, was all too accurate.

This was especially true of lines on the Southern Region, where it was very much a case of the 'haves' and 'have nots'. The 'haves' were electrified. The 'have nots' did the best they could with ageing 0-6-0 and 0-4-4 tanks and a variety of venerable 0-6-0s. The Wainwright H, Adams 02 and Drummond M7 classes of 0-4-4 tank put in decades of work on the branches of Kent, Sussex, Hampshire, Dorset and Devon. The Havant to Hayling Island line, however, was monopolised to the end by Stroudley 'Terrier' tanks built in the 1870s. The weight limit on Langstone Bridge permitted nothing heavier.

The branches of East Anglia left some abiding images: a six-coupled, or 2-4-0 goods engine plodding across the fields and between the hedgerows with the daily pick-up goods; or a 2-4-2 tank pulling into a somnolent country halt with a couple of vintage Great Eastern coaches. Merely climbing aboard one of these vehicles, with its faded upholstery, sepia prints promoting the delights of east coast resorts, sagging luggage racks and well-worn leather window straps, was to travel back in time. The names – the Kelvedon & Tollesbury Light Railway, the Wisbech & Upwell Tramway – said it all.

Scotland could boast an abundance of what the guides would now call 'scenic routes'. There was the lovely ten-mile branch from Kirkcudbright to Castle Douglas, closed in May 1965. None was more dramatic than the Oban-Connel Ferry-Ballachulish line that hugged the banks of Loch Leven and Loch Linnhe and was worked, like so many Highland branches, by McIntosh 0-4-4 tanks of Caledonian Railway origin. These engines also supplied the motive power on the glorious run from Killin to Killin Junction, on the Callander to Oban line. Ominously, due to the sparse population in the area, the section from Killin to Loch Tay was closed as early as 1939.

The most north-easterly of North British Railway branches was that from Montrose to the fishing port of Inverbervie. It merited a daily

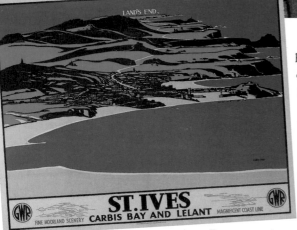

ST.IVES
CARBIS BAY AND LELANT MAGNIFICENT COAST LINE
GWR FINE MOORLAND SCENERY GWR

The terminus of the St Ives branch, photographed in 1957, with a Churchward Prairie tank about to depart with a three-coach train for St Erth, junction for the Plymouth-Penzance main line. Although the station here has been demolished, this Cornish branch – extolled in a GWR poster (left) – remains open for business.

pick-up goods until closure in 1967. Undoubtedly the most photogenic branch in the area was the seven-mile run from Dornoch to The Mound. This had been the domain of Drummond 0-4-4 tanks until the Civil Engineer revised the weight limit to accept BR Standard 2MT 2-6-0s. In June 1960, the final workings on the Dornoch branch were undertaken by – of all things – a pannier tank imported from the Western Region.

With such gems as the Cheddar route and the Lyme Regis branch, the West Country and Wales rivalled Scotland for photogenic lines. Comparing maps old and new reveals just how much has gone from ex-Great Western territory, and how towns such as Monmouth and Brecon were once railway 'hubs'. The cathedral city of Wells, in Somerset, once boasted three stations; Dowlais, in South Wales, had four. Malmesbury, in Wiltshire, lost its train service in 1951 but the Culm Valley line from Tiverton Junction, in Devon, to Hemyock was kept open by its milk traffic until 1973.

Like many GWR branches, the Culm Valley was home to the delightful 1400 class 0-4-2 tank engines, which were equipped for push-pull working. Charles Collett, originator of the 1400, put considerable effort into producing new motive power for the GWR's by-ways. Along with the 1400, he developed the 1600 class pannier tank which was a lighter version of the standard 5700 class. Another variant of the 5700, the 6400 class, was push-pull fitted. The 5600 class 0-6-2T was specifically designed for the steeply graded Welsh valley lines.

The territorial ambitions of, principally, the Midland Railway, ensured there were outposts of the LMSR deep in the heartlands of the LNER and GWR. A 26-mile ex-Midland tentacle meandered from Hereford along the River Wye to join the Cambrian Railway system at Three Cocks Junction. It closed in 1962. The Midland also built a line from Ashchurch, in Gloucestershire, through Tewkesbury and Upton-on-Severn to Malvern Wells. Victorian 0-6-0s were put out to grass there.

Interestingly, the seed from which the entire Midland tree grew was a minor branch line. The erstwhile Leicester & Swannington Railway ran from West Bridge, Leicester, to Desford Junction. Sadly, this historic line, built in 1832-33 by Robert Stephenson, closed in 1966.

To the east of Leicester, the town of Seaton boasted two celebrated London & North Western branches. The one to Uppingham ran for almost four miles and, in the late 1950s, was graced by handsome tank locomotives displaced from the London, Tilbury and Southend line. It closed in 1960, leaving the Seaton-Luffenham Junction (and on to Stamford, by way of the Midland) line as the last steam-operated push-pull service in Britain.

ON THE MOOR

One of the most famous and atmospheric of Great Western branches wound its way on to Dartmoor. It began life in September 1823 as the Plymouth & Dartmoor Railway set up to carry granite from the quarry at King's Tor. An Act of 1878 authorised its substitution by the Princetown Railway, which was completed in August 1883. Services were operated by the Great Western and ran to-and-from Horrabridge before the opening of a junction station at Yelverton in May 1885.

During the 1920s, three additional halts were built along the 10.5-mile route, at Burrator, Ingra Tor and King's Tor. Ten trains each weekday tackled the 1 in 40 climb to the terminus at Princetown, 1,373 feet above sea level. They mainly conveyed hikers and ramblers out to enjoy the scenery, but there was also traffic to-and-from another local attraction – the notorious Dartmoor Prison.

In the final years of steam haulage, Stanier, Fairburn and Ivatt tank engines were the mainstays of most ex-LMSR branches. Yet it had not been all that long since Webb and Aspinall 2-4-2Ts were in evidence all over north-west England, or Johnson 1P 0-4-4Ts were at work in West Yorkshire. The peculiar nature of some lines brought an extended lease of life for some

Dwarfed by its carriages, ex-LB&SCR Stroudley 'Terrier' tank No32662 leaves Havant with a Hayling Island branch service in July 1963. Under four months later, in November, the 4.5 mile south Hampshire line closed.

The charm of the country branch line is captured in this 1958 scene at Colyford Station, on the ex-L&SWR branch between Seaton Junction and the resort of Seaton, on the south Devon coast. Drummond M7 class 0-4-4T No30046 is ready to leave for Seaton Junction. The branch opened in March 1868 and closed in 1963. However, it is still possible to travel between Seaton, Colyford and Colyton on the Seaton Tramway.

SERVING RAJAHS AND THE RAF

A seven-mile branch from Kemble, on the Swindon to Gloucester line, to Tetbury opened in 1889. It was initially noteworthy for the intermediate stop of Rodmarton Platform. This was the first Great Western 'platform', a term it had borrowed from Scottish railways and which represented something between a simple unstaffed halt and a fully fledged station.

'Platforms' were longer than halts and usually were staffed by senior grade porters. They sold tickets and dealt with parcels and other traffic, such as milk.

At Tetbury, in the 1930s, the platform was lengthened to accommodate trains bringing wealthy Indian rajahs and their polo ponies to the Beaufort polo fields at Westonbirt.

At the end of that decade, in 1939, Jackaments Bridge Halt was opened for the benefit of a different set of high-fliers: Royal Air Force personnel based at the nearby Kemble aerodrome.

During the 1920s, the GWR employed the Tetbury branch as the test-bed for a new type of locomotive it hoped would improve branch line working. Built by the Sentinel Waggon Works and introduced in 1926, this vertical-boilered, gear-driven engine was not a success. However, the fortunes of the line were transformed with the introduction of diesel railbuses in the 1950s. Passenger numbers increased by 150 per cent but it was not enough to save the branch, which closed on 5 April 1964.

A SUFFOLK STORY

In 1900, mid-Suffolk was a sparsely populated area mainly given over to agriculture. The area's development was held back by poor transport links. Purely for the social benefits it would bring, a railway was a necessity. Predictably, this laudable notion found no takers among the major banks so local people resolved to undertake the project themselves.

Their plan was to build a line from Westerfield Junction, near Stowmarket, to Halesworth, between Saxmundham and Beccles. Things began well. In 1901, the Duke of Cambridge came to Westerfield to cut the first sod. The ceremony was attended by 600 guests, who enjoyed a fine lunch to the accompaniment of music from two regimental bands.

What the folk of Westerfield were unaware of was that the ever-expanding Midland Railway was supposedly seeking access to an east coast port. On hearing this, their fellow investors altered the route so that the railway would run from Haughley rather than Westerfield. Haughley was nearer to Cambridge, which was where any new line would have to connect with the existing Midland route from Kettering. The work at Westerfield was abandoned. Nevertheless, even with its junction at Haughley, the line lost money for all concerned. Building never progressed beyond Laxfield, some six miles short of the original target of Halesworth.

The Mid-Suffolk Light Railway enjoyed its moment of glory during World War II when it served nearby US Air Force bases. On 28 July 1952, however, the last passenger train ran from Haughley to Laxfield with ex-Great Eastern J15 0-6-0 No65447 in charge.

The following year, another J15 – No65404 – became the last locomotive to work over the line. It hauled the demolition train that lifted the track.

elderly tank engines long after their illustrious tender engine contemporaries had vanished. The running shed at Barrow Road, Bristol, for example, had to maintain a pair of ex-Lancashire & Yorkshire built 0-4-0 saddletanks of 1901 vintage – the diminutive 'Pugs' – solely to work the Avonside Wharf branch.

While some branches were curiosities, others could be spectacular. As the roads of the Lake District are clogged with tourist traffic, there must be regrets that the 40-mile long line from Penrith to Workington was allowed to close. In its last days, Troutbeck, Keswick, Braithwaite and Cockermouth were home to one of the last, and finest of branch line engines, the LMSR Ivatt 2MT 2-6-0.

However, if one type of locomotive epitomised the branch line scene, it was the Great Western Prairie tank that was originally developed by G.J. Churchward. Picture in the mind a green Prairie, a rake of chocolate-and-cream carriages, a neat country station bedecked with spring flowers, a porter going about his business, whistling, milk churns and a luggage trolley on the platform, and it was almost possible to believe that the England of *The Titfield Thunderbolt* had really once existed.

Push-pull fitted 6400 class 0-6-0 pannier tank No6412, coupled to a auto-trailer, approaches Standish with the 9.30am Chalford-Gloucester in August 1964. Many GW rural services were worked by these auto-trains. No6412 now operates on the West Somerset Railway.

TICKET TO RYDE

Untouched by modernisation, the railway system of the Isle of Wight could transport you across an era as well as across an island.

It was a melancholy occasion when, on New Year's Day 1966, Class 02 0-4-4T locomotive No14 *Fishbourne* took the very last steam-hauled train out of the resort of Shanklin. It was not just a sadness at the passing of a handsome class of passenger tank engines, or of a unique railway system. More, it was the uneasy feeling that, while some sections of the Isle of Wight's railways were superfluous to requirements, the eradication of all rail links to towns such as Cowes and Ventnor was a miscalculation that locals and visitors would come to regret.

The send-off given to Fishbourne was doubtless similar in style, if not mood, to the one that took place in 1862, when islanders enjoyed their first taste of rail travel. The four-and-a-half mile Cowes and Newport Railway offered a delightful trip alongside the River Medina, with trains headed by 2-2-2 tank engines built by Slaughter, Gruning & Company of Bristol.

In 1864, the Isle of Wight Eastern Railway (the 'Eastern' was later dropped) opened a line between Ryde and Shanklin. Two years later it was extended to Ventnor, a task that included boring a 1,312-yard tunnel between Wroxall and Ventnor. For motive power, the Eastern railway opted for a quartet of 2-4-0 tanks built by Beyer Peacock of Manchester and it was these engines that began the tradition of naming locomotives after places on the island. Ryde, Sandown, Shanklin and Ventnor subsequently were joined by Wroxall, Brading and Bonchurch.

Adams O2 class 0-4-4T NoW26 Whitwell storms away from Newport with the 2.18pm train from Ryde to Cowes on 13 November 1965. Built at the L&SWR's Nine Elms Works in 1891 as No210, this locomotive was among 23 O2 tanks shipped to the Isle of Wight by the Southern Railway, arriving in June 1925. It was also one of the last withdrawals, in 1966.

pier, carrying the railway to a new station at Ryde Pier Head. Though operated by the Isle of Wight railway companies, construction of the pier was financed from the mainland by a joint committee of the London & South Western and London, Brighton & South Coast Railways. Then, in 1882, the grandly named Brading Harbour Improvement and Railway Company opened a branch line from Brading to Bembridge. Five years later, in 1887, the Ryde & Newport and Cowes & Newport Railways merged to form the Isle of Wight Central Railway. Newport was established firmly as the hub of the system when, in 1889, the Freshwater, Yarmouth & Newport Railway opened, serving the less populated west-ern half of the island. For 25 years the FY&NR was content to let the Isle of Wight Central Railway supply its locomotives and rolling stock but a bitter dispute in 1913 forced a change of policy. Relations became so acrimonious that the IWCR refused the FY&NR access to its terminus at Newport, forcing the latter to build another station 100 yards down the line!

The FY&NR immediately acquired two sec-ond-hand engines for itself. The first, No1 Medina, was a Manning Wardle 0-6-0ST that had been employed on the mainland during con-struction of the Great Western/Great Central

Yet another railway company to set up business was the Isle of Wight (Newport Junction) Railway that, in 1875, inaugurated a cross-island line between Sandown and Shide. Four years later, it extended the short distance from Shide to Newport – and promptly went bankrupt! In its time, the IoW(NJ) bought just one locomotive and hired another.

Soon after the opening of the IoW(NJ)R, the Ryde & Newport Railway established a link between those two ports and, noting the success of the Beyer Peacock tanks elsewhere on the island, ordered two for itself. What a glorious sight they must have looked in the R&NR red liv-ery with their copper-capped chimneys and gleaming brass domes. They enjoyed working lives of nearly 50 years, No4 *Cowes* being retired in 1925 and No5 *Osborne* the following year.

Despite the bankruptcy of the Isle of Wight (Newport Junction) Railway, which was taken over as a joint operation by the Ryde & Newport and the Cowes & Newport Railways, the 1880s saw further significant developments of the island system. First, in 1880, came the opening of Ryde

MAKING THE WIGHT CHOICE

In the main, the island's enginemen enjoyed working on the Adams O2 tanks, although some engines were much pre-ferred to others. At one stage, before overhaul, NoW30 *Shorwell* became almost impossible to fire because of the thick coating of scale in its boiler. Maintaining steam pressure was a full-time job for any fireman. Conversely, NoW29 *Atherstone* was regarded as an exceptionally good machine after its post-war overhaul at East-leigh and could be trusted to cope with an extra coach over the normal load.

Mr White, the signalman at Havenstreet on the Newport-Ryde line, exchanges single-line tokens with the fireman of O2 class 0-4-4T NoW24 Calbourne as it draws into the station with the 9.30am from Cowes on 31 August 1965. Havenstreet is now the home both to today's Isle of Wight Steam Railway, and to Calbourne, the sole survivor of the once 60-strong O2s.

Joint line. More significantly, the second locomotive was one of eight ex London Brighton & South Coast Railway Stroudley A1/A1X 0-6-0 tanks that saw service on the Isle of Wight over a 48 year period from 1899. The island's connection with these famous engines – the much loved 'Terriers' – is still evident today on the Isle of Wight Steam Railway.

The final link in the island system was completed by the Newport, Godshill & St Lawrence Railway, which perceived a need for a direct link between Ventnor and Newport. This it achieved by establishing a new station at Ventnor West and connecting with the Sandown Newport line just east of Merstone. Building southwards, it reached St Lawrence Halt in 1897 and Ventnor in 1900. The line was worked by the IWCR until 1913 when it was absorbed by the Central company.

Several other schemes for railways on the island never came to fruition. One was for a tunnel beneath the Solent to link up with the L&SWR at Lymington. It is interesting to speculate how that might have changed the course of the Isle of Wight railway story. The principal reason for the system retaining its period charm was the cost of ferrying new equipment across the water.

Consequently the Southern Railway inherited a motley bunch of locomotives when it took over the island's railways in 1923. There were 19 in all, the largest group being the Beyer Peacock 2-4-0 tanks. Some of these had accumulated over five decades' service. Twenty years earlier, the Isle of Wight Central Railway had contemplated buying surplus William Adams designed 02 0-4-4 tanks from the London & South Western but the plan came to nothing. However, the suitability of these engines was never in doubt and, in 1923, enough were available to restock the Isle of Wight fleet. Not that the 02 was a new design: it had been introduced in 1889.

The first two 02s arrived at Ryde Pier Head in May 1923 and were unloaded with the assistance of the Admiralty's floating crane. (In 1925, the Southern installed its floating crane at Medina Wharf to assist in transferring stock to and from the mainland.) Two further 02s arrived in 1924 as 'kits of parts' and were reassembled by fitters bought over from Eastleigh Works. By 1928, a further ten engines were at work and, during the 1930s and 1940s, 02s were sent to the island as and when required to replace life expired engines. In total, there were 21 in service at nationalisation in 1948 and these were joined by two more a year later.

VICTORIA'S STATION

Queen Victoria's stays at her favourite home, Osborne House, brought royal patronage to the Isle of Wight railways. The Queen herself encouraged the building of a private station at Whippingham, on the Ryde-Newport line and, in her journal noted her first journey by train on the island. This occurred on 11 February 1888, when the Queen visited the Royal National Hospital for Consumption at Ventnor. The entry indicates that Her Majesty was well satisfied with the railway service.

After the inevitable downturn during World War II, by 1950 tourism was again booming on the Isle of Wight. Some three million visitors came each year, with up to 60,000 arriving at Ryde on summer Saturdays. This, together with local traffic, ensured the 02 tanks were kept busy. Over summer weekends, the early hours would find the depot at Ryde St John's Road a hive of activity. Twenty-six crews would report for duty and a succession of engines would run off-shed, the first at 2.50am Saturday morning. After collecting its train, it would make for Ryde Pier Head ready to form the 4.05am departure for Ventnor. Throughout the day, locomotives returned for ash clearance and refuelling. However, the first line closures were only two years away and, in 1955, the first of the island's 02s was retired.

The final eleven 02s saw out the last year of steam operation, 1966, and two survived into 1967 to work engineers' trains on the Ryde to Shanklin line. This was the only stretch of the once-extensive Isle of Wight system to be spared the axe by British Railways and the decision was taken to electrify it. Continuing the century-old pattern, the motive power was again second-hand: ex-London Transport tube trains.

Just one 02 survives, NoW24 *Calbourne*, and it can be seen – along with two of the island's Stroudley 'Terriers' – at work on the Isle of Wight Steam Railway, running between Smallbrook Junction and Wootton.

Ferries were used to transport locomotives and rolling stock across the Solent to-and-from the Isle of Wight. Here, Adams O2 0-4-4 tank No211 is taking to the water. Having entered L&SWR service on the mainland in 1892, No211 was despatched to the island in 1923, where it was unloaded courtesy of the Admiralty's floating crane. It subsequently became NoW20 Shanklin.

THE CROSS-COUNTRY RUN

They crossed the high hills, hugged the river valleys, and connected country towns in search of often elusive customers. But one thing the cross-country lines never lacked was character.

One of the many fine structures on the Settle-Carlisle line, Batty Moss Viaduct at Ribblehead. In September 1971, it was still conveying the Class 47 diesel hauled 'Motorail' between Kensington Olympia, in London, and Perth.

These days the term 'cross-country' generally describes routes other than those radiating from London that link the cities of Scotland, the north-east and the north-west with the Midlands, Wales, East Anglia, the West Country and the south coast. These, however, are simply main lines that avoid the capital. The true cross-country line shuns cities. Instead it links country towns and coastal resorts, villages and hamlets, sometimes in ways that owe more to the politics of 19th century railway building than the convenience of the travelling public. Lines were built because gaining a railway connection was considered a matter of civic pride. Others were constructed to bridge a gap in the network and reap the passenger and freight traffic eager to use the new link. Such traffic rarely existed in the anticipated quantities.

Often the attraction of a cross-country route lay in its air of independence, something that no amalgamation, or even nationalisation could eradicate. The most celebrated of English cross-country routes was the Somerset and Dorset, but there were others of similar character: the Didcot, Newbury & Southampton; the Midland & South Western Junction Railway; the trans-Pennine Stainmore route; and the Midland & Great Northern Joint Railway.

The Somerset & Dorset was the product of a merger between the Dorset Central and Somerset Central Railways. Thanks to connections on to Burnham-on-Sea and Bournemouth, it hoped for

a profitable traffic between the Bristol and English Channels. This did not happen, but it did have the output of the Somerset coalfield to sustain it. The S&D sought to improve its fortunes by building a line between Evercreech and Bath, which gave it onward access to Bristol and the Midlands. Completed in 1874, the route made a bold crossing of the Mendip Hills with tunnels and viaducts, and – inevitably – some stiff gradients. It was costly to build and expensive to operate, and the company went into bankruptcy.

Attracted by its north-south links, the S&D was leased by the Midland and London & South Western Railways, who formed a new company, the Somerset & Dorset Joint Railway. From the mid-1880s, holiday expresses from the north and the Midlands to south coast became a feature of S&D operations but when such through traffic ceased in 1964, local traffic was insufficient to halt its decline. The Somerset & Dorset closed for business in March 1966.

Another magnificent route across the high hills was that between Darlington, Barnard Castle, Kirkby Stephen, Tebay and Penrith, which surmounted the Pennines at Stainmore, 1,370 feet

above sea level. Here was a line with a clear purpose. It linked the ports of the North Sea with those of the Irish Sea and united the industries of the north-west with those of the north-east. Coal and coke from Durham and Northumberland travelled west to the ironworks of Workington and Whitehaven, while Cumbrian ore fuelled the blast furnaces of Tyneside and Teesside. From a railway viewpoint, the line supplied a useful link between the East and West Coast Main Lines, at Darlington and Tebay respectively.

The Stainmore route was carried over two imposing viaducts, at Deepdale, west of Barnard Castle, and at Belah, east of Kirkby Stephen. The latter was an extraordinary structure, built in the trestle style favoured in North America. Along

SNOWDONIA
LONDON MIDLAND AND SCOTTISH RAILWAY

This 1930s poster extolling the splendour of Snowdonia was produced for the LMSR, which had access to North Wales thanks to its inheritance of ex-LNWR lines to Blaenau Ffestiniog, Caernavon and Llanberis, at the foot of Snowdon.

LMS THE ENGLISH LAKES
SCAFELL AND WASTWATER

its 1,040 feet length, the columns making up its 16 spans were connected by a lattice-work of horizontal and diagonal tiebars. Moreover, at 196 feet, Belah was the loftiest viaduct in England.

Although nominally independent, the Stainmore line was worked from its opening in 1861 by the Stockton & Darlington Railway, and subsequently by the North Eastern Railway. At the turn of the century, mineral trains travelled the line day and night but, after World War II, freight traffic declined and closure followed in 1962. Regrettably, the majestic iron viaducts were demolished.

Similarly, little now remains of Scotland's most famous cross-country line, the so-called 'Waverley Route' running between Edinburgh and Carlisle. Its construction owed more to the fierce competition between the Caledonian and North British Railways than to commercial necessity. To take on the Caledonian, which ran from Carlisle to Edinburgh by way of Carstairs, the NBR elected to lay tracks over 43 miles from the border city to Hawick. Here, they would meet the NBR's existing line from Edinburgh to Hawick, which took in Galashiels and St Boswells. Construction, however, was dogged by problems and bad weather, and the line was completed a year late and £400,000 over budget.

The 'Waverley Route', which climbed to 1,006 feet above sea level at Whitrope Summit, ran through inhospitable and largely uninhabited country that generated little intermediate traffic. Even during its best years, annual revenue from many of its stations was counted in hundreds rather than thousands of pounds. Protests were voiced, but it should have surprised no one when the line closed in January 1969. A more debatable Scottish closure was that of the direct route from Dumfries to Stranraer by way of Castle Douglas. After modest beginnings, the line prospered following the introduction of through sleeper services from Euston and the increase in ferry services to Ireland. The route also saw intense traffic during both world wars. Yet, since its closure in 1965, reaching Stranraer by rail from the south has meant travelling in a vast loop by way of Glasgow and Ayr.

Reaching into the heart of Norfolk did not require the feats of engineering encountered in the Pennines or the Scottish Borders. Thanks mainly to the Great Eastern Railway and its constituent companies, the county had one of the best rural railway networks in Britain. However, this did not deter the Great Northern Railway and the ever predatory Midland Railway from seeking a share of the traffic. In 1893 they formed the Midland & Great Northern Joint Railway to take over a predominantly rural network encompassing King's Lynn, Fakenham, Norwich, Cromer and Great Yarmouth. Connections to the MR and GNR main lines were made through Wisbech and Peterborough. Along with the main line between King's Lynn and Great Yarmouth, the M&GNR gained branches from Melton Constable to Norwich and Cromer. Melton Constable, a small, remote village, found itself the hub of this network and boasted a locomotive depot and workshops. However, the M&GNR empire began to shrink in the 1950s, and with passenger services ceasing by the end of the 1960s, Melton Constable returned to its earlier tranquillity and anonymity. Something of the old atmosphere that characterised M&GNJR services can be sampled today on the North Norfolk Railway, which operates over ex-M&GNJR metals between Sheringham and Holt.

The same is true of the preserved Llangollen Railway and Bala Lake Railway, the sole surviving sections of the Great Western's line along the Vale of Llangollen between Ruabon, Bala and Barmouth. This only became GWR property over its entire length in 1923. Until then, trains from Ruabon stopped at Dolgellau where the GWR met its rival, the Cambrian Railway. The latter owned the Dolgellau to Barmouth section and was in no mood to share it. Insanely, passengers and freight had to change trains to continue to the coast, which explains why revenues from the line were consistently modest.

Despite the growth of tourism in 1930s, the line failed to realise its potential. Flood damage closed the Barmouth Junction to Llangollen section in 1965, and closure of the stretch from Llangollen to Ruabon followed in 1968.

Many such cross-country routes were axed during the 1960s, although a number escaped despite being on Dr Beeching's list. Now generally single tracked, with bus shelters instead of station buildings, and 'Sprinter' units providing a semblance of a service, they somehow survive even though they are hopelessly uneconomic. One reason for their existence is the current political unpopularity of railway closures. Another is the enthusiasm and determination shown both by railway staff and local support groups.

Top: It may be 2 April, but snow still lies thick at Cockermouth as a diesel multiple unit arrives forming the 9.25am from Workington to Penrith and Carlisle. The Workington-Keswick section closed soon after.

Above: On the Somerset & Dorset Joint line in pre-nationalisation days, 1922-built Midland Railway 4F 0-6-0 No4558 approaches Midsomer Norton & Welton with a passenger service.

5
GOING AWAY BY TRAIN

*A day by the sea or a works outing; the start
of a family holiday — invariably the
excitement began with a train ride.*

TO THE SEASIDE

Time was when, for the majority of Britons, going on holiday meant travelling by train. How many childhood memories centre on trips to the seaside, whether for the annual family holiday or just a day out?

The 13-coach 'Cornish Riviera Express', hauled by a 'King' class 4-6-0, heads for Paddington packed with returning holidaymakers. Navigating the sea wall in south Devon, the train is about to enter Parson Tunnel, on the approach to Dawlish.

The train journey was part of the excitement, especially if riding behind a 'big' engine was a rarity. For the adults, it meant an escape from the daily routine, time away from the usual surroundings of factories, mills, teeming back streets or dreary suburbs. Workers in the Lancashire cotton towns headed for Blackpool, Lytham, St Annes, Southport and Morecambe. From Liverpool, it was a relatively short journey to Rhyl or Llandudno on the north Wales coast. Across the Pennines, the citizens of Leeds and Bradford would head for Scarborough, Bridlington and Filey. Glaswegians could inhale the sea air along the Ayrshire coast while the

resort towns of Fife offered similar rest and recuperation to the people of Edinburgh. The West Country and the Cambrian coast of mid-Wales became accessible to Midlanders.

Londoners were spoilt for choice with a host of resorts strung along the south and east coasts, from Weymouth to Eastbourne, and Southend to Great Yarmouth. They could also sample the attractions of the Kent coast at Margate, Ramsgate or Herne Bay, or down a plate of whelks on the world's longest pier at Southend-on-Sea. The more adventurous would head for Norfolk and visit Cromer, Sheringham or King's Lynn. Two innovations were central to this

opening up of Britain's coastline to everyone. One was the introduction of paid holidays; the other was the coming of the railway.

As early as the 1830s, the Kilmarnock & Troon Railway was credited with establishing Troon as a fashionable sea-bathing destination. The first main line railways to take holiday traffic seriously were, unsurprisingly, those to Brighton and Southampton while the majority of lines contented themselves with laying on extra trains for specific events: race meetings, market days, fairs and the like. However, railway companies were soon actively involved in the development of seaside resorts: Saltburn, in North Yorkshire, and Hunstanton in Norfolk were prime examples. At Cleethorpes, the Manchester, Sheffield & Lincolnshire Railway (later the Great Central) built a promenade with gardens, baths and refreshment rooms and bought the pier! In 1844, the Railway Chronicle noted that train excursions had become "our chief national amusement" and,

by 1850, Blackpool, Southport, Weston-Super-Mare, Eastbourne and Torquay were all connected by rail. By 1914, you could take a train to almost 200 coastal resorts, towns and villages.

Not all holidaymakers, however, opted for the seaside and trains also served popular inland destinations such as the spa towns of Bath, Buxton, Droitwich, Tunbridge Wells, Malvern and Leamington. For those who had neither the time nor the money to take long holidays, there were day and half-day trips to places closer to home. The Great Eastern Railway built a branch that took Londoners to the edge of Epping Forest,

Above: Enjoying an east coast summer.
Below: Beach life as portrayed by artist, Tom Purvis (1888-1957).

EAST COAST JOYS
travel by L·N·E·R
TO THE DRIER SIDE OF BRITAIN

Above: Class 40 (English Electric Type 4) 2,000hp
1Co-Co1 diesel-electric No40031 prepares to depart
Blackpool North with a return working to Glasgow and
Edinburgh on 31 July 1976. To the right, classmate
No40017 is in charge of a Manchester train.
Right: A poster commissioned by the Southern Railway
in 1936 which has been endlessly imitated.

at Chingford, and on one Easter Monday no less than 180,000 people took advantage of the facility. The South Eastern Railway inaugurated day trips to France and, in the period 1900-09, the London Brighton & South Coast Railway issued around 19 million excursion tickets. Half-day excursions alone accounted for over ten per cent of its passenger receipts. However, believing they lowered the social tone of the town, not all residents of seaside resorts welcomed this influx of jolly punters from the cities. Bournemouth was notably snooty in this respect.

Railways also catered for the more active holidaymaker. Cheap tickets allowing travel to one station and return from another were offered to cyclists and ramblers. Between 1905 and 1914, the Great Western operated a 'ramblers' special' from Paddington to five stations east of Swindon, enabling walkers to explore the scenic delights of the Vale of the White Horse.

After World War I, the railways' monopoly of holiday traffic began to be challenged by the growth in private motoring and by the advent of motor coaches. The railways countered this threat by lowering fares and, in an era when dual carriageways, let alone motorways, were unheard of, exploited their speed advantage. This was the period that saw the introduction of some of the most famous 'named' expresses. 'The Atlantic Coast Express' connected London with

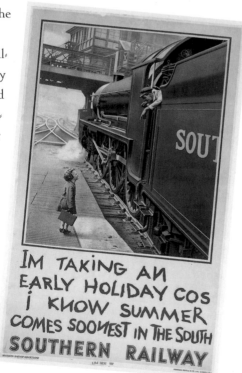

IM TAKING AN EARLY HOLIDAY COS i KNOW SUMMER COMES SOONEST IN THE SOUTH SOUTHERN RAILWAY

Homeward bound, with bucket-and-spade, after a day at the seaside. Cheap day (as well as half-day) excursions to coastal resorts were enjoyed by millions during the 1950s and 1960s.

BREWERY BEANO

The first railway excursion to be organised by a non-railway individual took place in 1841. It conveyed 570 people the 12 miles from Leicester to Loughborough where they attended a temperance meeting. The promoter of this outing was Thomas Cook who went on to found the world's most famous travel agency.

It is unlikely, however, that temperance was much in evidence when, in the summer of 1904, a Burton-on-Trent brewery staged a workers' outing to Liverpool. The whole operation must have taken quite some organising as no less than 17 special trains were required, the first leaving Burton at 4.00am, the last at 6.50am. The 101-mile journey took an average of two-and-three-quarter hours, which meant that the early risers could catch the first ferry of the day across to the Wirral and enjoy the pleasures of New Brighton.

Since the return trains did not begin setting out from Liverpool Central until 8.00pm, there was time for the more adventurous day-trippers to take a steamer to Douglas and spend a couple of hours on the Isle of Man. The last return train deposited its weary and, doubtless, bleary cargo at Burton around 1.40am the following morning. Apart from the optional trip to the Isle of Man, the entire cost of this beano was met by the brewery.

the coast of north Devon, while 'The Torbay Express' and 'The Devonian' served the south of the county. 'The Lakes Express' conveyed you from Euston to the shore of Lake Windermere, while 'The Cambrian Coast Express' ran trains west from Paddington to Aberystwyth and Pwllheli. There were many other holiday orientated services, including sumptuous Pullman trains such as 'The Bournemouth Belle' and 'The Queen of Scots'.

Following the outbreak of war in 1939, nearly all such prestige services were suspended, some never to return. A number of excursion and holiday services were revived under British Railways (trains serving Butlin's, for example) but the growing competition from road and air transport was irresistible. One by one the named trains disappeared. If they survive today, it is only as a barely noticeable footnote in the timetable or a perfunctory sticker on a carriage window.

TOURING BY TRAIN

Trains transformed tourism. The pleasures enjoyed by a privileged few became accessible to almost everyone and, by the end of the 19th century, leisure travel was big business. Trains brought large numbers of people to previously remote areas such as Scotland, Cornwall, the Yorkshire Dales and the Lake District. Not all residents approved of the influx of visitors: the poet, William Wordsworth, wrote in verse the effect of railways on his beloved Lakeland.

Unsurprisingly, the railway companies saw things differently. They used every means to promote tourism, from special excursion fares to commissioning posters from leading artists. Guidebooks, such as the 'Holiday Haunts' series, were published. Inclusive tours were offered combining rail travel, hotel accommodation and outings by coach or steamship. The Caledonian Railway advertised over 100 tours in Scotland but faced stiff competition from the North British and from the Midland, which liked to sell itself as the 'Tourist Route to Scotland'. In Wales, the Cambrian Railway similarly promoted the delights of their principality.

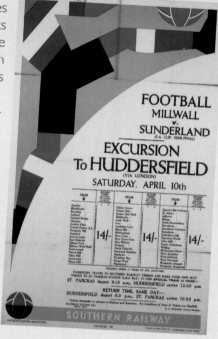

The railways tailored services to specific groups, such as school parties and youth groups. The Southern Railway ran race specials to racecourses such as Ascot, Goodwood and Epsom. Special trains conveyed supporters to Wembley Stadium for FA Cup and Rugby League Challenge Cup Finals.

By its nature, tourist traffic was seasonal and summer Saturdays on the Great Western and Southern would see every available item of rolling stock pressed into service. However, the railways' monopoly came under challenge from coaches and cars. After World War II, additional competition came from package holidays to overseas destinations, and the 1960s saw many holiday resorts lose their train service. For those spared the axe, such as Scarborough, disused sidings and empty platforms are silent reminders of better days.

Left: The Southern Railway encourages Millwall fans to attend their club's FA Cup semi-final against Sunderland on 10 April 1937. They lost, and Sunderland went on to win the trophy.

Below: Newbury, seen here in 1905, was one of two racecourses with adjacent Great Western stations, the other being Cheltenham. That at Newbury remains in use.

TRAINS AND BOATS

A luxurious journey to Paris, the final leg of an Atlantic voyage, or the connection to a crossing to Ireland, the boat train took many guises.

'Battle of Britain' class Pacific No21C156 Croydon pilots an unidentified 4-4-0 on the Continent-bound 'Night Ferry' at Victoria on 15 November 1947. The heavy sleeping and dining cars often required double-heading.

The term 'boat train' invariably conjures images of the 'Golden Arrow' Pullman, or the exotic 'Night Ferry' with its dark blue Wagons Lits sleeping cars. Yet these were simply the most celebrated among a surprisingly large number of boat trains that served Britain's ports. Since 1848, when the 'Irish Mail' first ran between London and Holyhead, there have been trains timed to connect with ships sailing to Ireland, the Channel Islands, the Isle of Man, Continental Europe and beyond.

With the channel ports of Dover, Folkestone, Newhaven, Southampton and Weymouth in its territory, the Southern Railway (from 1948, Region) was most closely associated with boat trains. It offered, as the Southern's publicity

termed it, the 'Short Sea Route', from London Victoria to Calais and Boulogne. Alternatively, the Southern could ferry you from Newhaven to Dieppe, or provide a more leisurely overnight journey from Southampton to Le Havre, leaving London Waterloo at 9.00pm and arriving in Paris at 10.15am.

Waterloo was also the starting point for trains connecting with the ocean liners that called at Southampton. During the 1950s, half of Britain's ocean-going passenger traffic with the rest of the world passed through the docks there. Annually, around 3,900 boat trains arrived at Southampton, including 400 for the Channel Islands ferries. The docks could also expect some 75 troop trains. In the opposite direction, over 2,700 boat trains left for London. Between midnight and 8.00am on the night of 12/13 September 1957, a record was set after ten ships docked at Southampton disembarking over 5,600 passengers. The most boat trains in a single night, twelve, left for London.

The Southern Region's blanket name for trains serving the great liners was the prosaic 'Ocean Liner Express'. However, in 1952, it concluded that certain ships and shipping lines merited individual treatment. 'The Cunarder', for example, conveyed passengers for the liners *Queen Mary* and *Queen Elizabeth* and 'The Statesman' for the *United States*. There were too many, though, to name them all. During a typical summer month in the 1950s, over 150 'Ocean Liner Expresses' were run. On just one day – 5 July 1959 – 13 trains ran in to connect up with seven liners.

The classic images of the boat train, however, remained the 'Golden Arrow' and the 'Night Ferry'. Inaugurated on 15 May 1929 as a first class-only, all-Pullman service, the 'Golden Arrow' left London Victoria each day at 11.00am. At Dover, passengers boarded a specially built steamer and sailed for Calais. There, the equivalent French railways (SNCF) train, the 'Flèche d'Or', was waiting to depart for Paris, reaching the Gare du Nord at 5.35pm.

Though suspended during World War II, the 'Golden Arrow' was restored to the timetable on

15 April 1946 and enjoyed immense popularity. It was hauled by locomotives based at Stewarts Lane depot, Battersea, usually a Bulleid 'light Pacific' or, after 1951, by one of two new 'Britannia' Pacifics based there, No70004 *William Shakespeare* or No70014 *Iron Duke*.

The return sailing docked at Folkestone where the Pullmans waited on the harbour branch. Here, the weight limits barring Pacifics from the line inadvertently created one of the spectacles of the steam age. With exhausts like cannon fire, two or three ancient tank engines pulled and propelled the Pullmans up the 1 in 30 gradient to Folkestone Junction where a Bulleid or 'Britannia' would be standing serenely to take the train on to London. In its later years, the train was entrusted to one of the Southern Region's 2,500hp Bo-Bo electric locomotives. In the end the 'Golden

All of the 'big four' companies are represented in this 1932 poster, produced at a time when overseas holidays were still a novelty and mainly for the wealthy. Artist Irwin Brown distilled the continent's attractions: eating, drinking and entertainment.

VIP TREATMENT

After its Wagons Lits rolled off the ship at Dover, the 'Night Ferry' was always scheduled to run non-stop to Victoria. The same was true of the London-Paris service. The train is recorded as having made an unscheduled stop on just one occasion, and that was on the evening of 16 December 1951. Instructions were issued to the Pullman conductor to take a bottle of whisky and a siphon of soda to an unoccupied sleeping compartment. Then, to the surprise of the train staff, the 'Night Ferry' pulled to a halt at Sevenoaks Tubs Hill Station in Kent. Those on board were similarly perplexed by the security presence at the station, which was clearly off-limits to passengers – except one. A familiar figure climbed aboard and went into the unoccupied compartment where he doubtless poured a large scotch and soda and lit a cigar. For Prime Minister, Winston Churchill, who had been staying at his home of Chartwell, near Sevenoaks, it was the most convenient and civilised way of journeying to a meeting in Paris.

ALL AT SEA

Almost from the beginning, railway companies owned and operated ships, and were responsible for the growth of ports such as Hull and Southampton. The majority of the vessels were ferries of one kind or another, but railways also ran pleasure steamers, such as those on the River Clyde.

On its formation in 1923, the Southern Railway inherited a fleet of 21 cross-Channel ships and 25 smaller boats. Swiftly concluding that the fleet needed modernising, it ordered three new ferries. The *Isle of Thanet* and *Maid of Kent* took up duties on the 'Short Sea Route' to Calais and Boulogne in 1925, while in 1929 the *Canterbury* was allocated specifically to the 'Golden Arrow' service. In 1931, the Southern introduced the Autocarrier for travellers taking cars across to France, the vehicles being craned on and off the ship.

There was accommodation on the ship for 35 cars, with charges varying from £1 17s 6d (£1.88) to £5 according to wheelbase. The drive-on car ferries first appeared in 1939, on the Stranraer-Larne route. However, it took until 1952 to augment the cross-Channel fleet, when *Lord Warden* entered into service between Dover and Boulogne.

Above: Evening at Portsmouth Harbour, on 14 July 1968, with two Isle of Wight ferries: the paddle steamer Ryde *and MV Shanklin (nearest camera).*

Arrow' lost its glamour, and most of its passengers, to the airlines. It passed into history at the end of the summer 1972 timetable.

The 'Night Ferry', a through service between London Victoria and Paris, was notable as the only example of Continental-built passenger rolling stock running on British tracks. New train ferry terminals were constructed at Dover and Dunkerque, three new ferries built, and a modified version of the French Wagon Lit produced to suit the British loading gauge. The ferries could each carry 12 coaches, positioned on four tracks and shackled to the deck with chains.

Inaugurated on 14 October 1936, from the outset the 'Night Ferry' was an exceptionally heavy train. In the early 1960s, when the load had reached 19 vehicles, it was – at 800 tons – the heaviest passenger train in Britain. The Wagons Lits, with their French attendants, were augmented by restaurant and kitchen cars, and by carriages for passengers without sleeping berths. The 'Night Ferry' outlived the 'Golden Arrow' by eight years, last running on 31 October 1980.

The LNER, and subsequently the Eastern Region, looked to the North Sea ports for boat train traffic. A number of services, most famously the 'Hook Continental', ran between London Liverpool Street and Harwich Parkeston Quay. Here, they connected with sailings to-and-from the Hook of Holland, Zeebrugge in Belgium, and Esbjerg in Denmark. It was the Eastern Region that operated undoubtedly the most unusual boat train, the unofficially titled 'North Country Continental'.

On leaving Harwich, it crossed East Anglia to March, in Cambridgeshire, where two coaches were detached for Birmingham (by way of Peterborough, Leicester and Nuneaton). The train then continued to Lincoln where one portion went forward to Sheffield, Manchester and Liverpool, and the other to Doncaster and York.

Further along the east coast trains connected with sailings to Scandinavia from the Tyne Commission Quay down river from Newcastle, while other boat trains served Immingham on Humberside.

On the west coast, the Great Western's principal boat train service connected with sailings from Fishguard to Rosslare in Ireland. LMSR boat trains also combined with ferries to Ireland, those from Holyhead to Dun Laoghaire and between Stranraer and Larne. Though Southampton gradually captured much of the trans-Atlantic business, Liverpool remained the destination for many ships from the United States and Canada. In the port's heyday, the London & North Western ran a four-hour luxury express from Liverpool Riverside to Euston, a train so exclusive it did not appear in the timetable.

Luxury was not a description that could be applied to the trains that linked London St Pancras with Tilbury, on the Thames Estuary. They were a legacy of the Midland Railway's involvement with the London, Tilbury & Southend Railway. Composed of ordinary coaching stock, and usually entrusted to nothing more glamorous than a Fowler 4F 0-6-0 or an Ivatt 4MT 2-6-0, they first circumnavigated north London before joining the LT&SR at Barking. Among the ships they served were those laden with British migrants heading for Australia.

GO BY THE BOOK

Only the sketchiest of information on cross-Channel services was included in the Southern Railway's main timetable. The traveller to Europe needed the 'Continental Handbook', a volume that could excite the imagination simply with its index of destinations, details of connecting services, map of Continental main lines and itineraries of 'Famous International Expresses'. In matter-of-fact fashion, one timetable was headed routinely 'London-China-Japan by Trans-Siberian Railway'.

In addition, there was reassurance for the novice tourist, which extended to portraits of the company's interpreters. They could be consulted at the Gare du Nord and Gare St Lazare in Paris, and at Basle, Brussels, Cologne and Le Havre.

Above: A collaboration between France's Chemin de Fer du Nord (Northern Railway) and Britain's Southern Railway c1930 to promote cross-Channel services within France (la traversée la plus courte – the shortest crossing).

Left: The Golden Arrow arrives at Dover Marine on 30 May 1961 behind rebuilt 'West Country' Pacific No34100 Appledore.

COMMUTING BY TRAIN

Urban and suburban systems not only cater
for the commuting classes but played a
significant role in creating them.

ALONG SUBURBAN LINES

Railways played a key role in suburban development around Britain's large cities. Improved services, often as a consequence of electrification, strengthened the dependence of commuters on trains.

Hats and raincoats are the order of the day as commuters crowd aboard a city-bound train. Some things have never changed...

The existence, or even the promise of a suburban railway link was frequently instrumental in the creation of residential areas, such as those to the south of London. The development of Surbiton, in west Surrey, over the past century has stemmed from being only a 20 minute ride from Waterloo. An increasing distance between home and workplace became a feature of communities throughout Britain, but was particularly pronounced in the London area. It was propelled (and in the case of the property-developing Metropolitan Railway, facilitated) by extensions of the underground railway network, and by the spread of electrified lines south of the Thames.

Similarly, the Great Eastern Railway encouraged development in north-east London. As the so-called 'Northern Heights' of Barnet and beyond

became desirable places to live, the Great Northern had to build new suburban facilities at King's Cross to meet the demand. In contrast, until around 1900 the GWR, Midland and L&NWR had done little to cultivate suburban traffic from west and north-west of the capital but found they could ill afford to ignore this new 'commuting class'. (Not that the term 'commuter' was in use then. It was imported from the United States and not used widely until the 1960s.) Growth continued after World War I and around 70 new stations were opened in London's suburbs between 1920 and 1940.

In other areas, journeys to work were generally shorter and the relationship between railways and suburban expansion was less conspicuous. Trams and buses remained the principal means of getting into and out of town. Eventually, though, every large city welcomed a local railway service. People travelled to work from, for example, Harrogate to Bradford and Leeds, from Southport and Lytham to Liverpool, and from Solihull to Birmingham.

The benefits of suburban electrification were not confined to the London area. In 1903, Liverpool's Mersey Railway became the first British railway to switch from steam to electric operation. Electrification was subsequently extended to the Wirral, Southport and Ormskirk lines. In the Manchester area, the Lancashire & Yorkshire Railway electrified its line to Bury in 1916, while, in 1930, an expanding suburban traffic justified electrifying the Altrincham route. In the Newcastle area, the North Tyneside system was an early electrification project. This was followed, in 1938, by the electrification of lines on the south bank of the Tyne.

Outside London, Glasgow boasted the largest passenger network in Britain. By 1897, 15.75 million passengers annually were using its Central station. However, in many areas, the city's tram and bus systems competed successfully with rail services, one reason perhaps why it took until 1960 for the first of Glasgow's railways to benefit from electrification.

JUST THE TICKETS

The season ticket and the workman's ticket were two trademarks of suburban travel. From around 1900, railway companies fostered their season ticket business. During World War I season ticket sales soared, notably after the big fare increases imposed by government order in 1917. Between the wars season tickets, particularly those sold at bargain rates, continued to grow in popularity. Electrification and consequent improvements in services all drew passengers, especially on the Southern Railway.

Interestingly, it was only in 1917 that a bye-law was introduced requiring season tickets to be shown on demand. Previously, the relatively small number of season ticket holders had been familiar to staff at their local stations.

Railways introduced reduced-fare workmen's trains for those going to work in the early morning and returning at night. In the 1860s, permission for the Great Eastern to extend its line into Liverpool Street was conditional on the running of workmen's trains from Edmonton and Walthamstow at a return fare of two pence. By 1899, 104 such trains conveyed 23,000 passengers each weekday. Some workmen's trains took people out of the city, an example being those travelling out of Birmingham to the Cadbury's confectionery factory at Bournville.

In 1913, workmen's trains made 25 million journeys. By 1938, this figure had risen to 328 million. However, workmen's fares were phased out after nationalisation.

A CAPITAL SYSTEM

Its logo is recognised everywhere and, for a long time, London's underground railway system was also regarded as the finest in the world.

When the first section of the Metropolitan Railway opened on 10 January 1863, it became the first railway in the world to pass under the streets of a city. The original route ran from Bishop's Road, next to Paddington Station, to Farringdon Street, near Smithfield market. One of the purposes of the line was to allow Great Western Railway services to run beyond Paddington to the edge of the City of London. To that end, the track was laid to a mixed gauge: 7-feet for GWR broad gauge trains, standard gauge for the rest. In the event, a dispute between the Metropolitan and the GWR resulted in the broad gauge rails being lifted in 1869.

The previous year, the Metropolitan had gained a companion. The Metropolitan District Railway (invariably abbreviated to the District Railway to avoid confusion with its peer) opened between South Kensington and Westminster on Christmas Eve 1868. By July 1871, it had reached Mansion House. Meanwhile, the Metropolitan was extending slowly eastwards with the aim of meeting up with the District and forming a 'circle' line. However, as relations between the companies deteriorated, the project suffered and the Inner Circle was not completed until 1884.

The Metropolitan was built by the 'cut-and-cover' method, which involved making a cutting, adding walls and arches, and then replacing whatever had been above (usually a road surface). As well as being a relatively cheap method of construction it was — without a reliable tunnelling machine — the only practical option. When James Henry Greathead developed just such a machine (the 'Greathead Shield') the way was open for railways to burrow under the very heart of a city.

LONDON TRANSPORT—

A somewhat surreal commission by London Transport, a comparison between the LT 'bullseye' logo and Saturn.

The yard at London Transport's Neasden depot in 1957, home to Metropolitan Line units and, represented by the train fourth from right, Bakerloo Line tube stock. LT's Neasden power station dominates the skyline behind.

These 'tube' railways, however, would require a new form of motive power. Despite crude attempts at ventilation and the use of locomotives equipped with apparatus that condensed the exhaust and returned it as water to the sidetanks, journeys on the Metropolitan could be made very unpleasant by smoke and steam. On a wholly enclosed 'tube' line, passengers would be asphyxiated.

The solution was provided by the German engineer Ernst Werner von Siemens, who demonstrated that electric motors could be used to power trains, and so opened the way for railways to be built deep underground. London's – and the world's – first 'tube' was the City & South London, which opened in December 1890 between King William Street and Stockwell, a

distance of 1.25 miles. The C&SL had its problems (its cramped carriages were compared to padded cells), but it paved the way for the host of tube lines constructed during the 1900s.

In 1900, the first section of the Central London Railway was opened between Shepherds Bush

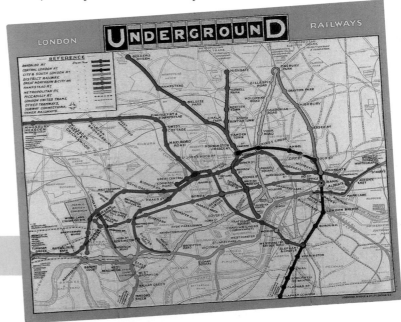

Strap-hanging on the tube; today, only the fashions have changed.

and Bank, a distance of 5.75 miles. At first its services were hauled by electric locomotives, but in 1903 self-powered electric trains were introduced, with driving cabins in the end cars. These were forerunners of all subsequent tube train designs. The Central London reached Liverpool Street in 1912 and was then extended to Stratford and Leyton in the east and Ruislip in the west. Subsequently, its trains ran over what were then LNER tracks to Epping and Hainault. With 51.25 route miles of track, it became the largest of the underground lines, with a journey length of 34 miles between West Ruislip and Epping. The Central London (renamed the Central Line in 1937) also instigated the first 'flat fare' policy. It became known as the 'tuppeny tube', since a twopence ticket covered all journeys.

In 1902 the London Electric Railways Company (known as the Underground Group and made up of both existing and projected lines) was incorporated. It was an important step towards developing the integrated underground system that, in the main, has served London well these past 100 years. Among its first tasks was the electrification of the steam-powered lines, which began in 1903. The one significant 'underground' railway to avoid integration was the Metropolitan, which regarded itself as a main line with an inner-city link. It was also the only 'underground' railway to handle significant quantities of freight and parcels traffic. By 1892, it had extended to Aylesbury,

38 miles from the capital. Not content with that, it laid a further 15 miles of track to meet up with the L&NWR's Oxford to Bletchley line at Verney Junction. To demonstrate its status, between 1910 and 1939, it included Pullman cars, named Galatea and Mayflower, on certain services between Baker Street and Verney Junction. Supplements were payable: sixpence as far as Rickmansworth, one shilling beyond.

However, the Metropolitan's ambition did not extend to complete electrification. While the rest of the system was electrified by 1908, the Metropolitan remained steam-worked north of Harrow-on-the-Hill. The traction changeover point later moved north to Rickmansworth but the section between Rickmansworth and Amersham was not electrified until 1961.

In 1914, the Underground Group acquired financial control of the Central London and City & South London Railways. The latter subsequently became the Northern Line and, in 1926, was extended to Morden, in the heart of suburban Surrey. It was a rare Underground foray south of the Thames, since the area was amply catered for by the extensive Southern Railway overground network.

The development of tube lines, alongside bus, tram and suburban train services, leading up to World War I turned Londoners into the most mobile citizenry in the world. It was during the 1930s, however, that the underground system reached its zenith. On 1 July 1933, the London Passenger Transport Board came into being, establishing the model of a municipal transport system. Its chairman, Lord Ashfield, and his number two, Frank Pick, succeeded in integrating all public transport in the capital – tubes, buses, trams and, later, trolleybuses. They emphasised this unity of service with an overall design plan that extended to station architecture, maps, signs, poster art and typography and was embodied in the universally recognisable 'line-and-circle' logo.

An ambitious programme of tube extensions got underway during the 1930s, part of which was delayed by the outbreak of World War II and

ELECTRIC PERSONALITIES

Before the introduction of multiple units, Metropolitan Line trains between Aldgate, Baker Street and Rickmansworth were hauled by the smart, maroon-liveried Bo-Bo locomotives. Twenty were built by the Metropolitan Carriage & Wagon Co. between 1904 and 1907 and equipped with four 300 horsepower motors and a novel form of electro-magnetic slow-speed control for shunting work. Two separate braking systems were fitted, vacuum and Westinghouse compressed air, and the maximum speed was 65mph. The entire class underwent rebuilding by Metropolitan Vickers between 1921 and 1923.

All 20 locomotives bore the names of characters and personalities associated with London and locations in Metropolitan Railway territory. These ranged from Sherlock Holmes of Baker Street and Thomas Lord of cricket ground fame, to Beaconsfield's Benjamin Disraeli and Lord Byron, sometime pupil at Harrow School. The majority were withdrawn in 1962 but two of the class have survived. No5, named after the Civil War parliamentarian John Hampden, resides in the London Transport Museum, Covent Garden; No12, which celebrates the 18th century actress Sarah Siddons, has been a regular participant in gala events on the underground in recent years.

Above: Having exchanged steam for electric haulage, an Aylesbury-Baker Street service leaves Rickmansworth behind Metropolitan Railway Bo-Bo No8 Sherlock Holmes.

completed in the late 1940s. After these projects were completed the system was not enlarged for over two decades, apart from the electrification of some outlying sections. It was only in 1969 that the light blue of the Victoria Line was added to the colours of the underground map.

SOUTHERN ELECTRIC

Between 1925 and 1939 the Southern Railway revolutionised suburban services in south-east England. With justification, it boasted it was responsible for the 'world's greatest suburban electrification'.

Compared to Germany and the United States, Britain's railways were slow to introduce electrification. In 1900, although there were 348 miles of street tramways as well as the London Underground employing electric traction, just 74 miles of railway had been electrified. The overall situation changed little until after World War II.

However, during the 1920s and 1930s, one company did commit itself to an ambitious programme of electrification and that was the Southern Railway. The Southern handled by far the largest number of London-bound commuters, and they contributed significantly to the 75 per cent of the railway's revenue that came from passenger traffic. Competition from new

tramways, together with the growth of commuter traffic, had been the spur for the first railway electrification in south London. In 1909, the London, Brighton & South Coast Railway electrified the loop line that linked Victoria with London Bridge, by way of Denmark Hill. The system, based on German technology and publicised as the 'Elevated Electric', employed overhead conductor wires energised at 6,700 volts dc. During 1911-12, electrification was extended to the lines from Victoria to Crystal Palace via Streatham Hill, and to Peckham Rye and Tulse Hill.

The London & South Western Railway had experienced similar growth in passenger numbers and similarly opted for electrification. However, it chose a different system from the LB&SCR. In

Pictured approaching Clapham Junction, four-car multiple unit No4526 was assembled from ex-LB&SCR steam-hauled stock. Alphabetical destination headcodes were subsequently replaced by numbers.

1915/16, the L&SWR electrified its lines from Waterloo to Wimbledon, Richmond and Shepperton at 660 volts dc. The current was carried in a conductor rail laid alongside the running tracks and collected by 'shoes' attached to the motor coach bogies. These first L&SWR electric trains were made up of three vehicles, with motor coaches either side of a trailer car.

After the 1923 Grouping, the chairman of the newly created Southern Railway, Sir Herbert Walker, gave his backing to a large/scale programme of electrification. The question was which, if either, of the two existing systems it should adopt. Alfred Raworth, late of the South Eastern Railway, was placed in charge of the project. He probably recognised that the overhead system had the edge technically, but the third rail option was cheaper and he knew that would appeal to his cash/strapped employers. In 1926, the Southern committed to the third rail system and, by 1929, all the ex/LB&SCR electrified lines had been converted.

By 1930, with the third rail extended to Windsor, Guildford, Orpington and Gravesend, the SR announced that the remaining 36 miles from Coulsdon to Brighton would be electrified. The plan amounted to a complete modernisation of the line. Stations, track and signalling were all to be upgraded.

Electric trains to Brighton and Worthing began operating on New Year's Day 1933. The non/stop services were advertised as 'On the hour, in the hour' and were provided by six/car units, each including a Pullman car for first class passengers. Electrification was extended to Eastbourne in 1935, Portsmouth in 1937, Chichester in 1938 and the Medway towns in 1939. Everywhere there were dramatic improvements in journey times and service frequency. Southern Electric proved popular not only with commuters, but with holidaymakers and other leisure travellers.

Although the electrification programme was halted during World War II, in 1948 the nationalised Southern Region still inherited over 700 miles of electrified routes. Further electrification

had to wait until the 1960s, reaching the Kent coast ports and resorts in 1961.

It can be assumed that widespread electrification spelled an early end for steam traction on the Southern. Paradoxically, the Waterloo to Bournemouth line hosted some of Britain's last steam/hauled services. Its Bulleid Pacifics and BR Standards were only displaced by electric multiple units, operating on 750 volts dc, in July 1967.

DOUBLE VISION

Forever the innovator, the Southern Railway's Oliver Bulleid saw double-decker trains as a possible solution to the problem of overcrowding on rush-hour services. However, loading gauge constraints precluded a simple two-tier design. Instead the compartments were dovetailed, with those at the lower level linked to the upper level by a short staircase. Capacity was increased by over 30 per cent, enabling a four-car unit to seat 552 passengers. Only after two prototype units entered service on the London to Dartford line in mid-1949 did the practical drawbacks become apparent. It took longer for passengers to board and leave the train, so delaying other services. People also found the carriages claustrophobic. The idea was rejected in favour of the obvious conventional solutions: extended platforms and longer trains. Nevertheless, the prototypes, Nos4001 and 4002, remained in service until 1971.

Below: One of the Southern's experimental double-decker units. Introduced in November 1949 on the busy north Kent line, increased capacity was offset by drawbacks such as restricted headroom.

THE CITY SLICKERS

It took some equally smart operators to get the City of London's money men to and from their offices each day.

The safety valves of Class N7/3 0-6-2 tank No69701 lift as it awaits departure from Liverpool Street. These robust, 65-ton engines originated as a Great Eastern Railway design in 1914 but it was the LNER that built the class in quantity. One N7, BR No69621, survives in the care of the East Anglian Railway Museum.

The Great Eastern Railway's terminus at Liverpool Street had two distinct areas, west and east, divided by a roadway. From the former area, trains left for Hertford, Cambridge and Kings Lynn, while the latter served Chelmsford, Colchester, Ipswich and Norwich. Additionally, both sides handled suburban services from north and east London, Hertfordshire and Essex. The 18 platforms may have been adequate for all this traffic, but immediately outside the station the operating department faced a permanent obstacle. All the tracks had to dovetail into just three pairs of running lines. The bottleneck was created by the presence of a major road – Bishopsgate – to one side and the viaduct carrying the North London Railway to the other.

Despite this complication, at the turn of the century Liverpool Street was successfully managing the most intensive (and punctual) suburban service in Britain. In 1901, the Great Eastern was responsible for more individual passenger journeys than any other railway. By 1912, a total of 1,230 train movements into and out of Liverpool Street took place each weekday. Between 7.00am and 8.00am, 24 services arrived from Enfield, Chingford, Walthamstow, Palace Gates and Lower Edmonton. During the evening peak, between 6.00pm and 8.00pm, 33 packed trains were despatched from the west side platforms alone. All this was achieved with manual signalling and a fleet of moderately-powered locomotives.

The zenith of the GER's north London suburban service came after 1920, under chairman Sir Henry Thornton. It was clear that further capacity was needed and experience south of the Thames had demonstrated that could be brought about through electrification. There was a price, of course – in the GER's case around £3 million. Luckily for Thornton, he had a brilliant operations man on his management team, F.V. Russell.

Russell argued that, through modifications to the track layout at key points and improvements in signalling and operating practices, the line capacity could be increased dramatically. Moreover, it could be done at a fraction of the expense of electrification. It cost the Great Eastern just £85,000 to implement Russell's proposals yet it was able to expand the evening peak service from Liverpool Street's west side by 25 per cent. The improvement to the morning timetable was even more remarkable – 75 per cent more trains ran between 8.00am and 10.00am.

Among Russell's ideas were additional signalling to cut the headway between trains and a re-arrangement of the tracks in order to give non-conflicting paths for incoming and outgoing trains at Liverpool Street. Additionally, each platform was provided with an engine dock. Similar changes, albeit on a reduced scale, were made at Enfield Town, Walthamstow and Chingford.

The service became known as 'The Jazz', partly thanks to the popularity of the then-new American musical genre but also because of the bright, 'jazzy' colours applied to the doortops of the carriages to indicate the different classes of accommodation.

Maintaining the 'Jazz' service placed onerous responsibilities on staff. The working timetable (the one used by railway personnel rather than that produced for the public) was calculated to the nearest half-minute. Even the slightest delay could have serious repercussions. With 16 stops, for example, on the journey to Enfield Town, this meant engine crews had to be as adept at stopping and starting from stations as running between them. The schedules were too tight to

offer the slightest chance of recovery from poor driving or firing.

Without doubt, a key factor in enabling Great Eastern's suburban tank engines to maintain those schedules was the fitting of the Westinghouse compressed air brake. It was responsive, quick-acting and could be operated with great precision. The characteristic 'pant' of the Westinghouse pump remained a feature of these north London services up to 1960, when electric multiple units replaced the GER/LNER L77/N7 class 0-6-2 tank locomotives.

To the end, the N7s put in reliable, nippy performances. Giving them their head on the longer runs to Hertford East or Bishops Stortford could produce 60mph sprints along the flatlands of the Lea Valley. In many respects, they were the ideal inner-suburban tank engines and the timings they achieved on the Enfield and Chingford lines still compare favourably with today's electrics.

A rush-hour arrival on the Bishopsgate side of Liverpool Street. These platforms served the Essex suburbs with trains to Romford, Shenfield, Chelmsford and Southend-on-Sea. Electrification on the overhead system at 1,500v DC reached Shenfield in 1949 and was extended to Chelmsford and Southend in 1956.

7 FAMOUS LOCOMOTIVES

Forty locomotive designs whose celebrity didn't come solely from being revolutionary, super-powerful or breaking records

A LOOK ALONG THE LINE

From a 'Duchess' to a 'Deltic', an A4 to a 'Brush 4', our line of classic locomotives reflects six decades of triumph and transition.

To the travel writer, H.V. Morton, a steam locomotive was a "poem in steel". A more apt description for British passenger locomotives of the late 19th century would be hard to find. With their flowing lines, ornate liveries, gleaming brasswork and minimum of external piping, they were elegance itself. The large diameter driving wheels of a typical 4-4-0 made them quick, too. Their pulling power, however, was comparatively modest. This was of little consequence so long as trains remained short and light in weight. When the trains changed, the engines had to as well. Style remained important, but speed and power now took centre-stage. The 20th century saw a further term enter the locomotive lexicon: standardisation.

Wooden coaches were superseded by heavier, steel-bodied vehicles. Additionally, continuous braking – the application of compressed-air or vacuum brakes to every wheel – allowed longer trains to run safely at speed. Importantly, there were plenty of passengers to fill those trains. The need for bigger, more powerful locomotives was met by engineers such as the Great Northern Railway's Henry Ivatt, whose Atlantics of 1902 open our survey.

With its trailing axle supporting a larger firebox, the 4-4-2, or Atlantic, type was a logical development of the 4-4-0. Larger fireboxes sustained larger boilers. These produced more steam and generated more power.

Another important factor as trains grew heavier was adhesion – essentially, the ability of a locomotive to grip the rail. This saw the appearance of the 4-6-0, with greater adhesion coming from its third set of driving wheels. The 4-6-0 reached Britain in 1894, and found favour with, among others, George Jackson Churchward of the Great Western Railway. It would go on to become the most numerous British passenger and mixed traffic type, with thousands being built up until the mid-1950s.

Churchward was the outstanding locomotive engineer of his age. Between 1903 and 1911 he equipped the GWR with a fleet of locomotives significantly in advance of those on any other British railway. Churchward's ideas – such as the standardisation of components, – influenced all

Churchward's 'Star' class 4-cylinder 4-6-0 inaugurated a new era in express passenger engine design. Production began at the Great Western Railway's Swindon workshops in 1907, with No4022 – seen here departing Paddington in March 1939 – being delivered in June 1909.

The 4-cylinder 'Princess Coronation' class Pacifics, introduced in 1937, were the LMSR's response to the record-breaking streamliners of the LNER. The first members of the class sported a bathtub-like shroud with decorative 'speed whiskers', and were designated to haul the prestige 'Coronation Scot' between London and Scotland. On a wintry December day in 1938, the regular 1.30pm departure leaves Euston. It was scheduled to reach Glasgow at 8.00pm.

subsequent locomotive development in Britain. However, he was not alone in seeking to make the steam locomotive more efficient.

There were many ideas for improving efficiency, some worthwhile, others plain quirky. Undoubtedly, the most significant technical development was superheating—raising the temperature and volume of steam through the application of additional heat as it passes between the boiler and cylinders. This allows more work to be obtained from the steam, so reducing fuel consumption. Superheated locomotives can generate up to 25 per cent more power than their non-superheated equivalents. Two German engineers – August von Borries and Wilhelm Schmidt – led the way in superheater development, their ideas eagerly taken up by British designers.

The 1923 'Grouping' had a significant effect on locomotive development. With Midland Railway personnel dominating the largest of the 'big four' rail companies, the London, Midland & Scottish, a decade of near stagnation resulted as its 'small engine' policy held sway in this region. The Southern Railway appointed the competent and well-qualified Richard Maunsell to direct motive power matters, but he was often frustrated in his efforts to modernise and standardise the SR's ageing locomotive fleet because the Southern invested most of its resources in electrification.

Nevertheless, between 1925 and 1930, Maunsell was allowed to update the Southern's express passenger fleet with some fine locomotives, among them the 'King Arthur' and 'Lord Nelson' 4-6-0s and, arguably his masterpiece, the 'Schools', the last 4-4-0 to be built in Britain.

With Nigel Gresley at the helm, the London & North Eastern Railway began building Britain's first production series of Pacifics in 1922. In many respects, the 4-6-2, or Pacific, type was the ideal express passenger locomotive. The leading four-wheel bogie supplied guidance and stability at speed; the six driving wheels delivered that speed, along with adhesion and power; and the trailing truck supported a large firebox that helped generate this power. Gresley's design was the first of a new breed of fast-running and – by British standards – 'big engines', which threatened the pre-eminence of GWR's fleet of 4-6-0s.

The kind of advances pursued by Churchward and Gresley not only helped produce 'fliers' but enhanced the performance of freight locomotives. Nonetheless, Britain's railways remained the only ones in the world that developed bigger and more powerful express passenger engines than freight engines. Freight remained largely entrusted to elderly 0-6-0s and 0-8-0s. Only the Great Western, Great Central and Great Northern invested in more modern 2-8-0s.

From the mid-1920s, increasing fuel costs highlighted the need for even greater efficiency and the work of the French engineer, André Chapelon, was vital here. His techniques of eliminating pressure losses were shown to increase power and efficiency by up to 40 per cent. Chapelon's principles were first adopted by Gresley, and later by Oliver Bulleid of the Southern Railway and William Stanier on the LMSR. Stanier's main task, however, was to restock the LMSR fleet with modern locomotives. This he achieved with a series of sound designs such as the Class 5 4-6-0, 8F 2-8-0, 4MT 2-6-4 tank and the 'Princess Coronation' Pacific. Even before the outbreak of war, the emphasis was shifting towards simplicity, flexibility and

When built by the English Electric company in 1955, the 3,300 horsepower 'Deltic' was the most powerful single-unit diesel locomotive in the world. In six years the prototype ran over 400,000 miles on both the West and East Coast Main Lines. Its success led to 22 production 'Deltics' being built in 1961-62 for east coast express haulage.

ease of maintenance. War only accelerated the process, producing locomotives so devoid of frills that they became known as 'Austerities'. There were exceptions. On the Southern Railway, Oliver Bulleid designed two classes of Pacific that incorporated all manner of advanced ideas. Unfortunately, not all the innovations worked in practice. The 'Merchant Navies', 'West Countries' and 'Battle of Britains' may have been a driver's dream but they could also be a fitter's nightmare.

In 1951 the first of the BR Standard designs, the 'Britannia' Pacific, appeared. Eleven more followed, some good, some indifferent. Most were based on proven practice, usually derived from the LMSR. There was no call for innovation and only two of the designs departed from the norm. One was the solitary Class 8 Pacific, No71000 *Duke of Gloucester*, a flawed orphan prevented from fulfilling its potential. The other was the outstanding 9F 2-10-0 freight engine. Here, at least, was a fitting climax to the story of the British steam locomotive.

By the time the last of the 9Fs was delivered in 1960, British Railways was taking delivery of a host of diesel locomotive classes. In direct contrast to steam traction, there had been minimal experience with diesels. During the 1930s, the LMSR had developed a competent diesel-electric shunter and the Great Western had enjoyed some success with a series of diesel railcars. After World War II, the LMSR and the Southern devised designs for main-line diesel locomotives but only three were in service when the railways were nationalised in 1948.

This pattern was not to alter greatly until after 1955, when the British Railways Modernisation Plan was drawn up. The Plan sounded the death knell for steam traction and outlined its replacement by a mixture of diesel classes and electrification. There was to have been a period of evaluation (and, with hindsight, unquestionably there should have been). Instead, in the rush to eliminate steam, orders were hastily placed for a wide range of diesel types. There was no option

other than to use existing engine designs, irrespective of whether they would meet the criteria laid down in the Modernisation Plan. In most cases, they did not.

By 1962, British Railways was operating 19 classes of main-line diesel, including five that employed a different transmission system from the rest (the Western Region's diesel-hydraulics). So much for standardisation. Most of the classes were underpowered, some were hopelessly unreliable, and a couple were next-to-useless. Nevertheless, several did prove their worth, most notably the 'Brush 4' that has remained in service to this day. A handful – the 'Warships', 'Westerns', 'Deltics', 'Peaks' and English Electric Type 4s – even came to earn the admiration and affection of dyed-in-the-wool steam enthusiasts.

Appropriately photographed at sunset, No92208 was a representative of the final class of British main line steam locomotives, the magnificent 2-cylinder 9F 2-10-0 of 1954. Built at Swindon in June 1959, it was withdrawn from Carlisle Kingmoor depot just eight years later, in October 1967.

WHEN ATLANTICS MADE WAVES

A logical development of the internationally acclaimed 4-4-0, the 4-4-2, or 'Atlantic', type made its debut in the United States in 1888. Its additional trailing truck not only supported a larger firebox but also improved the locomotive's riding. Ten years later, the Great Northern Railway's Henry Ivatt introduced the Atlantic to Britain.

Appointed head of the Great Northern's locomotive department in 1896, Henry Ivatt faced the task of replacing the venerable Patrick Stirling. His predecessor, who had died in office aged 75, was revered not only for the performance of his locomotives but their looks. 'Artistry in metal' was one summation of Stirling's single-wheelers (locomotives with a single pair of large-diameter driving wheels). By the turn of the century, however, these elegant locomotives were being taxed by increasing train loadings on the East Coast line. Seeking the greater power and adhesion such loadings demanded, Ivatt looked to America for a solution. He found it in the 4-4-2 design, or the Atlantic type, which was quickly displacing the 4-4-0 on many American railroads. His counterpart on the Lancashire & Yorkshire Railway, John Aspinall, also saw the potential of the Atlantics and had begun working on a 4-4-2 design.

Possibly to gain the honour of being the first British railway to employ a 4-4-2, the GNR gave high priority to the construction of the first of the Ivatt Atlantics. Numbered 990 and named *Henry Oakley* (the incumbent General Manager of the Great Northern Railway) it was outshopped from Doncaster works in 1898, beating Aspinall's prototype by a few months. Ivatt placed great emphasis on boiler design and opted for a large capacity vessel with a much greater steam-raising capacity than Stirling's single-wheelers. The first production Atlantics entered service in 1900 and proved fast, lively runners — so lively that Ivatt

had to advise his drivers to rein in their steeds. There were stretches of uneven track between London and Doncaster where, at high speed, they displayed an alarming tendency to 'rock and roll'! Despite this Ivatt's Atlantics were used to head an accelerated service between London and Grantham and, in 1903, one of then covered this 105-mile-route in just 104 minutes, a run that included a top speed of 69 mph. Such performances made the Atlantics attractive, exciting engines and GNR publicity capitalised on their appeal.

One drawback of Ivatt's design was that the relatively small cylinders were inadequate for the boiler. These first Atlantics had to be worked at undesirable and uneconomic rates by the enginemen in order to achieve expected performance — in other words, they had to be thrashed. Considering this, surprise was expressed when Ivatt unveiled his 'large Atlantic' in 1902. It had a boiler — for its time — of startling proportions, but this fed steam to a chassis where the valve gear and cylinder size were unchanged. That this unbalanced, over-boilered locomotive worked at all spoke volumes for the efficiency of the cylinders in using steam, allied to an excellent blast-pipe and chimney arrangement.

Ivatt's successor, Nigel Gresley, was mindful of the engines' deficiencies and ordered the fitting of superheaters to the 'large Atlantics'. It was a move that both brought an immediate improvement to their performance and, during the 1920s when teething troubles sidelined Gresley's new

One of Henry Ivatt's 'Large Atlantics', No291, speeds through Hadley Wood. When this photograph was taken in 1909, the locomotive was just five years old, having been outshopped from Doncaster Works in June 1904. It remained in traffic until April 1945.

Pacifics, enabled the large Atlantics to assume their role. Striving to maintain the Pacifics' accelerated East Coast schedules resulted in some remarkable performances.

Finally displaced from the heavier trains in the late 1920s, the Ivatt Atlantics found fresh admirers on the LNER's lightly-loaded Pullman services to Harrogate and Sheffield, and on the notorious Cambridge 'beer trains'. The Ivatt Atlantics did not last long in British Railways service. A final run from Kings Cross to Doncaster took place on 24 November 1950 and,

at its conclusion, the last working Ivatt Atlantic, No294 (BR No62822) went for scrap. Thankfully, by then, the two prototypes, Class C1 No251 and C2 No990, had been preserved. In September 1953, they double-headed the 'Plant Centenarian' specials marking the centenary of Doncaster works — the 'Plant' as it was known to generations of railway workers. These were to be the last main-line appearances of locomotives that, while falling just short of greatness, had few rivals when it came to glamour.

THE CRIMSON RAMBLERS

Compounding — a means of obtaining more work from each charge of steam entering a locomotive's cylinders — had several devotees among British engineers. The efforts of the Midland Railway's Samuel Johnson were among the most successful, and certainly the longest-lived.

The sight of a Midland compound piloting a Stanier 4-6-0 became commonplace in LMSR and BR days. Leading 'Jubilee' class No5562 Alberta, Class 4 4-4-0 No1045 passes Ais Gill summit at the head of the 2.45pm ex-Carlisle on 27 July 1939.

Samuel Johnson introduced compounding to the Midland Railway in 1902, with a design based on a three-cylinder layout employed by the North Eastern Railway. In this arrangement, two outside low-pressure cylinders were fed by a single high-pressure cylinder situated between the frames, where it had to compete for space — not always successfully — with three sets of valve gear.

Johnson's successor, Richard Deeley, refined the design (chiefly by the addition of superheating) and produced engines that proved ideal for the comparatively light, but tightly scheduled train-loads that characterised Midland passenger services. The combination of a deep maroon livery, and their widespread use across the sprawling Midland network, earned the compounds the nickame of 'Crimson Ramblers'.

Although acknowledged as successes within their limitations, the decision by the LMSR — which absorbed the Midland in 1923 — to adopt the 'Midland Compound' as its standard express

passenger locomotive astonished many observers. Agreed, in comparative trials, the compound had scored over its principal rival, the London & North Western's 'Prince of Wales' class. Evidence suggests, however, that the choice was more a reflection of ex-Midland managerial dominance within the LMSR hierarchy.

Construction of the compounds continued apace and only tailed off after 1927, when LMSR began to take delivery of new 'Royal Scot' 4-6-0s. In all, 240 4P compound 4-4-0s were constructed, the last in 1932. The Midland workshops at Derby accounted for most, with orders placed additionally with the North British Locomotive Company and Vulcan Foundry.

The Midland compounds were useful and responsive locomotives, economical on fuel, but dependent on sympathetic driving and firing. As a result, when operating outside traditional Midland territory, they frequently suffered at the hands of inexperienced crews. The technique for starting, for example, was far from easy to master. Ultimately, however, the Achilles heel of these engines was not their complexity, but their inability to cope with increasing train lengths. This shortcoming contributed to the costly practice of double-heading (two locomotives hauling one train) that characterised so many of the LMSR's operations and remained commonplace in the British Railways era.

In this respect, the compounds epitomised the short-sightedness of Midland Railway and, through its all-pervasive influence, early LMSR locomotive policy. Nevertheless, despite their limitations, they remained at work until 1961. One example survives, Midland Railway No1000. This compound enjoyed main-line outings in the 1960s, and again in the late 1970s and early 1980s, but currently resides at the National Railway Museum, York.

Undergoing a boiler washout at Derby, Class 4 compound 4-4-0 No1043 was built at the same location in March 1909 and put in exactly 42 years' service. The 3-cylinder Midland 4-4-0s were arguably the most successful British compound design built in any quantity.

COMPOUND INTEREST

Compounding had been employed to make more efficient use of the power of steam since the mid-nineteenth century. However, these were stationary engines not constrained by the confined area and mechanical complexity of the steam locomotive. Unlike more common 'simple' locomotives, compounds are equipped with both high- and low-pressure cylinders. The former receive the normal charge of high-pressure steam from the boiler, but do not exhaust it in the usual way. Instead, that steam – now at reduced pressure – is used again in a low-pressure cylinder (or cylinders). Originally compounding was seen as a method of fully utilising steam that, because of imperfect valve performance, was being exhausted before all its power had been extracted. The performance of compound locomotives varied widely. They were notably successful in France, but in Britain results, to say the least, were uneven. Francis Webb's 4-4-0 and 0-8-0 compounds for the London & North Western Railway were irredeemably flawed, but the Worsdell brothers – Thomas and Wilson – did better with their much simpler designs for the North Eastern Railway. However, it was designers working for the Midland Railway, beginning with Samuel Waite Johnson, who managed to profitably overcame the practical obstacles to using compounding.

THE CENTURY-MAKER

Was the Great Western's City of Truro *the first thing on earth to attain a speed of 100 miles per hour? Despite the doubts, the point-to-point timings of its 1904 run were remarkable as well as indisputable. They suggest a machine in the vanguard of locomotive engineering. Paradoxically, the 'Cities' were something of an anachronism.*

In the late 1950s, Great Western 4-4-0 No3440 City of Truro was returned to work for enthusiast specials. At Southampton Terminus on 23 May 1957, it has appropriate company in ex-L&SWR T9 4-4-0 No30285.

Locomotive No3440 *City of Truro* is about to mark two centenaries. The first, in May 2003, is of its construction at Swindon works. The following year sees the 100th anniversary of the run where *Truro* is said to have become the first locomotive to attain 100mph.

The claim, by railway commentator Charles Rous-Marten, remains controversial. It is not his integrity that is questioned, simply the accuracy of his stopwatch. Few doubt, though, that this engine, a hybrid of old and new ideas, was at least capable of the feat.

The gestation of the 'City' class began in September 1902. The GWR's newly-appointed Locomotive Superintendent, George Jackson Churchward, rebuilt 'Atbara' class 4-4-0 No3405 *Mauritius* with his new Standard No4 taper boiler. Did he want to 'road-test' the new steam raiser, or did he consider the original boiler inadequate? Whatever the reason, it was a move that was to influence all subsequent Great Western locomotive design.

Following trials with *Mauritius*, an order was placed with Swindon works for ten similar locomotives, all for delivery during 1903. Though powerful by Great Western standards, the newcomers were lightweights when compared with contemporary designs such as the Great Northern's Ivatt Atlantics and the North Eastern Railway's Worsdell 4-4-0s. Another anachronistic feature of the 'City's design was its four-coupled, double-framed format. By the early 1900s double frames had been rejected by most locomotive engineers because they were heavier and more expensive to fabricate than their single counterparts. They did, however, have the advantage of allowing a greater area of bearing surface, so reducing the chance of overheated axleboxes when working at high speed. Wedding this mechanical robustness to a powerful steam-raiser such as the Churchward boiler resulted in a 'flier'.

Not long after its debut, the class was putting in startling performances. On 14 July 1903, *City of Bath* was in charge of a train that included two coaches conveying the Prince and Princess of Wales from Paddington to Plymouth. The train took just 92 minutes to cover the 106.9 miles to Bath, and arrived in Plymouth 37 minutes early, having averaged 63.2mph over the 240 miles.

Though the 'Cities' have a lasting place in railway history, their working lives were comparatively short. Displaced from express work by Churchward's new 4-4-2 and 4-6-0 designs, they found employment on secondary routes. The first withdrawals came after just 24 years' service and, by 1931, just two remained, *City of Truro* being one of them. Its survival owed little to the GWR,

however, whose General Manager, James Milne, declared that he 'did not consider the engine of outstanding importance'. To its credit, the LNER disagreed and offered to display *City of Truro* in its York museum. Since that time, the record-breaker has been overhauled twice to working order, most recently in 1985 to mark the 150th anniversary of the formation of the GWR. Plans are underway to ensure it is back in steam to mark the centenary of its 100mph triumph.

FIRST WITH THE POST

Behind *City of Truro's* record-breaking was the Great Western's desire to be first with the post. It competed with the London & South Western Railway for mail traffic offloaded from trans-Atlantic liners docking at Plymouth. Given that the L&SWR route to London was 15 miles shorter, the GWR had to rely on speed. On 9 May 1904, it was actively seeking to publicise its new service between Plymouth and the capital. The 'Ocean Mails Express' normally carried no passengers but the GWR made a point of asking along the writer, Charles Rous-Marten. Clearly something special was planned.

At 8.00am the Norddeutscher Lloyd liner *Kromprinz Wilhelm* dropped anchor in Plymouth Sound en route from New York to northern Germany. Its UK-bound cargo was offloaded into five postal vans, adding up to a train weight of around 148 tons. At the head of the rake was No3440 *City of Truro*, a surprising choice since classmates Nos3433 *City of Bath* and 3442 *City of Exeter* were reputed to be faster engines. It soon became apparent that was not the opinion of driver Moses Clements.

Fifty-five minutes out of Plymouth, *City of Truro* was flying through Exeter. There now followed 30 miles of high-speed running, culminating in what Rous-Marten described as the 'hurricane descent' of Wellington bank in Somerset. Over one quarter-mile, he claimed to have logged a time of eight-and-four-fifths seconds, corresponding to a speed of 102.3 miles per hour. But with the best will — and stopwatch — in the world, it was impossible to be quite that accurate and even the publicity hungry Great Western withheld full publication of Rous-Marten's log for 18 years. It has to be remembered, too, that for many, the very notion of travelling at 100 miles an hour would have been terrifying!

With its coal running low, *City of Truro* was replaced at Bristol, after having averaged 72.7mph over the 44 mile journey from Taunton. The new engine, No3065 *Duke of Connaught*, took the train on to Paddington, and completing the 240-mile journey in 3 hours 47 minutes.

A FIRST FOR FREIGHT

Transitional would be the broad description of George Jackson Churchward's first locomotive designs. Then, in 1903, he broke new ground with a prototype that was to become the forerunner of a new breed of British freight locomotive, the 2-8-0.

Sunday visits in the 1950s and 60s to locomotive depots serving the East Midlands and South Yorkshire coalfields brought home the scale of railway freight operations. There were seemingly endless rows of Stanier 8Fs at Toton, 'Austerities' at Colwick and LNER 04s at Mexborough, all simmering under the smoke haze and waiting to resume duties come Monday morning. In the early 1900s, the picture was the same on Teesside and Tyneside, in West Yorkshire and East Lancashire, in Cheshire and Derbyshire, and in South Wales where the story of these 2-8-0 freight classes began.

Eight-coupled tank and tender engines, notably the Webb 0-8-0s of the L&NWR and the Aspinall 0-8-0s of the Lancashire & Yorkshire Railway, had been around for some years. In South Wales, the Vale of Neath and Barry Railways used 0-8-0 and 0-8-2 tank engines. To Churchward, however, goes the credit for adding a front pony truck and producing Britain's first 2-8-0, thirty-seven years after the type had made its debut in the United States. Since 1866, the coal-carrying Lehigh Valley Railroad of Pennsylvania had used 2-8-0s to haul 300 ton trains on grades as steep as 1 in 40. With its leading pony truck, or guiding wheels, the 2-8-0 offered greater stability and better weight distribution than an 0-8-0. For Churchward, ever receptive to new ideas, what worked in Pennsylvania would work in Pontypool.

With South Wales coal and iron ore traffic in mind, Churchward provided for a heavy freight locomotive in his planned range of 'standard' locomotive types. Built at Swindon in June 1903, the doyen of the class, No97, shared several components with another prototype, the 2-cylinder 4-6-0 No98. These included the tapered boiler and Belpaire firebox that would become trademark features of all subsequent Great Western tender locomotives.

Production of the 2800 class 2-8-0s got underway in 1905, with a number of modifications resulting from trials with No97. An enlargement of the cylinder diameter and an increase in boiler pressure lifted the tractive effort by a good margin. Superheating was incorporated into the class from 1909, with No2808 the first to be 'retro-fitted'.

The 84 2800s built under Churchward remained the Great Western's principal long-haul freight locomotives throughout the 1920s and 1930s. Although 35 years had elapsed since the

FUEL FOR THOUGHT

Between 1945 and 1947, post-war coal shortages saw 20 of the 2800s – along with many locomotives from the other railway companies – converted to oil-burning. The experiment was eagerly backed by the government, but this enthusiasm waned once extra maintenance costs were calculated and the bill arrived for the imported oil. The scheme was abandoned in 1948, the year that saw one of the 2-8-0s, No3803, emerge remarkably successfully from trials against more modern freight engines, including the LMSR 8F 2-8-0 and the WD 2-8-0 and 2-10-0. Such was their suitability for the task that it took the appearance in 1954 of the British Railways 9F 2-10-0 to displace the Great Western 2-8-0s from their main role of heavy mineral haulage. Even then, there was still work for the class up to the end of steam on the Western Region in 1965.

appearance of No97, little updating was needed when Churchward's successor, Charles Collett, added to that figure. Construction of the Collett version, designated the 2884 class, began in 1938 and by 1942 had taken the number of 2-8-0s to

165. The total remained intact until 1958 when the prototype – now numbered 2800 – became the first to be withdrawn. Sixteen of the 2800/2884 classes have survived but, to date, only two have been restored to working order.

A GREAT SERVANT TO ALL

The story of John Robinson's heavy freight 2-8-0 for the Great Central Railway is an extraordinary one. It encompasses at least nine countries, five engine builders, eight main line railway companies, five rebuildings and two world wars.

Such a colourful history was not anticipated when, in 1910, the still-youthful Great Central Railway decided it needed a more powerful class of freight engine. The principal motivation was the impending opening of its vast new docks complex at Immingham on Humberside. The GCR rightly anticipated a huge increase in coal and other mineral traffic through the port and a need for engines to handle it. The job of designing these machines went to its Chief Mechanical Engineer, the Newcastle-born John George Robinson.

The first of the 8K class 2-8-0s was outshopped from the Great Central Railway's Gorton (Manchester) workshops in September 1911. It was essentially a superheated and extended version of an earlier Robinson freight design, the 8A class 0-8-0 of 1902. Alongside the Gorton-built engines, orders were placed with the North British Locomotive Company of Glasgow and with Kitson's of Leeds. As a consequence of this, by June 1914 — two months before the outbreak of World War I — 126 2-8-0s were in traffic. Robust and uncomplicated, the 8K steamed well and proved outstandingly reliable, qualities obviously appreciated by the wartime Ministry of Munitions.

By 1916, the Ministry had requisitioned some 600 locomotives from Britain's railway companies. With no end to the conflict in sight, it now decided to build rather than borrow. Not only was the Robinson 2-8-0 a proven design, it enjoyed powerful backing from Sir Sam Fay, a GCR manager who was appointed the government's Director of War Transport.

Deliveries of the new engines, which were handed over to the Railway Operating Division (ROD) of the Royal Engineers, began in September 1917. A total of 305 2-8-0s saw service on the Western Front and production continued until 1920 — two years after hostilities ceased — at wartime production levels in order to maintain employment in the factories. As a result, the government ended up owning 521 surplus locomotives. Its first attempt to sell them was only modestly successful, which was not surprising as it was asking £12,000 for second-hand engines that had cost between £6,000 and £8,000 to build.

At the head of a westbound freight for Gorton, an O4/8 class 2-8-0, No63841, passes under the wires of the trans-Pennine electrified route between Manchester and Sheffield at Guide Bridge.

The next scheme to offload the remaining 468 engines met with a more enthusiastic response. They were advertised for hire and a host of companies took up the offer. Then, in 1921, the hire agreements were abruptly terminated and the locomotives recalled. If the intention was to force companies into buying the engines, the ploy failed and they languished in dumps around the country. By 1923, with its asset deteriorating and devaluing, the government reluctantly settled for whatever prices it could obtain. The majority of the ex-ROD locomotives were bought by the Great Western, London & North Western, and London & North Eastern Railways (who modified the design of the 8K and reclassified it to 04). Some found more exotic homes. A batch went to colliery railways in China, and 13 were acquired for a similar role in New South Wales, Australia, where they remained at work until 1973.

In 1941, 92 of the Robinson 2-8-0s were again requisitioned for war service. This time, however, there was a drawback: the LNER's modifications had robbed the class of its essential uniformity. The War Department switched its allegiance to the LMSR's 8F 2-8-0, but not before a number of the Robinson engines had been despatched to the Middle East. They ended up working in Egypt, Palestine, Syria, Iraq and Iran, with a few reaching the Soviet Union.

After World War II, the home-based Robinson 2-8-0s were generally confined to former GCR routes. Withdrawals began in 1958 and were completed in 1966, with the exception of No63601 (GCR No102) which was set aside for the National Collection. In 1995, the locomotive was placed in the care of today's Great Central Railway, in Leicestershire, where it has been restored to working order.

With the familiar clocktower in the background, O4/1 class 2-8-0 No 63605 runs tender-first through Wakefield Westgate with coal empties from Wrenthorpe yard bound for the Barnsley area. Built by the Great Central at its Gorton (Manchester) works in June 1913 it lasted In traffic until August 1962. Its 4,000 gallon tender appears filled to its six tons coal capacity.

THE GLORY OF THE GLENS

If one locomotive type represented the 'Scottish school' of design, it was the 4-4-0.
Among the most celebrated were the 'Glens' of the North British Railway.

Speedy, sturdy and flexible enough to cope with their severe gradients and sharp curves, all five of the pre-grouping Scottish railways counted upon 4-4-0s as 'maid-of-all-work' passenger engines. The 4-4-0 was introduced to Scotland in 1862 by the Great North of Scotland Railway and, by 1921, there were 826 in service north of the border.

The largest stock (213) belonged to the North British Railway, where William Paton Reid became Locomotive Superintendent in 1906. That year, the first of five 4-4-0s designed by him were outshopped from the company's Cowlairs workshops in Glasgow. Further batches followed between 1909 and 1912, among them the so-called 'Scotts' – sixteen engines named after characters from the novels of Sir Walter Scott.

The culmination of Reid's development of the 4-4-0 emerged from Cowlairs in September 1913 – officially the K class, but destined to become revered by railway enthusiasts as the 'Glens'. Essentially, the 'Glens' were a superheated version of one of Reid's earlier designs and were built specifically to work the taxing West Highland line between Glasgow, Crianlarich, Fort William and Mallaig. Initially, only nine examples were built, but construction resumed in 1917 and continued off-and-on until September 1920, by which time the class numbered 32.

The free-steaming, free-running qualities of the 'Glens' ensured their popularity among footplate crews, while their versatility endeared them to the NBR's operating department. They were restricted, though, to a maximum load of 190 tons over the West Highland route, requiring regular double-heading. However, it is a tribute to the soundness of William Reid's design that the 'Glens', like the earlier 'Scotts', were left largely

A 13-coach Sunday excursion from Glasgow to Whitley Bay requires the services of two ex-North British Railway 'Glen' 4-4-0s, No9281 Glen Murran (leading) and No9256 Glen Douglas. Both were built at the NBR's Cowlairs workshops in Glasgow. Glen Douglas eventually regained its NBR dark green livery and number, and, as No256, it stayed available for special workings until 1965.

untouched during LNER ownership (the North British became part of the LNER at the 1923 grouping).

Although the 'Glens' found employment all over the NBR system, the largest contingent was always based at Eastfield depot in Glasgow to work the West Highland line. Several were also out-stationed at Fort William and Mallaig. Half the class remained Eastfield engines up to nationalisation in 1948, with the remainder principally divided between St Margaret's, Edinburgh, and Thornton Junction in Fife, from where they worked to Dundee.

All 99 Reid-designed 4-4-0s survived World War II and all but two of the 'Glens' joined the motive power roster of British Railways' Scottish Region in 1948. Three more were withdrawn in 1950 but the remaining 27 lasted until September 1958. By this time they were employed mainly on goods traffic, working out of the depots at Hawick, Keith and Kittybrewster, near Aberdeen. In early 1960, No62471 *Glen Falloch* and No62496 *Glen Loy* made a

memorable appearance on the BBC's 'Railway Roundabout', the first — and only — television magazine programme that has been broadcast specifically for railway enthusiasts. The latter engine, along with No62484 *Glen Lyon*, was the last of this much-loved class to be retired, from Eastfield in November 1961.

Hugging the northern shore of the Firth of Forth, between Culross and Kincardine, Glen Douglas heads a railtour along the line linking Dunfermline and Alloa.

SCOTTISH SWANSONG

Locomotive No62469 *Glen Douglas* was set aside for preservation in 1959 and, after repainting in its original North British olive green livery, was allocated to Dawsholm depot, Glasgow, to work specials. It was joined there by three other Scottish veterans, like the 'Glen' all in running order. They were Caledonian Railway 4-2-2 No123 of 1886, Highland Railway 'Jones Goods' 4-6-0 No103 of 1894 and Great North of Scotland Railway 4-4-0 No49 *Gordon Highlander* of 1920. The quartet enjoyed this swansong until 1965 when all were incarcerated in the Glasgow Museum of Transport. In 1992, *Glen Douglas* was moved to Bo'ness on the Firth of Forth for a proposed overhaul that would see it in steam to commemorate the centenary of the West Highland line in 1994. Ten years on, that overhaul is still anticipated.

A HORSE FOR A COURSE

The 'course' was the Somerset & Dorset Joint Railway, whose route between Bath and Bournemouth traversed the Mendip Hills. The 'horse' was a rugged 2-8-0 that took those hills in its stride.

In 1876, the cash-strapped Somerset & Dorset Railway relinquished its independence and settled for joint administration by the Midland and London & South Western Railways. Both railways wanted to keep the S&D as a going concern because its routes provided an essential link between the South Midlands and the Channel coast. Unfortunately, the Midland had nothing in its motive power fleet suited the line's long, and often severe gradients. Its medium-power 0-6-0s restricted the loads that could be hauled and invariably required a second engine as banking assistance. This added appreciably to operating costs, especially for the mineral traffic originating from the mines and quarries of the Mendip Hills.

The Locomotive Superintendent of the Somerset & Dorset Joint Railway (the name given to the combined enterprise), M.H. Ryan, argued for a locomotive tailored to the route. It took until 1914 for his wish to be granted. The Chief Mechanical Engineer of the Midland, Henry Fowler, asked his senior draughtsman at Derby, James Clayton, to devise a locomotive that could take heavy mineral trains over the Mendips unassisted. Given a free hand, Clayton broke significantly with Midland tradition to produce a powerful outside-cylinder 2-8-0.

In order to minimise production costs, the superheated boiler of an existing Midland compound 4-4-0 was fitted to the new 2-8-0, along with a Belpaire firebox and circular smokebox. To help boost power, outside Walschaerts valve gear was employed, with the cylinders inclined at 1 in 12 to avoid fouling platform faces. Conscious that the locomotives would be descending steep gradients with heavy loads, Clayton took no chances with the braking arrangements: there were three steam brake cylinders on the engine and another on the tender.

The first of the S&DJR 2-8-0s, No80, entered traffic in March 1914. That year, Derby delivered a further five and they quickly proved their worth. The eight-coupled wheelbase made for a sure-footed steed and the power available far out-stripped that of the resident 0-6-0s.

The Midland's operating department did conduct trials with the S&D 2-8-0s elsewhere (on Nottingham-London coal trains for example) but they were mystifyingly unable to replicate the performances put in over the Mendip Hills. One impediment was a prodigious appetite for coal – around 87lb per mile – and every attempt to produce a version of the 2-8-0 for general use foundered. Nevertheless, in 1925, the LMSR

LOCAL DIFFICULTIES

Although the Somerset & Dorset was wide enough for the 2-8-0s, in one important location it was far from strong enough – embarrassingly so.

Those entrusted with stipulating the engines' maximum axleweights checked against weight limits on every bridge on the line – except two. Unfortunately, these were on the access road to Bath locomotive depot and had to be strengthened before the 7Fs could be stabled there. Additionally, the engines were too long for the S&D's turntables and forced to do a great deal of tender-first running. Briefly, tender cabs were fitted to make this more agreeable but proved so draughty that crews preferred the traditional tarpaulin tender sheet. If fired on second-rate fuel, the engines' steaming was unpredictable – as one crew found out to its cost. They were overcome by smoke in the infernal confines of Coombe Down tunnel and only jolted out of their unconscious state when their uncontrolled engine derailed at Bath.

added to the number of S&D 2-8-0s by ordering five further examples from Robert Stephenson & Hawthorn. The first of this batch, SDJR No86, was exhibited at the Stockton & Darlington Railway centenary celebrations in 1925.

Eventually, vacuum brake gear was fitted to all eleven 7Fs allowing them to work passenger trains. (On summer weekends, every available engine was commandeered for holiday traffic on the Somerset & Dorset.) By the late 1950s, however, the 2-8-0s were being displaced by BR Standard types, particularly the 9F 2-10-0s (the only engines that could compete on the Mendip freight hauls). The 1914-built locomotives were retired between 1959 and 1962, but the 1925 examples lasted until 1963-64. Two have survived: No88 (BR No53808) on the West Somerset Railway, and No89 (BR No53809) at the Midland Railway Centre in Derbyshire. No88 has been one of the stalwarts of the West Somerset fleet over recent years, although at the time of writing was undergoing overhaul. During the 1980s, No89 enjoyed a number of main-line outings, mainly in the Midlands and the north but including a southern sojourn when it worked on the freight-only Andover-Ludgershall branch.

Somerset & Dorset Joint Railway No85 was the number six of the first batch of six 7F 2-8-0s that emerged from Derby in August 1914. In 1918, it underwent trials on the Midland main line between Toton and Brent but failed to impress. The tender cab, prominent here, was discarded by 1925.

THE 'ARTHURS' OF LEGEND

The names were heroic and frequently so were the performances. Yet the origins of the Southern's 'King Arthurs' are almost as curious as that of the mythical monarch.

The idea to name the class after figures from Arthurian legend came from John Blumenfeld Elliott, the Southern Railway's newly appointed Publicity Assistant. The company's trains served four counties – Cornwall, Hampshire, Somerset and Wiltshire – all of which had links (sometimes tenuous!) to the Arthurian legends.

Elliot's chairman, Sir Herbert Walker, suggested getting the view of the Chief Mechanical Engineer, Richard Maunsell. His response was terse: 'Tell Sir Herbert I have no objection, but I warn you it won't make any difference to the working of the engine!'

Maunsell, one imagines, was in no mood to appreciate Elliot's moment of inspiration. He was preoccupied with more basic concerns, such as how to update a fleet of 2,285 locomotives with an average age of 28 and divided among no less than 125 classes.

One of those classes was a 1918 design by Robert Urie for the London & South Western Railway, the N15. This 2-cylinder 4-6-0 appeared a sound design but, on the road, was liable to poor steaming. Despite their crews' best efforts, pressure fell steadily during journeys of any length, which may explain why only ten were built up to the end of 1919. Maunsell urgently needed the Urie N15s to perform and arranged tests to identify the cause of the steaming problems. These revealed that fitting the larger chimney and blastpipe employed on another of Urie's 4-6-0 locomotives, the H15, brought a substantial improvement. This, and other modifications to the draughting and the steam circuit, transformed the N15s into free-steaming, fast-running machines, which became known as the 'King Arthur' class.

Production of further new N15s was restricted by Southern's lack of cash, so Maunsell had to resort to creative measures in order to increase the size of the 'King Arthur' fleet. In 1925, he discovered that approval had been given three years earlier for the rebuilding of a batch of ten under-performing Drummond 4-6-0s; that rebuilding had never been implemented. He therefore converted these locomotives into N15s. Since only the tenders of the Drummond's were used, describing them as 'rebuilds' was solely for the benefit of the book-keepers.

On their own the original Urie engines and the 'rebuilt' N15s were not going to cope with the demands of the revised timetable for summer 1925, especially on the West of England line to Exeter and Plymouth. With no spare capacity in its workshops, the Southern placed an order for 20 'King Arthurs' – to Maunsell's modified

OFF THE RECORD

All depots were required to keep mileage record cards for their engines. These indicated when various examinations, of valves and pistons for example, were due. During the 1930s, nowhere were the 'Arthurs' better cared for than at Bournemouth depot where ex-fitter, Joe Elliot, was in charge. Joe believed his exceptionally high maintenance standards rendered mileage record cards redundant. Inevitably, the day came when officialdom, in the form of the Ministry of Transport inspector, demanded to see the non-existent records for a Bournemouth engine. After a while, 'records' were produced but their pristine condition aroused suspicion. An official paid Joe Elliot a surprise visit and demanded to examine the rest of these amazingly well preserved documents. Joe's conscientiousness in other areas appears to have spared him from nothing more than a severe dressing-down.

Maunsell N15 'King Arthur' class 4-6-0 No30793 Sir Ontzlake climbs Sole Street bank between Rochester and Meopham with a Margate-Victoria service in June 1955. Built at Eastleigh in March 1926, it was the first of a batch of 14 N15s intended for work on the Southern's Central Section. However, it spent much of its BR career based at Stewarts Lane depot in London, working the Kent Coast.

design – with the North British Locomotive Company of Glasgow. The engines were delivered in just three months and all were in service by July 1925. A follow-up order for a further ten of these 'Scotch Arthurs', as they were dubbed, was completed that October. The Arthurian 'Round Table' was completed during 1926-27 with the construction at Eastleigh of 14 more N15s, specifically for the Southern's Central Section.

Most of the 74 'King Arthurs' served southern England for over three decades. Their achievements were nicely summed up by H. Holcroft, one of Maunsell's design assistants. 'One could always measure up to a job,' he remarked.

A DIFFERENCE OF OPINION

The 'Arthurs' put in outstanding work on the London-Salisbury-Exeter route. On one occasion, the now-preserved No777 Sir Lamiel covered the 83.8 miles from Waterloo to Salisbury in 73 minutes, 13 minutes inside schedule.

Unfortunately, the efforts of driver, Fred Stickley, earned not praise from the Locomotive Running Superintendent, but a reprimand for recklessness. After receiving this dressing down, the crestfallen Stickley was escorted into the Chief Mechanical Engineer's office and congratulated on showing what an 'Arthur' could achieve. It would seem Maunsell thought the timetable compilers underestimated his engines.

THE SUPERHEATED DIRECTORS

Sporting their rich green and maroon livery, John Robinson's 'Director' 4-4-0s were among the most handsome engines, with an impressive performance to match their appearance.

Often described as an artist among locomotive engineers, John Robinson produced two unqualified masterpieces: the 8K 2-8-0 of 1911, and the 11E/11F 'Director' class 4-4-0s of 1913/1919.

Robinson's first class of 4-4-0s, the 11B, appeared in 1901, the year after he had joined the Great Central Railway as Locomotive Superintendent. He followed this design with other types of express passenger engine, all intended for the Manchester-Sheffield-Marylebone service, inaugurated with the opening of GCR's 'London Extension' in 1899. The most celebrated of the newcomers were the Atlantics of 1903; the most problematic of these being the 'Sir Sam Fay' class 4-6-0s of 1912.

Robinson's 'Directors' had firebox dimensions similar to those used in the 'Sir Sam Fay' 4-6-0s, but employed the shorter boiler of his first 4-4-0, the 11B, which was a much better steam-raiser, Far from representing a backward step, Robinson was a pioneer in the development of superheating – the most important technical advance of the period – and fitted superheaters in the 'Directors' from the outset. Added to that, they had first-rate boilers, with ample heating surfaces and steam capacity. These qualities enabled the 11E 'Director' to equal or better the 4-6-0s' performance on most trainloadings, and the 4-4-0 used less fuel in the process.

The first of the 'Directors', No429 *Sir Alexander Henderson,* was outshopped by the Great Central's Gorton works in 1913. A further nine engines followed in the same year but construction was not resumed until 1919, by which time the 11E had evolved into the 11F, also known as the 'Improved Director'. Most of the details of the 11E were retained, but the cabs were substantially improved and changes to the heating surfaces resulted in an even better steam-raising ability. The class came to dominate the Manchester-Marylebone expresses. Performances over the 103-mile stretch between Leicester and London were especially noteworthy, with near mile-a-minute runs on 300-ton trains a commonplace occurrence.

In 1922, 11F 4-4-0 No511 *Marne* became the last locomotive built under GC auspices before the company was absorbed into the newly created London & North Eastern Railway. It was not, however, to be the last of the 'Directors'. The LNER's Chief Mechanical Engineer, Nigel Gresley, ordered a further 24 of the Robinson 4-4-0s to meet a motive power shortage on the ex-North British lines in Scotland. This order was tangible evidence of Gresley's admiration for Robinson's engineering achievements.

Displaced from express work in the 1950s, the original Robinson engines served out their time on cross-country and stopping services, mainly working out of Sheffield. There seemed to be no reservations about rostering them for fairly heavy trains, even though they became ever more dilapidated. The last was retired in December 1960, but No506 (BR No62660) *Butler Henderson* was spared to represent this famous class in the National Collection. It is the sole surviving ex-Great Central passenger locomotive.

Class D11 'Improved Director' 4-4-0 No62660 Butler Henderson at Hare Park, on the GCR/GNR West Riding & Grimsby Joint line, at the head of a railtour organised by the Railway Correspondence and Travel Society on 21 September 1958.

LOCOMOTIVES TO REMEMBER

The directors whose names were immortalised by John Robinson's 4-4-0s were those of the Great Central Railway and over half the engines in the class honoured GCR board members. Three more locomotives took the names of members of the royal family.

Six of the 11F class, however, wore perhaps the most poignant names ever carried by British locomotives. These were towns and rivers of France and Belgium forever associated with some of the bloodiest episodes of World War I: the Somme, the Marne, Mons, Ypres, and Zeebrugge. A sixth engine, *Jutland*, commemorated the greatest sea battle of the conflict.

Additionally, one of Robinson's last express passenger engines for the GCR – a 9P 4-6-0 built in 1917 – was selected as a memorial to the company's employees killed in the war. The nameplate of No1165 *Valour* was inscribed: 'To the memory of GCR employees who gave their lives for their country 1914-1918.' Annually on Armistice Day up to 1938, it was customary for *Valour* – always turned out in immaculate condition – to work a special between Marylebone and Sheffield for a remembrance service. Regrettably, *Valour* went for scrap; only one of its nameplates survives, on display in the National Railway Museum.

WHAT MADE SCOTSMAN FLY?

*Like the champion racehorses from which they took their names
the Gresley A1/A3 Pacifics were thoroughbreds that stayed the course.*

American railroads had been building 4-6-2, or Pacific-type, locomotives since 1886. In Britain, however, there was little scope for such big engines, as the Great Western had demonstrated. Its No111 *The Great Bear* of 1908 – then the solitary British 4-6-2 – was more about prestige than practicality. Weight restrictions precluded it from working anywhere other than between Paddington and Bristol! Given such limitations, the GWR stayed loyal to the 4-6-0 type.

Gresley could have followed the example of Great Western and, for that matter, the other major railways in developing 4-6-0 designs. However, he was keen to retain the wide fireboxes that had proved so effective with Ivatt's Atlantics, and that dictated the use of a supporting trailing truck. Here lay the genesis of the Gresley Pacific.

On the Great Northern Railway, Nigel Gresley had been toying with the idea of a super-powerful passenger locomotive since 1915 but, with train loadings on the GNR seldom reaching 400 tons, there was no justification for such a machine. After World War I, that changed. Loadings of 400 tons-plus became commonplace and Gresley envisaged a time when 600 tons would be the norm on the East Coast Main Line. He resolved

Harnessed to a coal rail tender and carrying its final LNER number, Gresley A3 Pacific No41 Salmon Trout leaves Edinburgh Waverley with the 'Flying Scotsman' in August 1947. Doncaster-built, Salmon Trout entered traffic in December 1934 and was based in Edinburgh all its working life.

that future GNR locomotives would be a match for such loads, arguing that it was preferable to build engines that had ample capacity for the task rather than smaller designs that were constantly working at their limits. Gresley maintained that higher construction costs would be offset by long-term operating economies. It became known as the 'big engine' policy.

When designing his Pacifics, Gresley managed to balance the forces exerted by the movement of rods and pistons in the two outside cylinders by placing a third cylinder at the centre of the engine. All three cylinders drove on to the centre coupled axle, with Walschaerts gear driving the valves of the outside cylinders.

As the central cylinder was in a confined space, its valves were controlled by shafts linked to the outside cylinders. One rare misjudgement that Gresley made, however, was to install short-travel rather than long-travel valve gear to the central

Gresley A3 Pacific No60039 Sandwich, seen striding through Welwyn North at the head of a London-Leeds express on 29 September 1960, began its working life at Gateshead depot. Much of its career, though, was spent at Grantham and King's Cross.

cylinder, which diminished the steam power available to this cylinder. His faith in a steam pressure of only 180lbs/psi was also misplaced.

The order for two prototype Pacifics was issued in January 1921 and the first was completed the following March. Classified A1, No1470 *Great Northern*, caused quite a stir. It not only impressed with its size – huge by British standards – but also its sleek lines. Based at Doncaster shed, No1470 entered service in April and was joined by the second prototype, No1471, on 10 July. That day, the GNR ordered a further ten Pacifics.

The locomotives were designed for 600 ton trains and, on a test run on 3 September, No1471 *Sir Frederick Banbury* was put through its paces to see how it could cope with such a load. It took a

20 coach train from Kings Cross to Grantham, averaging 70mph on the level and reaching 45mph on the ascent of Stoke bank. No1471 was the last of the Pacifics to appear under Great Northern auspices. By the time the first production Pacific, No1472, rolled out of Doncaster in February 1923, the Great Northern Railway had been absorbed into one of the post-Grouping companies, the London & North Eastern. At the time, no one would have guessed that LNER No1472 was destined to become the most famous steam locomotive in the world – *Flying Scotsman*.

Even as the LNER was ordering more Pacifics, Gresley was being advised that their coal consumption was too high and that the valve settings needed re-thinking. He rejected the criticism and, during 1924 and 1925, Doncaster works and the North British Locomotive Company each produced 20 engines to the original specification. However, in 1925, the LNER's and Gresley's confidence was severely shaken. During exchange trials between a Gresley Pacific and a Great Western Railway 'Castle' class 4-6-0, the latter proved superior in almost every department. Not only did this smaller locomotive maintain the Pacific's schedules, it consumed 10 per cent less coal in the process. The results of this trial led to much head-scratching and experimentation.

In 1927, No2555 *Centenary* was equipped with redesigned long-travel valve gear and, on test, recorded a significantly reduced fuel consumption of over 10lb per mile – a saving of over a ton on the London to Newcastle run. Gresley immediately adopted the new valve gear for new Pacifics and existing engines were altered as they were overhauled. He also accepted that a higher steam pressure was needed and all new locomotives received boilers pressed to 220lb/psi and were fitted with larger superheaters. This warranted a new classification, and they became the A3 class. The original A1s received these new boilers when theirs fell due for renewal.

The Pacifics' improved coal consumption allowed the LNER to introduce non-stop running between London and Edinburgh – at 392.75

THE 'SCOTSMAN' STORY

By the time the last of the A3 Pacifics, No60052 *Prince Palatine*, was withdrawn in January 1966, the most famous member of the class, *Flying Scotsman*, had been bought privately from British Railways to begin a new, and equally eventful life in preservation.

Throughout its working life, *Scotsman* enjoyed celebrity status, even when relegated to routine duties on the ex-Great Central route, performed while it was based at Leicester Central. Withdrawn from Kings Cross shed in January 1963, the locomotive was bought amid great publicity by Alan Pegler, a businessman from Doncaster. Reverting it to its LNER guise of No4472 and repainted in lined apple green, *Scotsman* took railtours all over Britain during the mid- and late 1960s.

On 1 May 1968, the fortieth anniversary of its record-breaking London to Edinburgh non-stop run, *Scotsman* repeated the feat. It was the last time the 'Flying Scotsman' express was steam-hauled. Thanks to an agreement between Alan Pegler and British Railways, No4472 escaped the ban on steam traction imposed after August 1968.

However, Mr Pegler had more ambitious plans for the engine and it undertook a tour of the United States. Since that time, ownership of *Flying Scotsman* has twice changed hands and, in 1988/89, it ventured even further afield, touring Australia. While there, it set a world record for non-stop haulage by a steam locomotive.

After a major – and very expensive – overhaul during the late 1990s, the perpetually popular *Flying Scotsman* continues to be regularly employed on main-line railtours, principally in southern England.

miles the longest non-stop journey in the world. The 10.00am from Kings Cross – the famous 'Flying Scotsman' – was inaugurated on 1 May 1928, hauled, appropriately, by *Flying Scotsman*, by now renumbered 4472. Corridor tenders connected to the first coach of the train permitted crew changes during the journey

No4472 hit the headlines again on 30 November 1934 when it achieved the first authenticated 100mph by a steam locomotive. The following year, classmate No2750 *Papyrus* touched 108mph on a high-speed trial between London and Newcastle, still the world record for a non-streamlined locomotive. The LNER certainly got it right when it named the majority of

A1/A3 Pacifics after winners of the horse-racing classics, even if some of the appellations (*Pretty Polly*, *Blink Bonny* and *Captain Cuttle* spring to mind) appeared bizarre.

After World War II, the 78-strong A1/A3 Pacifics remained a mainstay of east coast express passenger services. In 1957 – 20 years after A3 No2751 *Humorist* had shown the benefits of the device – they were given a new lease of life by the fitting of Kylchap double blastpipes and chimneys. It took until 1958 for the problem of drifting smoke to be rectified with the fitting of trough-style smoke deflectors. That year saw the first withdrawal of an A3, No60104 *Solario*, but most were retired between 1962 and 1964.

THE 'CASTLES' OF THE WEST

One of the undisputed classics among steam locomotives, for 40 years the 'Castles' were the mainstay of GWR and, after 1948, BR Western Region express passenger services.

Responsibility for the 'Castle' lay with Charles Collett, who succeeded G.J. Churchward as the GWR's Chief Mechanical Engineer on 1 January 1922.

Before his retirement, Churchward had anticipated that more powerful passenger engines were needed, but his proposals were ruled out by weight restrictions. By the time Collett took over the reins, increased train loadings on the holiday routes to the West Country in the post war years were pushing GWR's fleet of 70 'Star' class 4-6-0s (introduced in 1907) to their limit. Clearly a

more powerful express passenger locomotive was needed urgently.

Collett set about producing the required design with characteristic pragmatism. For the new engines to be built within the specified time and to meet with Churchward's programme of standardisation among locomotive types, they had to use as many standard components as possible. Continuing weight restrictions on the West of England main line between London and Plymouth also limited Collett's options. The obvious solution was to create a more powerful version of the proven 'Star'. A larger boiler and increased cylinder diameter gave him the extra output required, some ten per cent more than the 'Star', but without infringing the Civil Engineer's 20 tons axleweight limit. Extending the frame length allowed a bigger firebox and, to the delight of engine crews, a more spacious cab to be fitted. The 4073, or 'Castle' class, was unveiled in July 1923, boasting a tractive effort of 31,625lb, eclipsing the 29,835lb of LNER's new passenger locomotive, the A1 Pacific.

At the British Empire Exhibition of 1924, Great Western 'Castle' class 4-6-0 No4073 *Caerphilly Castle*, was put on display close to LNER Pacific No4472 *Flying Scotsman* in the Palace of Engineering at Wembley and was

Collett 4073 'Castle' class 4-6-0 No7013 Bristol Castle, with double chimney, races along the Great Western main line near Maidenhead in October 1962. It began life in April 1924 as No4082 Windsor Castle but exchanged identities with the original Bristol Castle in February 1952 so an appropriately-named engine was available for the funeral train of King George VI.

PEER PRESSURE

Upon his retirement as Prime Minister in 1937, Stanley Baldwin was given a peerage. Since both he and his father had been board members of the GWR, the company acknowledged this by renaming 'Castle' No5063 *Earl Baldwin*.

This seemingly innocuous act caused great consternation among certain other members of the peerage. It was not that they resented Baldwin being honoured in this way, simply that their names were attached not to glamorous express 4-6-0s, but to 4-4-0 rebuilds more likely to be found pottering about mid-Wales. The GWR soothed bruised egos by transferring the names of the 20 earls to 'Castles' Nos5043-62, in some instances renaming a locomotive only five months after it was built.

In a more dignified renaming exercise, between October 1940 and January 1941, the names of 12 other 'Castles' were replaced by those of Royal Air Force aeroplanes made famous by war: Spitfire, Hurricane and Blenheim among them.

A modest turn for 'Castle' No5079 Lysander as it starts away from Kingswear with a local train for Exeter in September 1953. Outshopped from Swindon in May 1939, No5079 was one of the 'Castles' renamed (from Lydford Castle) in honour of famous World War II aircraft.

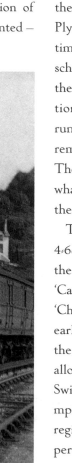

promoted as the most powerful passenger locomotive in Britain. Calculated solely on tractive effort, the claim was undeniable. In so public an arena, the debate this claim provoked between the representatives of two proud, and publicity-conscious railway companies can be imagined. It led them to resolving the burning question of which was the superior design where it counted – on the track.

Comparative test runs took place both on the East Coast main line between Kings Cross and Grantham and between Paddington and Plymouth. The selected LNER Pacifics and GWR 'Castles' ran well but everyone – including LNER's Nigel Gresley – became convinced of the GWR engine's overall superiority. On the Plymouth run, for example, while the Pacific kept time, the 'Castle' was clipping 15 minutes off the schedule. It was not solely the haulage capacity of the 'Castle' that impressed, or its smart acceleration and appetite for sustained high-speed running, but its striking economy. This was so remarkable that the findings were questioned. The LNER, nevertheless, soon put into practice what it had learned from the experience of seeing the 'Castle' in action.

The performances of the Collett's 'Castle' 4-6-0s soon became the stuff of legend. Several of the GWR's crack expresses were entrusted to 'Castles'. These included the 'Bristolian' and the 'Cheltenham Flyer' which, during the 1920s and early 1930s, was the fastest scheduled service in the world. In the 1929 timetable, the 'Flyer' was allowed just 70 minutes for the 77.3 miles from Swindon to Paddington, an average speed of 66.2 mph. Even in their twilight years, 'Castles' were registering high-speed runs: speeds of 100 miles per hour and above were attained more than once at the head of enthusiast specials.

'Castle' No5064 Bishop's Castle races along with the 8.20am from Weston-Super-Mare to Paddington, April 1955.

In all, including conversions from some of the 'Star' 4-6-0s, 179 'Castles' were built over 28 years, with few changes to the original specification. The most significant modification was the fitting of 66 examples with double chimneys and improved superheaters. The last 'Castle', No7037, was not outshopped from Swindon Works until August 1950 and was appropriately named after its birthplace. The nameplates were officially unveiled by HRH Princess Elizabeth on 15 November that year during a visit to commemorate the golden jubilee of the borough.

Over four decades, the 'Castles' served the holiday resorts of the West Country, the ports of Bristol and Plymouth, the industrial centres of South Wales and the West Midlands, and the cathedral cities of Gloucester, Exeter, Hereford and Worcester. Fittingly, the last scheduled steam-hauled service from Paddington, the 4.15pm to Banbury on Friday, 11 June 1965, was entrusted to a 'Castle', No7029 *Clun Castle*.

This engine has been preserved and is one of eight surviving 'Castles'. These include the prototype, No4073 *Caerphilly Castle* and one of the victors in the 1925 trials, No4079 *Pendennis Castle*, which was repatriated to Britain in 2000 after over 20 years spent in Western Australia. Four of the others have hauled main-line excursions and two — No5029 *Nunney Castle* and No5051 *Drysllwyn Castle* — are currently passed for main-line running.

A KING AND HIS 'CASTLE'

The tenth member of the 'Castle' class, No4082, was completed at Swindon in April 1924, just in time to undertake a special duty. A visit to the works by King George V and Queen Mary was scheduled for 28 April and the GWR's publicity department made the most of the event. Its newest locomotive, No4082, was rostered to haul the royal train from Paddington and it was no surprise to find this engine carrying the nameplates *Windsor Castle*. Later, the King drove No4082 the short distance from the works to Swindon station.

Thereafter, *Windsor Castle* became the GWR's 'royal engine' and had the solemn honour of hauling George V's funeral train in 1936.

Windsor Castle was requested to perform a similar role in February 1952, this time to convey the coffin of King George VI from Paddington to Windsor. Unfortunately, it was undergoing repair but the simple expedient of switching names and numbers saved the day. No4082 exchanged identities with No7013 *Bristol Castle*. The engines never reverted to their original guises.

THE DERBY FAVOURITES

If two locomotive types could be said to typify the character of the Midland Railway and the philosophy of its Derby-based engineers, they would be the six-coupled goods and shunting engines.

In 1911, the Midland Railway's Chief Mechanical Engineer, Henry Fowler, updated a type that had been the mainstay of the company's freight operations since the 1860s — the six-coupled goods engine. Two inside-cylinder 4F 0-6-0s, Nos3835 and 3836, emerged from Derby works with an innovation: superheaters.

Unfortunately, a long-standing design weakness was perpetuated: inadequate axle bearing surfaces. These undersized axleboxes were forever prone to overheating.

Both prototypes were allocated to Saltley shed in Birmingham and tested on passenger as well as goods work. In the summer of 1912, comparative trials were undertaken with two saturated (i.e. non-superheated) 0-6-0s to measure coal and water consumption. Although they required running repairs, Nos3835 and 3836 achieved worthwhile fuel savings.

Despite this success, five years passed before the Midland went into production. Doubtless the delay was due in part to the outbreak of war in 1914, and to the fact that the company already had a stock of 1,495 0-6-0 tender engines, amounting to around 50 per cent of its fleet.

A batch of 15 Fowler 4F 0-6-0s appeared in 1917 and construction continued steadily up to the grouping in 1923. At that time 197 were in traffic. The prevailing Midland influence within the newly formed LMSR then ensured that, with only minor modifications, the design was adopted as its standard freight locomotive. More were built every year up until 1928. Bafflingly, throughout this period, no attempt appears to have been made to correct fundamental deficiencies of the design.

With the introduction of the 8F 2-8-0 in 1935, it would have been reasonable to assume that the LMSR's reliance on the 4F 0-6-0 would end. Instead, pressure from the operating department persuaded William Stanier to authorise the construction of a further 45 examples. It took the number of 4Fs built by the LMSR between 1924

Fowler 4F 0-6-0 No 43944 awaits departure from Shipley with a cross-country service from Paignton to Bradford. This was one of batch of 50 4Fs that the Midland contracted out to Armstrong Whitworth of Scotswood-on-Tyne. As MR No3944, it was delivered in 1921. Although primarily freight locomotives, the 4Fs were no strangers to passenger work .

4F 0-6-0 No43922 of Carlisle Kingmoor depot (12A) coasts away from Shields Junction with empty carriages for Glasgow's Gushetfaulds sidings. A product of Derby Works in 1920, No43922 was one of 197 4Fs in Midland Railway service at the grouping in 1923.

and 1937 to 575 and the class total to 772, all of which joined the British Railways list in 1948. They put in many more years' useful, if unspectacular, service, mainly in ex-Midland territory. However, since the Midland's tentacles extended into East Anglia, West Yorkshire, central Wales and the Bath, Bristol and Gloucester areas, the 4Fs travelled far and wide.

Withdrawals began in 1954, with the last retired in 1966. Four have been preserved, including the first 4F built for the LMSR, No4027 of 1924, as part of the National Collection. It, along with two others of the surviving quartet, Nos43924 and 44422, has worked in preservation but the fourth, No44123, awaits restoration.

The LMSR also took delivery of the first of its 3F shunting tanks in 1924. As with the 4F 0-6-0, they had Midland ancestry, the final development of a pattern originating from 1874. The attraction of the Midland format was that it was proven, and straightforward to maintain and operate. Only a few modifications were deemed necessary before orders were placed with three private contractors: Vulcan Foundry, the North British Locomotive Company and the Hunslet Engine Company.

Curiously, although the Derby drawing office produced the blueprint, its workshops built not a single member of the class. Of 422 delivered by 1930, just 15 were built by a LMSR works, that at Horwich, near Bolton.

Although half the class was scrapped between 1959 and 1964, the 3F tanks remained a vital part of LMSR and BR operations for almost 40 years. A handful of engines soldiered on into 1967 and ten escaped the torch altogether.

A HELPING HAND

The 3F tanks made a fine sight in the role of banking engines on the Lickey Incline between Birmingham and Bristol, often working in triplicate! In 1940, eight examples were commandeered by the War Department and saw service in France. A memorable outing occurred on Christmas Eve 1959, on the Somerset and Dorset route. A 'West Country' Pacific, at the head of the heavily loaded northbound train, was in trouble. The best Radstock depot could manage to despatch to assist it over the 1 in 50 incline to Binegar was a 3F tank. Yet, assist it did, although it was prevented from piloting the Pacific all the way through to Bath. Downhill running with such an unbalanced combination was considered unwise!

THE SOUTHERN'S SEA-DOGS

The Southern Railway boasted 'Britain's Most Powerful Locomotive' once in its 25-year history, and then for only ten months. More than this brief pre-eminence, though, distinguished the sixteen 'sea-dogs' of the 'Lord Nelson' class.

No850 Lord Nelson strides through Shorncliffe (between Folkestone and Ashford) in 1936 with a boat train for London Victoria.

A 4-cylinder express passenger 4-6-0 was envisaged in the plan to restock the Southern's ageing steam fleet devised by its Chief Mechanical Engineer, Richard Maunsell. The requirement for new engines, though, was too pressing to await its development, so in 1925 a reworking of the existing Urie 2-cylinder N15 4-6-0s — better known as the 'King Arthurs' — was undertaken instead. Despite their success, a more powerful locomotive was still needed if, as proposed, 500-ton holiday expresses were to maintain an average speed of 55mph. Maunsell's plan for a 4-cylinder alternative was resurrected.

In order to comply with the traffic department's insistence on a maximum axleloading of 21 tons, the design of this 4-6-0 became an ingenious exercise in weight saving—ranging from the use of high-tensile steels for the coupling and connecting rods to the machining of excess metal

from moving parts. The newcomer came in just under the limit, yet the increase in tractive effort was dramatic: 33,150lb compared to the 25,320lb of the 'Arthurs'. It was this statistic that, in 1926, gained the prototype of the 'Lord Nelson' class the tag of 'Britain's most powerful locomotive'.

In truth, there were not many duties on the Southern that called for such a mighty machine apart from the prestigious 'Golden Arrow' and 'Night Ferry' boat trains and the 'Bournemouth Belle' Pullman (all of which had 500-ton loadings). Acknowledging this, the production run of the Lord Nelson class was reduced from 30 engines to just 15.

As with the 'Arthurs', the choice of names was inspired. With its trains serving the Royal Navy dockyards at Chatham, Plymouth and Portsmouth, the Southern decided their new 4-6-0s should carry the names of famous British seafarers – Drake, Raleigh, Hood, Anson, Collingwood, Rodney, Frobisher, Hawkins – and starting, of course, with *Lord Nelson*. The oblong nameplates of the 'Arthurs' were deemed too restrained. Instead large, curved gunmetal plates were fitted. Incongruously, given the emphasis on weight-saving, some of the longer ones – *Howard of Effingham*, for example – needed two men to lift them!

A feature of the 'Lord Nelson's' design was the setting of the cranks of the Walschaerts valve gear at 135 degrees to one another, instead of the more usual 90 degrees. This reduced the stress on axleboxes and motion parts and, in giving a more even torque, helped counter wheelslip on starting. Additionally, a more even draught was created on the fire, reducing the tendency for the blast to disturb the firebed when the engine was working hard. The most obvious effect of the crank setting was to double the number of beats for each revolution of the wheels from four to eight. However, despite these attributes and two years of painstaking trials undertaken on the prototype, the 'LNs' performance was frustratingly inconsistent. Their huge (33 square feet) grates required skilful firing if the engines were to steam

properly. To ensure they were handled by crews accustomed to their idiosyncrasies, the 16 'LNs' were always based at just four depots: Nine Elms and Stewarts Lane in London, Eastleigh in Hampshire and Bournemouth in Dorset.

During the 1930s, several attempts were made to tackle the foibles of the 'Nelsons'. Modifications included substituting the Belpaire firebox by the round-topped variety; fitting a 'Kylchap' double blastpipe and chimney; replacing the 6ft 7in diameter driving wheels with smaller ones of 6ft 3in; installing a larger boiler; and using conventional 90 degree crank settings. None of these experiments was extended to the whole class.

After Maunsell's retirement in 1937, his successor, Oliver Bulleid, finally attained a uniformity of performance from the 'Nelsons'. He achieved this primarily by fitting the class with the Lemaître five-jet multiple blastpipe, which improved airflow through the firegrate. Additionally, Bulleid redesigned the cylinders with larger and smoother steam passages and increased the diameter of the piston valves from eight inches to ten.

In this revised form, these 16 sea-dogs served for a further two decades. All were withdrawn from service between 1961 and 1962, with the last working Maunsell 'Arthur' outliving the 'Nelsons' by one month. By this time the doyen of the class, No30850 *Lord Nelson*, had become part of the National Collection.

THE THRONE OF KINGS

From the debut of No6000 King George V *in 1927, the Great Western's publicity department promoted the exploits of its 'King' class 4-6-0s. To this day, these regal engines command a loyalty that would gladden the heart of any real-life monarch.*

Were the Great Western 'Kings' a bold solution to a genuine need for more powerful locomotives, or an extravagant means of reclaiming lost prestige? The GWR's traffic department may have set its sights on running longer, heavier trains on its principal routes but overlooked some fundamental obstacles. For example, would station platforms be enlarged and trackwork remodelled to accommodate them? Then there was the GWR's apparent obsession with the 'most powerful locomotive in Britain' tag. Based on nominal tractive effort, its 'Castle' class 4-6-0s had been ousted from top spot in 1926 by the Southern Railway's 'Lord Nelsons'. The GWR's image-conscious general manager, Sir Felix Pole, wanted to reclaim the title, and do so emphatically. He insisted on a locomotive that would leave the competition trailing in its wake. Its tractive effort had to top the 'magic figure' of 40,000lb.

Such power came at a price, and that was an axleloading of 22.5 tons, two-and-a-half tons above the limit imposed by the GWR's Civil Engineer, J.C. Lloyd. The project could have foundered at that point had not consultations taken place between Lloyd and the Chief Mechanical Engineer, Charles Collett. Only then did it emerge that all the GWR's main-line overbridges had been progressively upgraded to accept a maximum loading of 22 tons. With Lloyd agreeing to the further half-ton required, the way was clear for Collett to produce what initially was known as the 'Supercastle'.

The original intention had been to introduce the new engines in the summer of 1927 but, with the first drawings not prepared until late 1926, this was delayed to the autumn. It then emerged that Sir Felix Pole had committed the prototype to appearing at the Fair of the Iron Horse, which began on 24 September. There was just one difficulty – the event was to be staged across the Atlantic, as a celebration of the centenary of the Baltimore & Ohio Railroad. Thanks to a good deal of round-the-clock working (completely new patterns had to be made for the driving wheels, for example), the first of the 4-6-0s, No6000, was ready by early June 1927. After trials and adjustments, it entered service on 29 June and made its first public appearance at Paddington two days

DOUBLE TRAGEDY

The most serious accident involving a 'King' class locomotive occurred during wartime, in the early hours of 4 November 1940. The 9.50pm express from Paddington to Penzance, with No6028 *King George VI* at its head, left Taunton at 3.43am. It had been signalled on to the down relief line to allow a late-running newspaper train to pass on the parallel main line.

Approaching Norton Fitzwarren, two miles west of Taunton, Driver Stacey made the error of misreading the signal for the main line, which was showing green, as his own. He had forgotten he was on the relief line and overruled the warning siren in the cab. Stacey only realised his mistake when the newspaper train overtook him. There was no time to brake. Travelling at 45mph, the Penzance express derailed on the trap points that protected the main line from the relief. Among the 27 fatalities was driver Stacey's fireman.

There was, though, a lot of sympathy for Stacey when it later emerged he had suffered a double tragedy. The previous night his house had been bombed, yet despite this he had reported for work as normal.

later. After running-in turns, on 20 July No6000 took charge of the 'Cornish Riviera Express' for the first time. That month, a further five engines rolled out of Swindon Works.

With GWR engines already bearing the names of abbeys, courts and castles, the expectation was that the new class would be named after British cathedrals. However, prompted by its impending American visit, it was decided something more patriotic was called for. Approval was obtained to use the names of English kings, beginning with the reigning monarch, King George V.

In traffic, the impact of the 'Kings' was immediate. They were the first engines able to take ten-coach trains over the Devon banks unaided, and allowed the schedule for the 'Cornish Riviera' to be rewritten. It was now allowed just four hours for the 225.5 miles from Paddington to Plymouth.

However, not all went smoothly for the 'Kings' – quite literally. Crews had reported instances of rough riding and excessive rolling before, on 10 August 1927, No6003 *King George IV* was derailed at speed, luckily without serious consequences. The cause was traced to the one truly novel aspect of the design: the plate-frame front bogie with its four independently sprung wheels. A cure was found by modifying the springing.

Between February and July 1928, Swindon out-shopped a further 14 'Kings' and the class of 30 was completed between May and August 1930. There was no call to add to that total since the engines were still confined to the London-Westbury-Taunton-Plymouth, London-Bristol Plymouth and London-Birmingham-Wolverhampton runs. It would be 20 years before they were allowed between Bristol and Shrewsbury and

Wearing its train reporting number of '153', and sporting a single chimney (a double one was not fitted until March 1957), 'King' class 4-6-0 No6025 King Henry III climbs Dainton bank, between Newton Abbot and Totnes, with the 3.30pm Paddington-Penzance, August 1956.

through the Severn Tunnel into South Wales.

The 'Kings' embodied the GWR's individuality and isolation. As the final development of the four-cylinder, six-coupled formula that began with Churchward's 'Stars' of 1906, they were magnificent locomotives. The price to pay for continuing that engineering lineage was that newer and potentially fruitful ideas on improving performance went untried.

During and after World War II, the 'Kings' were denied their regular diet of high-grade Welsh coal. As with many pedigree locomotives, their performances suffered. With fuel quality remaining variable, the alternative was to modify the engines in ways that would get more from what was available. A higher superheat temperature and better draughting were obvious first steps and, from 1955, all 30 were fitted with double chimneys and blastpipes and four-row superheaters. In this condition, they remained on front-rank duties until early 1962, recording a memorable swansong on the Paddington-Birmingham and Wolverhampton trains. These had been intensified to compensate for effects on

services resulting from electrification of the alternative route out of Euston.

All 30 'Kings' were retired between June and December 1962, although No6018 *King Henry VI* was steamed for a final time on 28 April 1963 to work a Stephenson Locomotive Society Special. Despite four months' idleness, it still registered over 90mph on several occasions. Upon withdrawal, ten of the class had come within 100,000 miles of completing a working mileage of two million.

Three of the 'Kings' reign still. No6000 *King George V* is on display at its birthplace, in the Swindon Railway Museum, and No6024 *King Edward I* may be seen in main-line action. No6023 *King Edward II*, once thought to be beyond restoration, has found a home and the expertise required for a rebuild at Didcot Railway Centre in Oxfordshire.

Far right: In 1971, after a three year ban, British Railways re-admitted steam locomotives to its main lines. The first outings of the new era, that October, were entrusted to the first of the GWR 'King' class 4-6-0s, No6000 King George V pictured here near Twyford.

Below: 'King' No6018 King Henry VI hustles through Sonning Cutting near Reading at the head of the 07.00 from Plymouth to Paddington on 3 April 1956. No6018 became one of the last four 'Kings' in traffic, being retired in December 1962.

ALL ABOARD

The transatlantic journey of No6000 *King George V* began at Cardiff Docks on 2 August 1927, when the locomotive was loaded on to the SS *Chicago City* of Bristol City Lines. The boiler and chassis had to be separated beforehand as none of the cranes was able to lift the complete engine on board.

The ship docked at Baltimore, Maryland, on 21 August and No6000 was moved to the Mount Clare workshops of the Baltimore & Ohio Railroad. There, it was reassembled by the accompanying team from Swindon, led by Charles Collett's Principal Assistant, William Stanier.

On 24 September, *King George V* had the honour of leading the B&O centenary procession of modern locomotives around the exhibition grounds. Riding on the running plate up by the smokebox was a young woman dressed as Britannia, her daily task until the show closed on 15 October. It must have been hot and dirty work!

The 'King' had impressed its hosts with its looks, but how would it perform? Two test runs were arranged over a 272-mile triangular route from Baltimore to Washington DC and on to Philadelphia, with a load of 543 tons. Despite indifferent quality coal, No6000 performed superbly, as did the crew, made up of Driver Young and Fireman Pearce of Old Oak Common depot in London. Speeds up to 75mph were recorded and reaching 23mph from a standing start on a 1 in 75 gradient showed the 'King' had muscle.

To commemorate the visit, the Baltimore & Ohio Railway company had some gold medallions produced, alloy replicas of which were fitted to the cabsides. They also added an archetypal American brass bell that has since adorned No6000's front bufferbeam – apart from on the couple of occasions when it has been stolen by some over-enthusiastic enthusiasts!

THE SAGA OF THE SCOTS

The LMSR took a gamble with the 'Royal Scots', building a class of vitally needed engines straight off the drawing board. Turning good engines into great ones, though, had nothing to do with luck.

No46115 Scots Guardsman heads a parcels train on the West Coast Main Line, near Carstairs, in April 1965. Built in 1928, No46115 starred in the famous documentary film Night Mail.

Act in haste, repent at leisure goes the saying. That was the price the LMSR could have paid when, in some desperation, it ordered 50 of a new and untried design of express passenger locomotive. There was no prototype, no trials and, significantly, scant involvement by its Chief Mechanical Engineer, Sir Henry Fowler. There was though, a little help from an unexpected source.

Fowler's solution to the LMSR's acute shortage of high-speed express power was to pursue the development of a 4-cylinder compound Pacific, a proposal that had originated with his predecessor, George Hughes. The project found few supporters within the LMSR management. Apparently without reference to Fowler, his superiors sought assistance from the Great Western Railway. One of the GWR's highly successful 'Castle' class

4-6-0s, No5000 *Launceston Castle*, went on loan and worked on the West Coast Main Line.

A year earlier, classmate No4079 *Pendennis Castle* had triumphed during comparative trials on the east coast and the outcome was similar. In both performance and economy, the 'Castle' was superior to anything the LMSR possessed. Committed to accelerating its Anglo-Scottish services in the 1927 summer timetable, the LMSR sought to place an order for 50 'Castles' with the GWR's Swindon Works. It was refused, ostensibly because the design would have had to be reworked to fit the more restrictive LMSR loading gauge.

This setback led the LMSR's motive power superintendent, James Anderson, to seek an alternative source of new locomotives. He had concluded (again, it would appear, without con-sulting Henry Fowler) that what was needed was a 3-cylinder, large-boilered 4-6-0 with the key attributes of a 'Castle'. Even if the GWR would not build the engines, thought Anderson, perhaps it would let the LMSR have a set of drawings. It

is said the request went unanswered. The Southern Railway, however, was more co-operative in sharing the secrets of its new 'Lord Nelson' 4-6-0 with the LMSR's draughtsmen at Derby. Coincidentally, the Southern's engineer Richard

FATAL FAILURE

The fame attached to *Royal Scot* contrasted with notoriety of the last of the class, No6170 *Fury*.

No6170 had started out in 1929 as an experiment combining the 'Royal Scot' chassis with the German Schmidt-Henschel boiler. This vessel produced steam at extremely high pressures and temperatures in two separate steam circuits. It then fed that steam to three compound cylinders. The aptly named *Fury*, however, had little opportunity to display its

abilities. At Carstairs, in February 1930, a firetube burst, killing one person on the footplate and seriously injuring another. The experiment was cut short and the engine placed in store, where it remained until 1934.

The chassis was then reclaimed and fitted with a newly developed taper boiler. Renumbered No6170 and named *British Legion*, in this guise the engine became the blueprint for William Stanier's wholesale rebuilding of the 'Royal Scots' nine years later.

Maunsell had incorporated many of the Swindon precepts in the 'Nelsons'.

Unfortunately for Anderson, none of his workshops had the capacity to deliver the engines in time. The task was accepted by the North British Locomotive Company and, in the race to get the new locomotive into production, much of the detail work was left to its Glasgow drawing office. In two major respects, however, the design was more typical of a Midland workshop as it incorporated a parallel boiler and Belpaire firebox.

Considering the agreement was signed as late as February 1927, NBL did well to deliver the first of the class on 14 July. It completed the 50 locomotives, ordered at a price of £7,725 apiece, by November 15. Given their unorthodox gestation, the new 4-6-0s proved remarkably problem-free and well able to deliver what was expected of them: to put the LMSR back in the business of high-speed travel between London and Scotland. On the strength of their success, 26 September 1927 saw the inaugural run of a new express service – the 'Royal Scot'. It was scheduled to run non-stop from Euston to Carlisle.

In October 1927, the LMSR began naming its new flagship locomotives. The doyen of the class, No6100, was named after the train service with which the class was associated, *Royal Scot*. The

remainder of the engines received an assortment of names. Half of these were revivals from long-gone London & North Western engines; the rest honoured regiments of the British army. Eventually, with three exceptions (*The Boy Scout, The Girl Guide* and *The Royal Air Force*) the whole class was 'called to the colours'.

The success of the 'Scots' led to the construction of a further 20 examples, this time at Derby Works. The first was delivered, on schedule, on 31 May 1930.

Convention demands that these 70 engines be described as the *Fowler* 'Royal Scots'. Sir Henry's input may have been negligible, but his was the name on the door of the Chief Mechanical Engineer's office. In truth, the greatest impact on the performance of the 'Scots' came from his successor, William Stanier. Immediately on joining the LMSR, Stanier addressed a problem of hot axleboxes that was plaguing the class. There had been 102 instances of this overheating problem during 1932 alone.

By making modifications to the coupled wheel axleboxes, Stanier began a process that was to transform an already excellent locomotive into arguably the finest express passenger 4-6-0 ever to run in Britain.

AMERICAN ADVENTURE

The high regard in which the 'Scots' were held became evident in 1933 when No6100 *Royal Scot* was selected as the LMSR's exhibit at the Century of Progress exhibition in Chicago. Subsequently, the locomotive (and its rake of LMSR coaches) undertook a seven-month, 11,194-mile tour of North America visiting, among other cities, San Francisco, Montreal, Vancouver, and Denver. The highlight was an unassisted climb of the Rocky Mountains.

Withdrawn in 1962, *Royal Scot* was bought for display at Butlin's holiday camp at Skegness on the Lincolnshire coast. Subsequently, it was secured by the late Alan Bloom for his Bressingham Steam Museum near Diss in Norfolk. It is there that *Royal Scot* – incorrectly liveried in LMSR crimson lake, given its rebuilt condition – continues to reside to this day.

Unfortunately, the chances of this famous locomotive steaming again seem slim.

Left: In rebuilt condition, with taper boiler and double chimney, 'Royal Scot' No46109 The Royal Engineer, passes Whitehall Junction, Leeds, with the northbound 'Thames Clyde Express' from London St Pancras to Glasgow St Enoch, via the Settle and Carlisle route.

Right: No6143 The South Staffordshire Regiment, Euston, 1937, just arrived with a West Coast express.

During the early 1940s, the decision was taken to renew the 'Scots' with taper boilers, double chimneys and blastpipes, new smokeboxes and new leading bogies. It would leave just the cab as the most visible surviving component from the original parallel-boiler design. There was, though, one obstacle to the scheme. It was conceived during World War II, at a time when expenditure on locomotives was expected to be allotted to mixed traffic and freight types, not express passenger classes. To skirt the ruling, the LMSR played semantics. The first ten rebuilds were described as 'conversions'. Presumably no-one asked 'conversions to what?' as they self-evidently remained passenger engines.

There was, however, a specific benefit from the rebuilding – a two-ton reduction in the axleloading. This change allowed the 'Scots' to work over the Leeds-Settle-Carlisle line, a route from which they previously had been barred that was now carrying a huge volume of wartime traffic.

Taken overall, the rebuilt 'Royal Scots' were highly economical machines, capable of handling the heaviest trains, and usually with some power in reserve. Under test, the 'Scots' delivered the highest power output per engine-ton of any British 4-6-0, outclassing the Great Western 'King' in drawbar horsepower.

Although rebuilding began in 1943, it was not completed until 1955. Withdrawals began seven years later, part of the wholesale cull of LMR 3-cylinder engines. *Royal Scot* was one of the first retirements, having covered 2,141,229 miles in a 35-year career. However, it was subsequently preserved, as was No46115 *Scots Guardsman*, the last of the class to be withdrawn in 1966. Neither is presently operational.

On the climb to Shap summit, No46166 London Rifle Brigade passes Scout Green at the head of a morning Manchester-Glasgow service, on Easter Saturday, 13 April 1963.

THE HALL'S CLAIM TO FAME

The fame of the Great Western 'Hall' came from being Britain's first 4-6-0 mixed traffic design, and for providing the inspiration for over 1,500 similar locomotives built up to 1957.

Alocomotive that was as adept at hauling fast freight as it was at pulling passenger trains remained somewhat of a novelty in the 1920s. George Jackson Churchward had anticipated the need for just a such a locomotive but his proposal to build one was defeated by the GWR's axleloading restrictions. As a consequence, when in January 1922 Charles Collett replaced Churchward, trainloadings had pushed the 4300 class 2-6-0s – the nearest thing to a general utility engine designed by Churchward – to their limit.

One suggestion was to rebuild a quantity of the 4300s as 4-6-0s. Instead Collett chose to modify another Churchward type, the 2-cylinder 'Saint' 4-6-0 of 1902. No2925 *Saint Martin* was selected for a conversion that principally involved exchanging its 6ft 8.5in diameter driving wheels for ones of 6ft 0in diameter.

Renumbered 4900, the rebuilt *Saint Martin* appeared in 1924 to undertake three years of trials. Further modifications were made during this period, including the fitting of outside steampipes and the realigning of the pitch of the taper boiler. The bogie wheel diameter was reduced by two inches, from 3ft 2in to 3ft 0in and the valve setting amended to give an increased travel of 7.25 inches. The overall weight of the locomotive had increased by 2.5 tons to 75 tons, but its tractive effort of 27,275lb compared favourably with the 24,935lb of the 'Saint'. Finally satisfied with No4900's performance, the GWR's operating department placed an order with Swindon Works and the first of the production series of 'Halls' entered service in 1928.

In what amounted to a further extended trial, the first fourteen were put to work on the strenuous proving ground of the Cornish main line. Success there was later repeated on other demanding sections of the GW network. Even before the first order for 80 had been completed, construction of a further 178 had been approved. By 1935, 150 were in service and the 259th and last 'Hall', No6958 *Oxburgh Hall*, was delivered in 1943. By this time, Collett had been replaced by Frederick Hawksworth who produced a modified version of the class. It remained in production until 1950, at which point 330 'Halls' and 'Modified Halls' were in traffic.

One of Hawksworth's reasons for amending the design was to better equip it for coping with the widely varying quality of coal available during World War II. A larger, three-row superheater was fitted, offering a higher superheat temperature. If anything, the coal supply situation worsened after the war, leading to an assessment of the viability of oil-firing. Starting with No5955 *Garth Hall* in 1946, the GWR converted 11 of the class to burn

On 22 September 1962, a well-groomed 4900 'Hall' class 4-6-0 No5992 Horton Hall, roars towards Cole, near Castle Cary, with an eastbound express. Here, a bridge carried the Somerset and Dorset line over the Great Western route to Westbury and Reading.

oil. This was not a success and all of them had reverted to coal-burning within four years.

Only one of the Collett 'Halls' failed to enter service with British Railways Western Region in 1948. No4911 *Bowden Hall* received a direct hit during a bombing raid on the Plymouth area in April 1941 and was judged beyond repair. Official withdrawals began in 1959 with the prototype *Saint Martin*. Adding the figure for its time as a 'Saint' to that as 'Hall' produced a remarkable total mileage of 2,092,500.

The 4900 class was rendered extinct in the final year of Western Region steam, 1965. Surprisingly for such a significant design, not a single example was selected for the National Collection. Eleven, however, were saved by various railways and societies. The Great Western Society at Didcot, has two, No5900 *Hinderton Hall* and No4942 *Maindy Hall*. In a final twist to the 'Hall' story, the latter is being rebuilt to represent the original 'Saint' class, none of which have survived. No5900 is one of five 'Halls' that have worked main-line specials in the past 20 years or so. The others are the Severn Valley Railway's No4930 *Hagley Hall*, the Birmingham Railway Museum's Nos4936 *Kinlet Hall* and 4965 *Rood Ashton Hall* and the Carnforth-based No5972 *Olton Hall*. No4920 *Dumbleton Hall* has also returned to working order, while four other ex-scrapyard 'Halls' await the completion of restoration work.

Where the GWR main line to the west meets the sea, 'Hall' class 4-6-0 No5959 Mawley Hall approaches Teignmouth with a westbound freight on 26 June 1959. The positioning of the two lamps on the front of the engine indicates an express goods.

ON THE 'SCHOOLS' RUN

The compact design of the 'Schools' was the Southern Railway's inspired solution to an apparently intractable problem of narrow tunnels.

Class V 'Schools' 4-4-0 No30928 Stowe climbs through Knockholt, between Orpington and Sevenoaks, with a southbound train on 15 January 1960.

Tunnels of unusually narrow bore are a peculiar feature of the line between Tunbridge Wells in Kent and Hastings on the Sussex coast. Locomotives and rolling stock conforming to the normal loading gauge width have only been able to pass through these tunnels for the past fifteen years following the reduction of the double track to a single line running through their centre. During the late 1920s, Hastings was a popular seaside resort and commuter traffic was growing in the surrounding area.

Consequently, Southern Railway was concerned that the limitations these tunnels placed on the size of locomotives they could use meant that the engines would not have sufficient power to cope with the increasing traffic loads.

In tackling this problem, Richard Maunsell produced what is generally agreed to be his most successful design, the Class V, or 'Schools' 4-4-0. Moreover, some commentators considered these engines the finest built by the Southern Railway in its 25-year existence. They were the last and

most powerful of the thousands of four-coupled express passenger engines built for Britain's railways since the 1850s. Maunsell tailored the 'Schools' to the Hastings line. The short frame length reduced the 'throw-over' on sharp curves (another characteristic of the route), and its curved profile fitted within the width restrictions imposed by the tunnels. Two outside cylinders of the required size, however, could not be accommodated. To produce a comparable power output, Maunsell chose a 3-cylinder layout, with the middle cylinder located between the frames.

A by-product of building such a compact, but powerful machine was a high axleloading (21 tons), calling for the reinforcement of the track along the entire Hastings line. Work was still underway when, between March and July 1930, Eastleigh Works delivered the first ten 4-4-0s. Allocated temporarily to other main lines in Kent and Hampshire, they turned in some breathtaking performances. This led Maunsell to conclude that the 4-4-0 could have broader applications and, by 1935, the class had been enlarged to 40 engines. Several were based on the Western Section where one of their prestige duties became leading the 'Bournemouth Limited'. This was allowed just 116 minutes for the 108-mile run from Waterloo, an average speed of 55.9mph.

By 1947, all but three of the 'Schools' had returned to their *alma mater* of the Hastings route. The exceptions were based at Brighton for cross-country services to Cardiff and Plymouth, which they hauled as far as Salisbury. After nationalisation, the entire class congregated on the Southern Region's Eastern Section, with the largest gatherings at two depots: Bricklayers Arms (London) and St Leonards, near Hastings. The remainder resided at either Dover or Ramsgate.

Made redundant in 1959 by the Kent coast electrification, and the introduction of a special class of narrow-bodied diesel multiple units on the Hastings services, the 'Schools' returned to the Central and Western Sections. Some ended their days back on the Bournemouth line. Others wandered the cross-country line between

'Schools' 4-4-0 No30936 Cranleigh of Bricklayers Arms shed (73B) brings a lengthy eastbound mixed goods through Penshurst, on the ex-SE&CR line between Redhill and Tonbridge, March 1960.

Reading, Guildford and Tonbridge. Following this, the 'Schools' were withdrawn over a two-year period beginning in January 1961. One, No925 *Cheltenham*, was reprieved for the National Collection, while two others were preserved privately. These were No30926 *Repton*, which was repatriated after a quarter-of-a-century in North America and now lives on the North Yorkshire Moors Railway, and No928 *Stowe* which inhabits more accustomed territory on the Bluebell Railway in East Sussex.

'SCHOOLS' OUTINGS

The naming of the Class V 4-4-0 was another masterstroke by Southern Railway's publicity department. A considerable number of private and public schools were located within the SR's boundaries. These included such famous establishments as Winchester, Lancing, Charterhouse, Dulwich, Sherborne and King's Canterbury. Many a parent and pupil travelled to-and-from these seats of learning by train. The Southern arranged for each school to 'adopt' its locomotive. New engines were sent to whichever stations were nearest the schools they honoured. Here, naming ceremonies would take place, with 'photo opportunities' that included delighted pupils polishing the nameplates and paintwork of 'their' engine.

The enlargement of the class saw schools outside southern England included. Among these were Cheltenham, Malvern, Marlborough and Rugby.

THE BIG RED ENGINES

No6200 The Princess Royal *was the first Stanier-designed locomotive to enter service on the London Midland & Scottish Railway. Its appearance marked the start of a momentous era, both for its designer, and for high-speed running on the West Coast route.*

The imposing length of its boiler is evident as the first of the prototype Stanier Pacifics, No6200 The Princess Royal, strides through Hatch End, in the north-west London suburbs, with the 5.30pm Euston-Liverpool on 5 July 1941.

By West Coast standards, the first LMSR Pacific, No6200, was a giant. It must have been a breathtaking sight emerging from the Crewe paintshop on 27 June 1933, gleaming in its crimson lake livery. However, its inaugural run between London Euston and Glasgow on 22 September 1933 was less than impressive.

Stanier had drawn on his experience with Great Western designs, with the 4-cylinder 'King' class 4-6-0 a clear inspiration. He copied its cylinder dimensions, driving wheel diameter, valve events and boiler pressure. Where he departed from the GW design was in the boiler and firebox, both of which he made much larger. The size of these components dictated a 4-6-2 arrangement rather than a 4-6-0, with the trailing truck supporting the rear of the locomotive. However, the use of low-degree superheat – established Great Western practice – was unsuited to the exceptionally large boiler. This, combined with a steam circuit that restricted the gas flow at certain points, left No6200 uncomfortably shy of steam.

'Princess Royal' class 4-6-2 No46204 Princess Louise of Edge Hill depot, Liverpool (8A), attracts interest as it waits to depart from Crewe on 25 November 1960. Outshopped from the nearby works in July 1935, apart from short spells based at Crewe North, No46204 was a Liverpool engine throughout its career. It was withdrawn in October 1961.

By the time work was underway to remedy this deficiency, a second prototype had entered traffic, No6201 *Princess Elizabeth* being outshopped from Crewe in November 1933. Boiler performance continued to concern William Stanier and his team and further production of the 'Princess Royals' was delayed until the summer of 1935.

These Pacifics were intended to supplement the 'Royal Scot' 4-6-0s on services between London and Glasgow. Though capable engines, the 'Scots' were being pushed to their limits and Stanier preferred to have power in reserve when handling 500-ton Anglo-Scottish expresses. Moreover, the newcomers were equipped to cover the entire 401 miles to Glasgow, eliminating time-consuming engine changes at Carlisle.

The introduction of the more powerful 'Princess Coronation' Pacifics in 1937 took the spotlight away from the 'Princess Royals', by now numbering 13 and including an experimental turbine-powered machine, the so-called 'Turbomotive'. During their remaining years they were based mainly at Camden (London), Crewe North, Edge Hill (Liverpool) and Carlisle Kingmoor depots. The appearance of Type 4 diesels on the West Coast saw the 'Princesses' spending periods in store during the 1950s. Although regularly reinstated to cover for motive power shortages, all (apart from No46202, wrecked beyond repair in the Harrow disaster of 1952) were withdrawn between October 1961 and November 1962. Two have been preserved, the record-breaking No6201 *Princess Elizabeth* and the first of the production engines, No46203 *Princess Margaret Rose*.

PRINCESS ROYALLY

Proof that earlier steaming problems of the 'Princesses' had been resolved was demonstrated emphatically by a record-breaking run between Euston and Glasgow undertaken by No6201 *Princess Elizabeth* on 16 November 1936. At the head of a seven coach train, loaded to 225 tons, it covered the 401 miles in an unprecedented five hours, 53 minutes and 38 seconds — an average speed of 68.1mph. What made the achievement all the more impressive was that driver T.J. Clark had to observe 50 speed restrictions along the way.

Despite stormy weather all along the west coast, the following day's return trip was even better. The formidable climbs of Beattock and Shap were surmounted at 70mph and, by Warrington, nine minutes had been clipped off the schedule. Average speed between Winsford and Coppenhall Junction was 90mph, with a maximum of 95mph. At its conclusion, the southbound run was nine-and-a-half minutes faster than the northbound.

A huge crowd greeted the train on its arrival at Euston and the crew were carried shoulder-high from the cab. That evening, driver Clark was interviewed on radio and subsequently became something of a national celebrity, even receiving a medal in the 1937 Honours List. Most importantly, though, Clark had clearly demonstrated that the LMSR could quite easily compete with its chief rival, the LNER, on the high-speed Anglo-Scottish passenger services.

THE BEAUTY OF A 'BLACK 5'

'A deuce of a good engine' was William Stanier's own assessment of his Class 5 4-6-0, the most numerous mixed-traffic locomotive to work on Britain's railways.

Encouraged by the success of the Great Western's 'Hall' 4-6-0s, William Stanier made a similar 'maid of all work' his highest priority upon joining the LMSR from Swindon in 1932. With its vast route mileage, wide variety of traffic and assortment of ageing pre-grouping classes, it was exactly the kind of 'standard' locomotive that the LMSR needed. That need was so great that an order for 50 was placed straight off the drawing board, with Crewe Works building 20 and Vulcan Foundry undertaking the construction of the remainder.

Unlike the 3-cylinder 'Jubilees', where hasty construction allowed serious design flaws to go unchecked, the 2-cylinder Class 5 4-6-0 was a success from the start. Its weight and length gave it virtually unrestricted access to the entire LMSR system. It could also deal with loose-coupled goods and fitted (i.e. fully vacuum-braked) freights as well as it handled semi-fast and even express passenger services.

The free-steaming qualities of the design, allied to Stanier's careful attention to valve settings,

A typical scene at Beattock Station, between Carlisle and Carstairs. Stanier 5MT 4-6-0 No45236, on a Crewe-Perth service, begins the climb while two other Stanier engines wait in the background on northbound goods trains, 8F 2-8-0 No48612 and, far right, 'Black 5' No44955.

In filthy condition, its exhaust blanketing the landscape, Stanier 5MT 4-6-0 No44802 approaches Birkett Tunnel on the climb from Kirkby Stephen to Ais Gill on the Settle and Carlisle line in August 1965. No44802 was built at Derby in 1944 and construction of the 'Black 5s' continued for a further seven years, by which point 842 were in traffic. Even though withdrawals began in 1961, August 1966 still found over 580 on British Railways' books. 'Black 5s' remained at work in the north-west up to the last day of BR steam, 11 August 1968.

enabled the Class 5s to comfortably reach speeds of around 90mph.

The first of the 'Black 5s' – as the class became dubbed – to be delivered was twenty-first in the numerical sequence, No5020, which was outshopped from Vulcan Foundry in August 1934; it was a further six months before the class leader, the now-preserved No5000, rolled out of Crewe. Orders for a further 75 5P5F 4-6-0s, as they were officially classified, followed. Then, in 1935, the LMSR was responsible for the largest single locomotive-building contract ever placed by a British railway company when it ordered 227 engines from Armstrong Whitworth on Tyneside.

By December 1938, there were 472 Class 5s in traffic. Wartime restrictions saw construction of the class halted until April 1943, when a further 20 examples were built at Derby. Thereafter, the LMSR workshops at Crewe, Derby and Horwich turned out batches every year until 1951. Engines built from 1945 onward were given a 49/48/47 or 46 prefix because all of the available 5XXX numbers had been used up (the first 'Patriot' 4-6-0 was No5500).

Stanier's successor, Charles Fairburn, left the design of the 'Black 5' largely unaltered but his replacement, George Ivatt, had other ideas. Ivatt,

who had been appointed Stanier's chief assistant in 1937, produced no less than eleven experimental versions of the Class 5. The modifications chiefly centred on assessing the value of roller bearings, both of Skefco and Timken manufacture, and replacing Walschaerts valve gear with the Caprotti variety. One locomotive, the now-preserved No44767 *George Stephenson*, was equipped with outside Stephenson's link motion valve gear. These later locomotives also incorporated devices that were to become obligatory on the BR Standard designs of the 1950s: self-cleaning smokeboxes, rocking grates and self-emptying ashpans. The Standard Class 5MT 4-6-0 of 1951 was no more than a modest reworking of the 'Black 5' design. This led the eminent commentator, O.S. Nock, to suggest that it might have been preferable for the ex-LMSR hierarchy of the Railway Executive to ignore accusations of bias and simply continue building the Stanier design. It had, after all, achieved a level of availability enjoyed by few other British steam locomotive

'Black 5' No45231, at Hest Bank, between Carnforth and Lancaster, on 10 July 1968 is one of 18 of the class to have been preserved. Home today is the Great Central Railway in Leicestershire.

classes. The 'Black 5' also had a remarkable record of reliability. The average mileage between general repairs for this class of locomotives was between 150,000 and 160,000, which made them highly economical.

Outside preservation, just four of the 842 Class 5s received names. All were Scottish-based engines and the quartet took the names of legendary Scottish regiments. Between 1936 and 1937, No5154 became *Lanarkshire Yeomanry*, No5156 *Ayrshire Yeomanry*, No5157 *The Glasgow*

Highlander and No5158 *Glasgow Yeomanry*. The last of the 'Black 5s' was built at Horwich Works in the spring of 1951. Ten years later, No45401 became the first to be withdrawn, and then only because of collision damage. Seven years later, on 4 August 1968, No45212 had the melancholy honour of hauling the last steam-hauled timetabled passenger train on British Railways. One week later, the final three 'Black 5s' — Nos44781, 44871 and 45110 — worked the '15 guinea' specials that ushered out the steam era. Like another Stanier engine, the 8F 2-8-0, the Class 5 4-6-0 had served British Railways from the day of its inception — 1 January 1948 — to the day it dispensed with standard-gauge steam traction. Eighteen 'Black 5s' escaped scrapping and, remarkably, only five of those have yet to see service in preservation.

Over recent years, 'Black 5s' have been a popular choice for main-line railtours. At the last count, seven have appeared at locations as far apart as Fort William, on the West Highland, to Brighton, on the south coast.

WHO'S COUNTING?

The Stanier Class 5 4-6-0 was one of the most numerous British locomotive classes. Between 1934 and 1951, 842 of these mixed traffic engines were built.

This total was exceeded only by the DX class 0-6-0s of the London & North Western of which there were 957 (built between 1858 and 1874), the 863 5700 class 0-6-0 pannier tanks of the GWR (1929-1950) and — if overseas-based examples are included — the 852 of another Stanier design, the 8F 2-8-0 (1935-1946).

Other British classes to be built in great numbers included the Great Central 8K 2-8-0 of 1911 (666 produced by various manufacturers up to 1919); the GWR 4300 class 2-6-0 (342 built 1911-1932); the LMSR 3F 0-6-0T (422 delivered 1924-1930); the LMSR Hughes/Fowler Mogul (245 built 1926-1932); the GWR 4900 'Hall' (1928) and 6959 'Modified Hall' (1944) classes (a total of 330 engines); the LNER B1 4-6-0 of 1942 (410 examples); the Hunslet 'Austerity' 0-6-0 saddletank (484 produced between 1943 and 1964); the BR Standard 9F 2-10-0 (251 engines, 1954-1960); and the War Department 'Austerity' 2-8-0, 733 of which entered the stock of British Railways.

THE MAGNIFICENT MIKADOS

*The first (and only) British eight-coupled express passenger locomotive was the
LNER's P2 2-8-2 – or Mikado – of 1934.*

Nigel Gresley consistently attempted to find an exact solution to the problems presented by LNER's operating department. In 1925, he built a pair of 2-8-2 freight engines (Class P1) expressly for the demanding Peterborough-London coal traffic. They took 100-wagon trains in their stride. Unfortunately, the project was self-defeating: sidings and passing loops were too short to accommodate 100-wagon trains so nothing was gained. A decade on, history repeated itself.

For gradients, the toughest section of the East Coast main line is the 130 miles between Edinburgh and Aberdeen. Gresley's A1/A3 Pacifics were restricted to loads of around 450 tons on the Aberdeen run which meant that sleeping car trains of 500 tons-plus had to be double-headed. LNER did not gladly tolerate double-heading and in order to avoid it pursued a 'big engine' policy that led Gresley to design and then to build a handful of mighty Mikados (2-8-2s), especially for the Edinburgh-Aberdeen line. With an eight-coupled wheelbase, these machines would have some 20 per cent more adhesion than the Pacifics and, to match the high adhesive weight, the tractive effort – at 43,462lb

– would be the greatest of any British express passenger class.

Classified P2, Doncaster Works outshopped the prototype Mikado in 1934, a semi-streamlined 3-cylinder design. The details of No2001 *Cock o' the North* revealed a significant French influence. It was fitted with the French-designed ACFI boiler feedwater heater (surprisingly, given the mixed results previously obtained with such gadgets) and the draughting arrangement was similar to that advocated by the Paris-Orleans Railway's André Chapelon. Exhaust was discharged through twin blastpipes and a double chimney, an idea first outlined by the Finnish engineer, M.M. Kylala, in 1919 but subsequently refined by Chapelon. (This adoption of the Kylala-Chapelon 'Kylchap' device was to play an important role in the later success of Gresley's Pacifics.) The use of poppet valves activated by a rotating camshaft was another unusual feature, and No2001 was the first engine to sport the trademark Gresley chime whistle.

On test, No2001 regularly attained 85mph – a previously unheard of speed for an eight-coupled engine. The most remarkable trial run took place on 19 June 1934, with No2001 in charge of a 650-ton train from Kings Cross to Barkston, just south of Grantham. Northbound, the climb to Stoke summit is a lengthy one that peaks at 1 in 178. Nevertheless, it was only on the final approach that the heavily loaded 2-8-2 – developing over 2,000 horsepower at the drawbar – dipped below 60mph.

In December 1934, this pride of the LNER visited France. The reasons were threefold. The first was to acknowledge the part played by French engineers, such as Chapelon, in the design. Secondly, No2001 was to undergo static trials on

No2001 Cock o' the North *awaits departure from King's Cross with a demonstration run. The locomotive was out-shopped from Doncaster the previous month.*

the testing plant at Vitry-sur-Seine and, thirdly, Gresley wanted to demonstrate the case for building a similar plant in Britain. Test runs did take place between Tours and Orleans but proved little. Incompatibility between the LNER vacuum brake and the French Westinghouse air brake precluded No2001 from hauling passenger trains. It had to perform with nothing more than three dead engines in tow.

Meanwhile, a second 2-8-2, No2002 *Earl Marischal*, had been built. Instead of poppet valves it employed the conventional LNER arrangement of piston valves driven by two sets of Walschaerts valve gear, with derived motion to the inside cylinder. Gresley may have felt it useful to draw comparisons between the two types, although he must have been aware that the cam gear of No2001 was wearing with worrying rapidity. For whatever reason, Walschaerts gear was preferred for the final four P2s, all built in 1936. These had a re-designed front end more akin to the streamlining of the A4 Pacifics, which had shown itself more effective in dealing with drift-

ing smoke. In 1937, Nos2001 and 2002 were similarly restyled, with the former's rotary cam valve gear replaced by the Walschaerts variety.

Once in action between Edinburgh and Aberdeen, the P2s left no doubt about their ability to haul lengthy passenger trains, and were usefully employed on fish trains, too. Unfortunately, few platforms in Scotland could accommodate trains of more than 15 coaches. Consequently, when a P2 was in charge of the kind of train length for which it was built, it invariably meant stopping twice at stations, disrupting schedules.

There were maintenance drawbacks, too, with heavy wear on the motion and bearings. Inadequate guiding force in the leading pony truck allied to the sharp curves of the line placed stress on the long wheelbase of the engines.

It was saddening, if unsurprising, that Gresley's successor, Edward Thompson, ordered the rebuilding of the 2-8-2s. Between 1943 and 1944, they re-emerged from Doncaster as ungainly 4-6-2s, almost unrecognisable from the impressive machines built there only a decade earlier.

The second P2 No2002 Earl Marischal appeared in October 1934 and was fitted with Gresley's standard conjugated valve gear.

FROM CREWE TO THE CASPIAN

Intended to modernise the LMSR's freight locomotive fleet, the Stanier 8F proved its worth much further afield, in both peace and war.

Despite handling more freight traffic than any other of the 'big four' post-grouping railways, the LMSR had kept faith with ageing and underpowered 0-8-0s and 0-6-0s for over a decade. Even its newest and most powerful machines, the articulated Beyer-Garratt 2-6-6-2Ts of 1927, had their flaws. Not surprisingly, therefore, a modern freight locomotive was integral to William Stanier's plans to restock the LMSR fleet.

There was nothing especially original about the design that Stanier came up with. Its clear inspiration was the Great Western's 2800 class 2-8-0 and it incorporated many features of Stanier's 5MT 4-6-0, the 'Black 5'.

Close-up of the smokebox, chimney and steampipes of a Stanier 8F, No48063, one of a batch of 54 built by Vulcan Foundry at Newton-le-Willows, Lancashire, in 1936. This design of 2-cylinder 2-8-0 filled the LMSR's need for a modern freight locomotive. It steamed well and rode well, and thrived on heavy hauls and tough gradients.

Introduced in 1935, the new locomotives — originally classified 7F — enjoyed immediate success. A well proportioned, free-steaming boiler was an essential component to this success, but the mechanical side of the design was equally sound. They were the type of well-equipped, easy-to-maintain engines that the LMSR urgently needed. A substantial increase in drawbar horsepower over other LMSR freight types at last enabled the operating department to run heavier trains at higher speeds. The climb through the Peak District with a 1,000-ton haul of limestone was well within their capabilities. Importantly, the 2-8-0s also rode well and could handle partially vacuum-braked freights at up to 50mph.

By 1939, 126 of what by then was classified the 8F 2-8-0, were in traffic. Numbered 8000-8125, only 57 were built at Crewe, the remainder being contracted out to Vulcan Foundry. However, World War II saw a dramatic rise in this relatively modest total. Following the earlier example of the Great Central's 8K 2-8-0, the Stanier 8F was chosen as Britain's 'engine of war'. The War Department had 208 constructed by Beyer Peacock and the North British Locomotive Company, and requisitioned a further 51 from the LMSR.

Few, if any, locomotives experienced more diverse lives. Some never got to turn a wheel: they were lost at sea when the ships carrying them were sunk. The majority, however, ended up working throughout the Middle East (where they were converted to oil-firing). Perhaps their most famous exploits came on the strategically vital link between the Persian Gulf and the Caspian Sea, moving supplies to the former Soviet Union to help combat the German invasion.

At home, given the 8F's wide route availability, the Railway Executive made it first choice to meet a wartime shortage of freight engines. Examples were built to government contracts by Great Western, LNE and Southern Railway workshops and were used throughout Britain. By 1946, 852 8Fs had been built, making it the fourth largest class of engines produced in Britain. There would have been even more had the War Department not decided, in 1943, that the 8F had become too costly and time-consuming to build and devised more basic alternatives, the 'Austerity' 2-8-0 and 2-10-0.

Following nationalisation in 1948, all British-based 8Fs were taken into the stock of the London Midland Region. A further 39 returned from overseas. Many, however, remained abroad and saw service with railways in Egypt, Iran, Iraq, Israel, Lebanon and Italy. Some Turkish-based 8Fs remained at work into the 1980s.

By 1957, British Railways' quota of 8Fs stood at 666 and, of the six BR regions, only the Southern had none on its books. They could be seen as far north as Perth, as far west as Plymouth and as far east as Norwich.

Although withdrawals began in 1962, around 150 8Fs survived into 1968. They had the melancholy honour of soldiering on until the final day of main-line steam traction – 4 August – when Nos 48318 and 48773 were retired from Burnley's Rose Grove depot. Seven ex-British Railways 8Fs survive in preservation and an eighth example has been repatriated from Turkey.

The Stanier 8F was built at GWR, LNER and SR workshops, as well as those of the LMSR. The LNER plant at Darlington outshopped No48730, seen climbing Shap on 15 April 1965, in 1945.

RUNAWAY HERO

On 9 February 1957, Stanier 8F No48188 left Buxton, Derbyshire, with a freight train. Suddenly, the pipe supplying steam to the braking system fractured, filling the cab with steam. The driver, John Axon, told his fireman to jump off the engine and apply as many of the wagons' handbrakes as he could. However, on the steep descent, this failed to halt the runaway.

Axon remained on the footplate, struggling to regain control. At Chapel-en-le-Frith, the 8F smashed into the rear of another goods train, killing Axon and the guard. For his courage and devotion to duty, Axon was posthumously awarded the George Cross. Radio's 'The Ballad of John Axon' was written in commemoration and, in 1981, Class 86 electric locomotive No86261 was named after him.

Despite sustaining extensive damage, No48188 was repaired fully and remained in service until 1966.

GRESLEY'S FLYING MACHINES

More than sixty years on, the record still stands: 126 miles per hour — over two miles every minute. Sir Nigel Gresley's A4 Pacifics were engines that took wing in more than one respect.

In the late 1930s, at stations on the line out of King's Cross, homegoing Londoners might linger a while on the platform. They would check their watches and, if it was around a quarter-to-six, listen out for a whistle. Not just any whistle, but the deep chime that announced the approach of something special.

Under its chief mechanical engineer, Nigel Gresley, the London & North Eastern Railway had recently introduced three train services that, for its wealthier travellers, set new standards for speed and luxury – the 'Silver Jubilee'. This departed from King's Cross at 5.30pm and would flash through north London, a blur of spiralling steam and silver-grey coaches. At its head would have been a member of one of the most celebrated classes of locomotive. To the LNER, they were simply the A4 Pacifics; generations of railway enthusiasts, however, had a more descriptive name for these streamlined fliers: 'Streaks'.

Streamlining was in vogue during the 1930s. On a visit to Germany in 1933, Nigel Gresley had been impressed by the streamlined 'Flying Hamburger' diesel train and the LNER considered buying similar units for an accelerated service between London and Newcastle-upon-Tyne. Then, on 3 March 1935, one of Gresley's A3 Pacifics, No2750 *Papyrus*, proved that steam traction remained capable of matching, and even bettering, the diesel's performance. It demonstrated that the envisaged four-hour timing was achievable with steam traction and, three weeks later, the LNER approved the building of streamlined train sets and the locomotives to haul them. By early September, the first of the A4s, No2509 *Silver Link*, was outshopped from the workshops at Doncaster. That month, on a press run to publicise the new 'Silver Jubilee' service, its speed of 112.5mph broke the British record.

For its first two weeks of operation, the train was hauled exclusively by No2509, which covered 5,366 miles in the process. It was then joined at King's Cross depot by two more silver-liveried A4s, while a third, No2511 *Silver King*, was based

WHAT'S IN A NAME?

Gresley's first series of Pacific-type locomotives, the A1 and A3 classes, were introduced in 1922 and were named after similarly fleet-footed creatures, the winners of horse races. In many cases, it proved a perfect combination: *Royal Lancer*, *Knight of the Thistle* and *Cameronian* struck the right note. However, the sight of *Sandwich*, *Spearmint*, *Blink Bonny*, *Pretty Polly* and *Captain Cuttle* nameplates, for example, adorning wheel splashers puzzled non-racegoers!

When it came to the A4s, the theme for the first four engines was self-recommending: silver trains and locomotives demanded 'silver' names, hence *Silver Link*, *Quicksilver*, *Silver King* and *Silver Fox*. Succeeding engines took the names of birds, apparently at the suggestion of Gresley's daughter. Again, there were some oddities: *Golden Eagle*, *Kingfisher*, *Sparrowhawk* and *Merlin* were fine, but *Woodcock*, *Gannet* and *Great Snipe* did not possess quite the same allure. Subsequently, a degree of renaming took place. While no one objected to Sir Nigel Gresley having one of his engines named after him, that eight – largely unsung – directors of the LNER were granted the same accolade was disheartening.

Other variations were more acceptable. Five A4s were named after the great territories of the British Empire: *Dominion of Canada*, *Empire of India*, *Commonwealth of Australia*, *Dominion of New Zealand* and – still active today – No60009 *Union of South Africa*. One of the final renamings took place in 1945 when, in recognition of his role as commander of the victorious Allied forces in World War II, engine No4496 exchanged *Golden Shuttle* for *Dwight D. Eisenhower*. After withdrawal in 1963, the locomotive was shipped to the United States and remains on display in Wisconsin.

on Tyneside, at Gateshead. The success, both of the A4s and the 'Silver Jubilee', persuaded the LNER to introduce two other streamliners, the 'Coronation' and the 'West Riding Limited' with seven new A4s rostered to work them. Garter blue was the livery chosen for these trains. In addition, a quantity of A4s was ordered for general service and these were painted in the standard LNER express passenger colour of apple green.

The twenty-first A4 constructed, No4498, also happened to be the one-hundredth Gresley Pacific and, on 26 November 1937, it was named after its designer. There was an irony to this. Gresley is said to have described the streamliners as a 'publicity stunt', yet appears to have favoured streamlining as a means of reducing air resistance and, therefore, getting more out of every ton of coal consumed. The key to the A4s' performance, however, was internal, not external. They benefited from experience with their predecessors, the 3-cylinder A1s and A3s, and from work done elsewhere, especially by the French engineer, André Chapelon. He had demonstrated the value of allowing steam to flow freely, and the steam passages of the A4 were as unrestricted as possible, from the driver's regulator valve to the chimney blastpipe. In March 1938, a new A4 became the first to be equipped with a device developed by Chapelon and a Finnish colleague, M.M. Kylala, the Kylchap double blastpipe and chimney. That locomotive was No4468 *Mallard*.

Wartime gave the A4s an opportunity to demonstrate that speed was not their only asset. Like the A3 Pacifics and V2 2-6-2s, they hauled huge loads the length of the east coast. On one occasion, an A4 took 850 tons up the bank out of King's Cross. During 1940, No4901 *Capercaillie*

No4465 Guillemot is pictured in original condition, with the driving wheel valances that were later removed from all the A4s to assist maintenance.

averaged 76mph with a 730-ton train for over 25 miles between York and Northallerton. After the War, despite the appearance of new express locomotives, the A4s remained in charge of prestige Anglo-Scottish expresses such as 'The Elizabethan' and 'The Talisman'. Appropriately, the record-breaking *Mallard* was at the head of the last steam-hauled 'Elizabethan' on 9 September 1961.

The first A4 to be withdrawn (apart from No4499, wrecked during the bombing of York locomotive depot in 1942) was *Silver Link* itself, in December 1962. Others enjoyed a 'Scottish swansong' working over the Glasgow-Aberdeen line and on the Waverley route between Carlisle and Edinburgh. The final three A4s were retired in September 1966, but six, including *Mallard* and No4498 *Sir Nigel Gresley*, have been preserved, four in Britain and two in North America.

The non-stop 'Elizabethan' between London King's Cross, Edinburgh Waverley and Aberdeen was introduced as a summer-only service in June 1953. For the inaugural northbound 'Elizabethan' of the 1960 timetable, on 13 June 1960, King's Cross shed turned out No60032 Gannet in immaculate condition.

AN UNBROKEN RECORD

Gresley had been concerned about the braking capacity of the A4 and, in conjunction with the Westinghouse company, had undertaken some high speed braking trials.

Ostensibly, the runs with *Mallard* on 3 July 1938 were a continuation of those trials, but as the LMS had recently snatched the British speed record with one of its new 'Princess Coronation' Pacifics the LNER wanted to reclaim it.

On the descent of Stoke bank in Grantham, Lincolnshire, driver, Joe Duddington, and fireman, Tommy Bray accelerated *Mallard* to 125mph – more than two miles a minute. For each of those minutes, the driving wheels went through over 500 revolutions and, at Milepost 90, the accompanying dynamometer car (a vehicle which carried measuring devices) recorded a new world-record of 126mph. The achievement made a legend of the A4, and celebrities of *Mallard*'s footplate crew.

WHEN 'V' EQUALLED VERSATILE

Many consider the mixed traffic V2 to be Nigel Gresley's masterpiece. It was certainly a willing workhorse, equally at home on express passenger and goods duties alike.

In the mid-1930s, rail freight was facing growing competition from road transport. To counter the challenge, the LNER inaugurated a fast, overnight Anglo-Scottish service that could convey anything from parcels to bulk loads. The LNER's publicity department gave the name 'Green Arrow' to what was a forerunner of today's container train. However, it called for a special breed of locomotive to handle both the loads and the schedules. While the Gresley A3 Pacifics might have proved suitable, they could not be spared from passenger duties.

In 1935, the LNER asked its Doncaster drawing office to work towards a new design for 'heavy long-distance work'. The outcome was a 2-6-2, or Prairie type. While such engines were popular in the United States (the nickname 'Prairie' came from their widespread use east of the Mississippi River), they were unusual in Britain. Here, the 2-6-2 wheel arrangement had been confined largely to tank locomotives.

Essentially, the newcomer was a variation of the A3. Gresley's trademark 3-cylinder configuration was retained, along with conjugated gear to the valves of the middle cylinder. The boiler was a shortened version of that used on the A3 and, with a 6ft 2in diameter, the driving wheels were six inches smaller. Initially, Doncaster built only

Gresley 3-cylinder V2 2-6-2 No60846 emerges at speed from the portal of Hadley Wood Tunnel, Hertfordshire, at the head of a summer extra bound for King's Cross. The V2 was designed as a fast freight engine but soon demonstrated it could handle passenger work equally well.

five of the new design – classified V2 – starting with the now-preserved No4771. Before long the locomotive was named after the fast freight service that inspired it: *Green Arrow*. Successful trials with this inaugural quintet led to both Doncaster and the former North Eastern Railway works at Darlington going into full production.

The V2s' free-steaming, free-running qualities met with the approval of the LNER's operating department. As hoped, they proved capable of working vacuum-braked freights at up to 60mph. There was a bonus: the V2s soon showed that they could ably deputise for the Gresley Pacifics on express passenger schedules. Indeed, in tip-top condition, a V2 could match a Pacific for sustained high-speed running. One was timed at 93mph on the 'Yorkshire Pullman', while another V2 attained 101mph on a test train. However, these handsome thoroughbreds had one drawback. With a 22-ton axleloading, the V2s were barred from around 60 out of every 100 of the LNER's route miles. All the main lines to East Anglia, for example, were off-limits.

Whatever the V2s achieved in peacetime will always be eclipsed by their astonishing feats of haulage during World War II. As far as LNER enginemen were concerned, these were the engines that won the war, not the Stanier 8F or American S160. The V2s were undaunted by the 20 coach-plus trains – loads of over 700 tons – that became commonplace on the East Coast Main Line linking London to Edinburgh. On at least one occasion, a single V2 hauled 26 packed coaches from Peterborough to London. Given this incredible capability, it was not surprising that construction was allowed to continue through the war years.

They were the last Gresley-designed engines to be produced, the final examples – delivered in 1944 – bringing the total to 184.

The V2s performed equally competently for British Railways, making their mark on the 'Waverley' route between Carlisle and Edinburgh, and on the ex-Great Central main line between London Marylebone and Sheffield. However, as

with most Gresley designs, they were susceptible to inadequate maintenance. Like any other locomotive, they could be 'flogged', but performances suffered as wear took its toll on the complex valve gear, or if the valve settings were allowed to drift out of alignment. Poor track conditions could lead to problems – some resulting in derailments – for the swing-link self-centring suspension of the leading pony truck.

The V2s' swansong came on the Edinburgh-Aberdeen run, working alongside the last survivors from the A2 and A4 Pacifics. All 184 engines were withdrawn between 1962 and 1965, with only the doyen of the class – No60800 *Green Arrow* – spared the torch.

Lit by low winter sunlight, exhaust erupting from the chimney, V2 2-6-2 No60885 presents a thrilling sight, taking the main line at Ouston Junction at the head of a southbound freight.

CROWNING MOMENTS

'Coronation' Pacifics tackling Shap or Beattock banks at the head of Glasgow-bound expresses remain the most potent images of Stanier locomotives. They represented the zenith of 4-cylinder locomotive development in Britain.

In November 1936, the heroic efforts of one of the prototype 'Princess Royal' Pacifics, No6201 *Princess Elizabeth*, had demonstrated that the Euston to Glasgow run could be completed in under six hours. The downside was that the LMSR was under-equipped to capitalise on the achievement. In contrast to the 80-plus Gresley Pacifics then working on the rival LNER, it had but a dozen engines of equivalent ability. To challenge the LNER's pre-eminence in high-speed services between London and Scotland required a fleet of engines of, for the LMSR, unprecedented power. Those engines were William Stanier's 'Princess Coronation' Pacifics.

Lessons learned from the 'Princess Royals' were applied. The heating surface of the 40-element superheater was greater than that of any other British locomotive. The boiler was much improved and cylinder layout modified, with the inside cylinder valves operated by rocking shafts working off the outside valve spindle crossheads. The grate area was enlarged to an enormous 50 square feet and the driving wheel diameter increased by three inches to 6ft 9in (an advantage when running at speed, if not in restraining wheelslip upon starting).

Most visibly, the first ten engines, like the LNER's A4 Pacifics, were streamlined. Nos6220-24 sported a deep blue livery with four horizontal silver stripes running the length of the engine and tender. On the next five examples, the livery was changed to crimson, with gold 'speed whiskers'. Aerodynamically, the value of this 'upturned bathtub'-like shape was questionable. Generally, streamlining is only effective on a long, continuous high-speed run and, on the West Coast main line, there were few opportunities for that. It was, though, very fashionable.

Unveiled in June 1937, No6220 *Coronation* promptly set a new British speed record of 114mph on its trial run. On the return leg, the 158 miles between Crewe and Euston were covered in 119 minutes, an average of 79.7mph. There were several peaks of 90mph plus, and 100mph was maintained for some distance.

The following month, the LMSR launched its 'Coronation Scot' service, using the new Pacifics to keep six-hour London-Glasgow schedules on a regular basis. The blue-and-silver streamliners were rostered for the duty, with coaching stock to match. Their crimson-and-gold classmates were handed other Anglo-Scottish turns and certain Merseyside expresses. The next batch of 'Coronation' Pacifics, Nos6230-6234, emerged from Crewe Works without streamlining and, if anything, looked even more imposing. On test between Glasgow and Crewe, one of these double-chimney engines, No6234 *Duchess of Abercorn*, conclusively demonstrated that it was Britain's most powerful locomotive. Hauling a

The LMSR was keen to gain maximum publicity from its new streamliners and this included the making of a film. For two hours on the morning of Sunday 13 June 1937, the lines between Llandudno Junction and Colwyn Bay were closed to allow No6220 Coronation to be filmed with the 'Coronation Scot' coaching set. At one point (not seen here), there was parallel running with the LNWR 1911 'Coronation' train, hauled by 'George V' class 4-6-0 No25348, and with a Liverpool & Manchester Railway replica train hauled by the preserved 1838-built 0-4-2 Lion. It must have made a remarkable sight!

On 27 September 1961, 'Princess Coronation' class 4-6-2 No46254 City of Stoke-on-Trent waits for a banking locomotive before climbing Shap bank with a Birmingham to Glasgow train. Built at Crewe in September 1946, No46254 was withdrawn from Crewe North depot in September 1964. Its final recorded mileage was 1,103,041.

The second of the 'blue streamliners', No46221 Queen Elizabeth striding through the Clyde Valley near Carstairs in 1961. Withdrawn in May 1963, with a mileage of 1,387,893, it was cut up at its birthplace two months later.

train of 20 coaches weighing 605 tons, No6234 produced over 3,300 horsepower at the cylinders. At that point, the Pacific was climbing the 1 in 99 of Beattock bank at a steady 63mph. There was only one caveat — two firemen were needed to satisfy its appetite for coal.

Record-breaking, and high-speed luxury expresses such as the 'Coronation Scot' were abandoned during wartime. However, the prodigious haulage capacity of the 'Coronation' Pacifics guaranteed their continued usefulness and further construction was permitted. Reverting to the streamlined state, Nos6235-6248 were delivered

between 1939 and 1943, and nine more non-streamlined examples were constructed up to 1948. The final pair appeared under the aegis of Stanier's successor, George Ivatt, who made some modifications, fitting roller bearings and a 'Delta'-type trailing truck.

Over a four-year period, from 1945 until 1949, the streamlined casings were removed from all 38 Pacifics. It was deemed a hindrance to efficient maintenance. Moreover, the condition of the West Coast Main Line was such that a return to pre-war schedules was out of the question. In the ensuing years, the 'Coronations' appeared in no

FROM BROOKLYN TO BUTLIN'S

The reputation of the 'Coronation Scot' and its locomotives spread far-and-wide. The LMSR was invited to exhibit No6220 *Coronation* and a 'Coronation Scot' train at the World's Fair in New York in 1939. With No6220 unavailable, classmate No6229 was selected to take its place. Completed at Crewe Works on 7 September 1938, No6229 was renamed and renumbered and shipped to the United States on 20 January 1939. It covered 3,120 miles and toured 38 cities but was stranded in America by the outbreak of war that September. It seemed pointless to risk losing the disguised No6229 in the waters of the Atlantic and engine and train were placed in store.

By 1943, the shortage of motive power on the LMSR was so acute that it was considered worth the gamble to get the ensemble home. On 20 April 1943, No6229, now carrying its allotted name of *Duchess of Hamilton*, finally joined its classmates. Its relatively pristine mechanical condition must have presented a strong contrast to the over-worked state of Britain's wartime locomotives.

Shorn of its streamlining in January 1948, the *Duchess* became BR No46229 and remained on the stock list until February 1964. Thanks to an unlikely rescuer, it then became one of three survivors from the Stanier 'Coronations'. While No46235 *City of Birmingham* went on display in its eponymous city, *Duchess of Hamilton* and No46233 *Duchess of Sutherland* were bought by Butlin's holiday camps. No46229 went on display in Minehead, Somerset and No46233 at Ayr, in Scotland.

Butlin's eventually decided the engines were no longer a suitable attraction and, in 1974, No46229 was towed to Swindon Works for cosmetic restoration. It was then 'adopted' by an organisation known as the Friends of the National Railway Museum and through its efforts – fund-raising and volunteer labour – was in steam for the 'Rocket 150' event in 1980. The Friends then raised a further £225,000 for a second heavy overhaul in the late 1980s, ensuring that *Duchess of Hamilton* remained at work until 1998. It is now on static display at the National Railway Museum in York.

Currently the only working 'Princess Coronation' Pacific is the other ex-Butlin's example, No6233 *Duchess of Sutherland*. It returned to the main line for the first time in 37 years in 2001.

---

less than five colours: lined black, lined green, two shades of blue and, finally, lined maroon. In the late 1950s, the London Midland Region repainted 20 Pacifics in this striking lined maroon livery. They looked superb, and provided a splendid riposte to the miserable greyness of much of the post-war railway.

Based at Camden (London), Crewe North, Edge Hill (Liverpool), Carlisle and Polmadie (Glasgow), the 'Coronations' continued serving the West Coast until the early 1960s. As well as operating between Euston and Glasgow and Euston and Liverpool, they mainly worked between Crewe, Perth and Aberdeen and along the North Wales coast to Holyhead.

At the last, they simply ran out of work to do and places to go. The influx of English Electric Type 4 diesels and the spread of electrification north and south of Crewe spelled the end for the 'Coronations'. Their size precluded them from working 'under the wires' on electrified lines and a suggested transfer to the Bournemouth line of the Southern Region came to nothing.

All were withdrawn between 1962 and 1964, with No46256 *Sir William A. Stanier F.R.S.* the last to go in October 1964. Three 'Coronations' were eventually preserved. Sadly No46256 was scrapped despite an active campaign to save it.

The last of the 'Coronations', No46257 City of Salford, rolled out of Crewe on 19 May 1948. On a summer afternoon in 1960, it has steam to spare as it approaches Carlisle with an express from Scotland. It was withdrawn in September 1964 having covered 797,758 miles.

A FLAWED FLAGSHIP

Innovative, unorthodox, enigmatic — in many ways the Southern Railway's 'Merchant Navy' Pacific mirrored the personality of its designer, Oliver Bulleid.

The nameplate and American-style Bulleid-Firth-Brown driving wheel of still-streamlined 'Merchant Navy' class Pacific No35019 French Line CGT, photographed at Waterloo on 30 November 1957. It was withdrawn in 1965.

Born in New Zealand of British parents in 1882, Oliver Bulleid came to Britain on the death of his father in 1889. In 1901, he secured an apprenticeship with the Great Northern Railway at its Doncaster Works and, by 1907, had become assistant to the locomotive works manager. However, Bulleid wanted broader experience. In December of that year, he joined the French subsidiary of the American Westinghouse company, becoming assistant manager at its Freinville works near Paris. Four years later, Bulleid returned to the GNR as personal assistant to Nigel Gresley, who had taken over as Locomotive, Carriage & Wagon Superintendent. This appointment was the beginning of a close and mutually profitable association that spanned more than 25 years.

Bulleid continued as Gresley's assistant when, in 1923, the latter became Chief Mechanical Engineer of the newly formed LNER. Gresley gave him a wide brief, ranging from rolling stock design to locomotive testing and experimentation. The role suited Bulleid perfectly, giving him free rein to try out his ideas. He was also closely involved with Gresley's ground-breaking designs such as the P1 and P2 2-8-2s. The downside was that Bulleid was mostly isolated from the day-to-day practicalities of keeping locomotives running and this had consequences for his later work.

It appears Bulleid was taken aback when, in 1937, he was offered the post of Chief Mechanical Engineer of the Southern Railway. The Southern had placed its faith in electrification and few significant additions had been made to its stock of steam locomotives during the 1930s. One of Bulleid's first initiatives was to assess the performance of the Southern's principal main-line classes, the 'King Arthurs', 'Lord Nelsons' and 'Schools'. His footplate rides on all three prompted changes, particularly in the exhaust systems, although only a handful of engines were modified.

Bulleid concluded that there was limited benefit to be gained from tinkering with these existing designs. He commissioned a report on the state of the entire steam fleet and, from its findings, was able to persuade the Southern's directors of the need to invest in new locomotives. Unfortunately for Bulleid, this took place against a background

of wartime austerity. Although the climate of experiment that characterised his time on the LNER had changed to one of expediency, Bulleid was not to be deterred. He succeeded in gaining authority to produce what was summarised as a 'fast mixed-traffic locomotive'; the adjectives 'revolutionary' and 'unorthodox' were noticeably absent from that description. The first outlines, for innovative 2-8-2 or 4-8-2 designs, were overruled by the civil engineer on weight grounds, forcing Bulleid to revert to a more conventional 4-6-2 arrangement.

The emergence of the first of Bulleid's Pacifics from Eastleigh works on 17 February 1941, must have amazed and excited all who were there. The novelty started with the outer casing. It was described as 'air-smoothed' rather than streamlined and was ostensibly to allow the engines to be cleaned in carriage-washing plants. Then there were the distinctive wheels that resembled the American 'boxpok' pattern. Bulleid had developed the design in conjunction with the Sheffield steelmakers, Firth Brown, and they had jointly patented it. It was lighter than the traditional spoked wheel, but also stronger and gave all-round support to the outer tyre.

A further innovation was the use of electric lighting, not only for smokebox and bufferbeam headcode lamps and tail lights, but to assist maintenance by illuminating the injectors, driving

Rebuilt 'Merchant Navy' Pacific No35023 Holland-Afrika Line approaches Mortimer, on the line between Reading and Basingstoke, with the southbound 'Pines Express' on 13 November 1965.

Rebuilt 'Merchant Navy' No35022 Holland America Line *comes off the curve at Reading West to join the Western Region main line with the 10.50am Bournemouth to York service on 17 October 1964. No35022 had the distinction of hauling the last down 'Atlantic Coast Express' between Waterloo and Salisbury, on 4 September 1964, and became one of 11 'MNs' to be preserved.*

wheels, front bogie, trailing truck and mechanical lubricators. This was among the visible aspects of Bulleid's radical approach. The most controversial, however, was concealed beneath the outer shroud. In theory, Bulleid's notion of chain-driven valve gear operating within a totally enclosed oil bath and isolated from contamination was a fitter's dream. It should have been virtually maintenance-free. Sadly, in service, water oozing into the oil bath caused corrosion; the driving wheels slipped on oil that had seeped on to the track, and there were many occasions when oil leaks set fire to the boiler lagging.

The redeeming feature of the design was the boiler. With a working pressure of 280lb per square inch – higher than any other British locomotive – and a superheat temperature of 400°C, it was the finest steam-raiser ever developed in Britain. The firebox similarly broke new ground. Using all-welded steel rather than riveted copper brought savings in cost and weight. Additionally, steel overcame the expansion and contraction problems that would have arisen when a copper firebox was subjected to the levels of pressure and temperature Bulleid envisaged. The fabrication process, however, pushed contemporary welding technology to its limit. Within seven years, the first ten boilers had to have their fireboxes

replaced and X-ray inspections monitored the state of the welding in the others. At least welding repairs could be undertaken 'on shed'.

Highlighting the problems of the Bulleid Pacific, however, paints a misleading picture. Many of its features were outstanding: the smooth-riding trailing truck; the comfortable and well-protected cab; the excellent ashpan arrangement. Most importantly, in performance terms, it delivered everything Bulleid had promised.

Soon after the delivery of No21C1 (Bulleid liked the European system of incorporating an engine's wheel arrangement within its number), it was decided to name the new Pacifics the 'Merchant Navy' class. The class name was chosen to honour the companies, and personnel who served on their ships, as the Southern Railway had commercial ties with many of the shipping lines then facing U-boat attack in the Atlantic.

This tradition was maintained after World War II, when the 'Merchant Navies' came under the scrutiny of British Railways. While they excelled in the locomotive exchange trials held in 1948, the engine record cards told another story. Since its introduction, the 'MN' had undergone 165 modifications, despite which the engines still averaged 62 days out of traffic annually for examination and repair. Once Oliver Bulleid had

departed for a post with Irish Railways, a proposal to rebuild the Pacifics gained support. The arithmetic was indisputable. The cost of rebuilding each engine (£5,615) would be offset by a projected annual saving of £11,770 in fuel and oil. Elimination of the most trouble-prone features would also save on repair time and make the 'new' locomotives more available for active service. Since the class would be operating over the Weymouth and West of England main lines for the foreseeable future, there would be ample time to recoup the outlay (this target was achieved within four years as it happened).

Rebuilding the MNs included the replacement of the chain-driven valve gear by the Walschaerts variety, the removal of the air-smoothed casing and the substitution of the stovepipe chimney for a more conventional casting. Much else was replaced, but the supervising engineer, R.G. Jarvis, always maintained that the rebuilt Pacifics were 'still 90 per cent Bulleid'. Certainly the 'MNs' lost none of their capacity for fast running, exceeding the 100mph mark on occasion.

Scrapping began in 1964, but seven remained at work up to the last day of steam on the Southern Region, 9 July 1967. No35023 *Holland-Afrika Line* had the dubious honour of hauling the last steam working from London's Waterloo, the 8.30am to Weymouth. Eleven 'Merchant Navies' have escaped scrapping, with No35029 *Ellerman Lines* now at the National Railway Museum. Three have been restored, Nos35027 *Port Line*, 35005 *Canadian Pacific* and 35028 *Clan Line*, the last two to main-line condition.

Still with its air-smoothed casing, No35003 Royal Mail *heads the London-bound 'Atlantic Coast Express' between Gillingham (Dorset) and Semley on 21 August 1958. Rebuilding for the 1941-built Pacific came exactly one year later.* Royal Mail *spent many years based at Exmouth Junction but was a Nine Elms engine when withdrawn – with a mileage of 1,131,793 – in July 1967.*

THE STRANGEST THING

The six-wheel goods was the archetypal British locomotive, but the final development of the type could hardly have been less conventional.

The Southern Railway was first and foremost a passenger-carrying railway. The coming of war in 1939, however, altered that role. World War II brought a huge increase in freight traffic to the Channel ports that it was ill-equipped to handle. The problem was compounded by the fact that the Southern had invested heavily in electrification during the 1920s and 1930s and this had inevitably curtailed renewals of its steam fleet, particularly on the freight side. Its best engines were the S15 4-6-0s, but they numbered only 45; its newest were the 20 unremarkable Q class 0-6-0s of 1938. Responding to the challenge, the Southern's Chief Mechanical Engineer, Oliver Bulleid, set about designing a locomotive that could do the job.

Aware that weight restrictions would compromise the scope of any eight- or ten-coupled design, Bulleid instead produced what would prove to be the last and most powerful class of British 0-6-0, the remarkable Q1 of 1942. Wartime shortages dictated a need to save on materials as well as weight and this meant dispensing with almost all traditional embellishment, even wheel splashers and running boards. Weight savings were made by using 'boxpok' wheels, which were half the weight of the spoked variety, and by employing a material known as Idaglass for the boiler lagging. Since this could not bear weight, it was not wrapped around the boiler in the normal way but supported on the frames, so giving the Q1 its unorthodox appearance. The boiler itself was fed from a firegrate of 27sq ft area, the largest of any British 0-6-0. Throughout, to save weight and cost, fabrications were used instead of castings. The outcome was a locomotive developing over 30,000lb tractive effort but weighing only 51 tons 5 cwt — around 14 tons lighter than other classes of comparable power. To describe the Southern's Q1 0-6-0 as the ugliest locomotive ever built. — which some have done — is to miss the point. As with the WD 'Austerity' 2-8-0s and 2-10-0s, its appearance was dictated by circumstances, not aesthetics

Construction of the 40 Q1s was divided between the workshops at Brighton and Ashford, Kent, and all were delivered during 1942. They were expected to have a limited lifespan but instead served the Southern Railway and British Railways for two decades. Most of their work was undertaken in the South Western and Central sections, with engines based at Eastleigh in Hampshire, Three Bridges in Sussex and at Hither Green in south-east London. Homes to the largest contingents were Guildford, in Surrey, and Feltham in south-west London. The latter depot served the adjoining marshalling yard and its Q1s were employed mostly on goods trains over the North Downs line between Reading and Redhill, and on inter-regional freights. These took the Q1s across London to the Western Region goods yard at Acton, to the London Midland Region yards at Willesden and Cricklewood, and to the Eastern Region's freight complex at Temple Mills, near Stratford. Their startling appearance made for a striking contrast with conventional six-coupled goods engines.

The first Q1 to be scrapped was No33028, in February 1963; the last, Nos33006, 33020 and 33027, were withdrawn from Guildford in January 1966. Though the Q1 had its detractors, it was appropriate that the first of the class, NoC1 (33001), was selected to join the National Collection.

Among a clutch of Bulleid Q1 class 0-6-0s gathered around the coaling stage at Guildford shed, in Surrey, on 17 April 1963 are Nos33018 and 33035. The surviving Q1, NoC1, is part of the National Collection and has been on long-term loan to the Bluebell Railway in Sussex. Speed restrictions prevented drivers from verifying the verdict of one Southern engineman who, while regarding the Q1s as good engines, added that, once up to 50 or 60mph, 'They didn't half rock and roll!'

A HARD-WORKING CLASS

Unloved and uncared for, the 'Dub-Dees', as they were nicknamed, were never going to win a locomotive beauty contest. They were a product of wartime, but triumphantly soldiered on for more than 20 years.

Steam leaking from every joint, cabside numbers barely legible under the grime, a rhythmic 'clank-clunk' from the connecting rods, a rasping bark from the chimney and, tailing into the distance, a rake of coal wagons – this is the abiding image of the WD 2-8-0s in their British Railways days. That these 1940s workhorses were still around in the 1960s was in itself remarkable, since they started out as the world's first 'disposable' locomotives. It misses the point to dismiss them as ugly.

After D-Day, railways would be vital in supplying the Allied invasion forces. An intensive programme of locomotive construction was initiated by both the United States and Britain.

Simplicity of design and speed of assembly were keys, and the engines had to operate with the minimum of maintenance and on the poorest quality fuel. Britain contributed two types: a 2-8-0 and a 2-10-0 version that had a larger boiler, appreciably wider firebox and lower axle-loading. Orders were shared between Vulcan Foundry in Lancashire, and the North British Locomotive Company of Glasgow. Construction of the 2-8-0s began in January 1943, and of the 2-10-0s that December.

Beginning in August 1944, locomotives were ferried from Southampton to Dieppe to take up duties in France and Belgium. Some engines were diverted to the Middle East. Major General D.J. McMullen, the Allies' Director of Transportation commented:

'Everyone loves the 2-10-0. It is quite the best freight engine ever turned out in Great Britain and does well even on Belgian 'duff' which is more like porridge than coal!'

On 9 May 1945, the day after Germany's surrender, 2-10-0 No73755 became the 1,000th 'war locomotive' shipped to Europe. By September 1945, a total of 1,085 engines had been delivered, 935 of the eight-coupled variety and 150 ten-coupled.

The assumption was that they would be discarded once their task was completed. But the 'Austerities', as they became known, continued to perform useful work in peacetime. A batch of 2-10-0s was acquired by Hellenic Railways of Greece, where they were at work up to 1976. They were also employed in Egypt, Syria, France, Belgium, Sweden and in occupied Germany. Twelve of the 2-8-0s were shipped to Hong Kong and used on the Kowloon-Canton Railway. By far

THE MILITARY TYPE

No600 *Gordon* is the most celebrated surviving WD 2-10-0. It was completed in December 1943 at a cost of £12,500. Although it was never engaged in front-line service, *Gordon* has always been a 'military' engine. One of its greatest contributions was training Army footplate crews on the Longmoor Military Railway near Liss, in Hampshire. Between 1953 and 1955, it was overhauled at a cost to the Ministry of Defence of £8,644. It repaid some of that during the Suez Canal crisis of 1956, when it is known to have worked highly secret nocturnal trains between Longmoor and Southampton.

Gordon, which was named after General Charles George Gordon, better known as 'Gordon of Khartoum', was regularly used on enthusiasts' specials on the Longmoor system, appearing at the final open day, 5 July 1969.

Following the closure of the LMR, the Army asked the Transport Trust to find a suitable custodian for the engine (which, strictly speaking, remains MoD property). Its home for 30 years has been the Severn Valley Railway, but there have been excursions to Shildon for the Stockton & Darlington 125th anniversary cavalcade in 1975, and Rainhill for the 'Rocket 150' event in May 1980.

the largest number of 2‹10‹0s – 103 – went to The Netherlands where some continued working until the mid‹1950s.

In Britain, while 733 of the 2‹8‹0s saw service with British Railways, only 25 of the 2‹10‹0s were employed because they were too large for most routes. These 2‹10‹0s mostly spent their days on freight traffic in southern Scotland and all were retired between 1961 and 1962. The final 'Dub‹Dee' 2‹8‹0s working on BR were stationed at Normanton in Yorkshire, from where, in September 1967, No90682, became the last to be withdrawn.

Happily, at least four of the WD 2‹10‹0s have survived, among them the last of the Army engines, No600 *Gordon*. Two engines repa‹ triated from Greece have found homes on the North Yorkshire Moors Railway, No601 *Sturdee* and No3672 *Dame Vera Lynn*. That historic 1,000th engine, No73755, is on display in Utrecht, honouring the contribution made by its type to the revival of rail transport in The Netherlands after the war.

BASIC EQUIPMENT

The WD 2-8-0s were not the most sophisticated of engines. For example, the tender water 'gauge' consisted of a device called a 'walking stick'. This was a metal pipe with holes drilled along it at reg‹ ular intervals. When the pipe was turned through 90 degrees, the level of water in the tender was indicated by which of the holes water poured out of.

On the footplate, the WD 2-8-0s had a curious shuffling gait and, at their worst, would give the crew a thoroughly good shaking. But they were free-steaming, very reliable workhorses and perfectly suited to trundling along at 30mph with heavy, loose-coupled freights. Even at the lowest point of steam, crews could generally trust a WD 2-8-0, no matter how bad its condition, to get on and do the job satisfactorily.

WD 'Austerity' 2-8-0 No90092 shuffles through Beningborough, on the East Coast Main Line north of York, with a northbound parcels train. Built in October 1944, No90092 was loaned to the LNER in December 1945 and, at nationalisation, was based at Heaton shed on Tyneside. It was withdrawn from service at Hull Dairycoates in October 1965.

TRAVELLING LIGHT

Following on from his Merchant Navy class, Oliver Bullied developed a 'Light Pacific' that could be used on nearly all of the Southern Railway routes and went on to become their main passenger express locomotive.

The line to Bude and Padstow along the north coast of Cornwall was a Southern outpost in Great Western territory. It was also one of the lines from which Oliver Bulleid's 'Merchant Navy' Pacifics were barred because their axleloading of 21 tons was too heavy for the bridges. Such restrictions, allied to a general requirement for a modern, general-purpose passenger engine, were the factors in the development of a scaled-down version of the 'MN', dubbed the 'Light Pacific'.

Modifications aimed at saving weight and so maximising the locomotives' route availability were very successful. With an axleloading of just over 18 tons, the Light Pacifics had access to almost all the Southern system. Though smaller and lighter, these 'West Country' Pacifics, as they became known officially, shared many of the features and components of their bigger brethren, including the 'air-smoothed' casing, electric lighting, Bulleid-Firth-Brown wheels and chain-driven valve gear.

The first 'WC' Pacific entered service in May 1945 and over the following six years, it was augmented by a further 109 engines built at Brighton and Eastleigh. Production continued at rates of between one and four engines a month up to December 1948, after which deliveries slowed. In

A chance to compare original and rebuilt light Pacifics at Waterloo on April 24 1966. No34064 Fighter Command stands alongside rebuilt No34032 Camelford. Both are at the head of Weymouth-bound trains.

THE GREAT ESCAPE

Incredibly, no less than twenty 'West Country' and 'Battle of Britain' Pacifics have managed to elude the cutter's torch. No other class of ex-British Railways main-line locomotives has been able to retain so many survivors. Nine of them even remain in their original, air-smoothed condition. Similarly, nine have been returned to working order and the restoration of a further two locomotives is now approaching completion.

Among the working examples, Nos34016 *Bodmin*, No34027 *Taw Valley* and No34092 *City of Wells* have been responsible for several stirring main-line runs in recent years.

Adding the twenty 'Light Pacifics' to the eleven surviving 'Merchant Navy' 4-6-2s brings the total of Bulleid Pacifics preserved to thirty-one. Remarkably, this figure adds up to almost a quarter of the total that were constructed.

May 1950, British Railways halted construction with just one more locomotive on order. There was speculation that it was undergoing a major redesign in an attempt to counter the failings of some of Bulleid's more temperamental innovations. However, eight months later, No34110 66 Squadron emerged unaltered from Brighton works. Whether the Southern needed so many Pacifics remains open to question.

The snag with complex mechanisms such as Bulleid's chain-driven gear was that they demanded a level of maintenance that, in the 1950s, was hard to justify or sustain. Following on from a scheme to rebuild the 'Merchant Navies', the decision was taken in 1957 to apply similar treatment to 60 of the 'WC Pacifics'. As with the 'MNs', the principal changes were the substitution of Walschaerts valve gear and the removal of the air-smoothed casing. In its place, large, square smoke deflectors were fitted, giving the engines a strong resemblance to the BR Standard Pacifics.

Whatever the drawbacks of the original design, the performance of Bullied's Pacifics was always consistently outstanding. They will be remembered storming the banks at the head of boat trains for the Channel ports, speeding holidaymakers to the resort towns of the West Country, or handling heavy Kent Coast commuter trains. 'WC Pacifics' soldiered on until the last day of Southern steam in July 1967.

On Derby Day in June 1947, the royal train was entrusted to No21C157, then only three months old. Later named Biggin Hill, *the Pacific was withdrawn in May 1967.*

SEASIDE RESORTS AND SQUADRONS

As with the 'King Arthurs', 'Lord Nelsons' and 'Schools' classes, the Southern's astute publicity department came up with a winning naming policy for the new Pacifics. They were identified with cities, towns, villages and tourist spots in south-west England, beginning with Exeter, the name given to No21C101 in a ceremony held in the city on 10 July 1945.

However, in November 1946, by which time 48 'West Countries' were in traffic, the policy changed. Examples were beginning to appear regularly on the Central and Eastern Sections and names were selected which would have a particular resonance in the counties of Kent, Surrey and Sussex. Locomotives took the names of the Royal Air Force squadrons, airfields, aircraft and key personalities that only six years earlier had fought and won the Battle of Britain.

MR PEPPERCORN'S PACIFICS

The last classes of 4-6-2s to be designed pre-nationalisation were the work of the LNER's Arthur Peppercorn. They provided a fitting finale to the era of the East Coast Pacific.

A fine profile of Peppercorn A2 Pacific No60535 Hornet's Beauty working a southbound goods through Northallerton. The locomotive still awaits its British Railways 'lion-and-wheel' totem to be applied to the tender. From November 1949, No60535 spent its days in Scotland, chiefly at the Edinburgh depots of Haymarket and St Margaret's. It was withdrawn from Polmadie (Glasgow) in June 1965.

Appointed in July 1946, Arthur Peppercorn's time in charge of the LNER's locomotive affairs was brief. Nevertheless, in the 18 months before nationalisation, he produced three locomotive designs, two of which were Pacifics. Both improved on the work of Peppercorn's predecessor, Edward Thompson and, like their designer, enjoyed considerably greater popularity.

Edward Thompson's rebuilding of the first of the Gresley Pacifics, No4470 *Great Northern*, in 1945 had more to do with ego than efficiency. This hamfisted way of signifying the end of the Gresley era earned Thompson few friends. The rebuild was to be the basis of a new class of 4-6-2s that, judging by the prototype, would have been singularly lacklustre. It certainly failed to enthuse Thompson's subordinates at Doncaster Works. It is said the drawing office made sure the detail design work was prolonged past Thompson's retirement to allow his successor, Arthur Peppercorn, scope to make significant changes. Whether or not a conspiracy took place, Peppercorn's reworking produced one of the finest of British express locomotives, one well meriting its classification of A1.

Not all of Thompson's ideas were discarded. His arrangement of the steam circuit was astute, as was the fitting of a large firegrate. At 50 square feet, it generated ample power even from poor quality coal. In most other respects the A1 resembled the earlier of the Peppercorn Pacifics, the A2 of 1947. The principal difference was in the driving wheel diameter, which, at 6ft 8in was six inches greater than that of the A2. The A2's proven arrangement of cylinders and valve gear was adopted and the boilers were interchangeable between the classes. However, unlike the A2, all the Peppercorn A1s were equipped with double chimneys and blastpipes from the outset.

The first of the A1s emerged from Doncaster in August 1948. The Yorkshire workshop then shared construction with Darlington Works, in County Durham, which contributed 23 examples. All 49 A1s were completed by the end of 1949. Initially, the A1s were distributed the length of the East Coast Main Line, from Edinburgh to London. Examples were based at Kings Cross, Grantham, Doncaster and York. Sixteen were shared between two Tyneside depots, Heaton and Gateshead, and five were allocated to Haymarket, Edinburgh. A further five went to Copley Hill, Leeds, a depot that later became synonymous with the class. Immediately, they were put to work on the heaviest main-line expresses, replacing the Gresley V2 2-6-2s that had been used as a stopgap to cover the shortage of suitable engines.

Above all, the A1s were renowned for their reliability. By 1961, the class had accumulated 48 million miles, equivalent to 202 miles each calendar day. Such figures were unmatched by any other steam locomotives on British Railways. Some of the best performances were put in by a quintet of engines that, in a move to increase mileages between general repairs, were fitted with roller bearing axleboxes. Between 1949 and 1961, Nos60153-57 covered 4.8 million miles, with an average mileage between works overhauls of 120,000. In a single year, No60156 *Great Central* of King's Cross ran 96,000 miles.

At least one leading railwayman considered the Peppercorn A1s the best all-round British express

passenger locomotives but, by the summer of 1966, all 49 had gone for scrap. The last to be withdrawn was No60145 *Saint Mungo* of York, after a working life of just 17 years. However, their reputations endured and, in the early 1990s,

POTTED PEPPERCORN

Arthur Henry Peppercorn was born in 1889 and joined the Great Northern Railway in 1905, becoming Chief Mechanical Engineer of the LNER on 1 July 1946. By all accounts, Arthur Peppercorn was well liked by his colleagues. He was a modest and, in some ways, a shy man (the naming of A2 No525 after him was at the behest of LNER Chairman, Sir Ronald Matthews). For example, when he was awarded the OBE in the 1945 Birthday Honours he twice refused it because he was anxious about attending the ceremony at Buckingham Palace. Eventually the medal was sent by post!

Had his picture appeared in the newspapers, Peppercorn might have become a more recognisable figure. As it was, when he approached a footplate crew to ask what they thought of their locomotive – which just happened to be No525 *A.H. Peppercorn* – the fireman replied: 'You pick up the bloody shovel when you start and you don't put it down again 'till you get to your destination!' Instead of coming out with the 'Do you know who I am?' response, Peppercorn enjoyed telling the story against himself.

Shy to the last, Peppercorn wanted his retirement party in 1949 to be a quiet affair. However, his associates from the LNER were determined to show their appreciation and secretly arranged for the building of a superb model of No525 to commemorate the occasion. After the toasts, a curtain was pulled aside to reveal the gift. Peppercorn was overwhelmed by the gesture and, in tears, told his wife, 'They got me, Pat!'

the A1 Steam Locomotive Trust was formed to construct what would have been the fiftieth member of the class. With sponsorship and technical assistance from a host of companies, No60163 *Tornado* will be the first main-line steam locomotive built in Britain since 1960. Fittingly, this commemorative A1 is being assembled in Darlington, County Durham.

The first of the other class of Peppercorn Pacifics, the A2, was outshopped from Doncaster in December 1947. Numbered 525 and named *A.H. Peppercorn*, it represented a return to successful Gresley principles. However, the modernity of the design was also evident. A rocking grate, hopper ashpan and self-cleaning smokebox were all incorporated and – following the

example of Bulleid's Southern Railway Pacifics – the engines were fitted with electric lighting.

The A2s immediately displayed their qualities. They were fast, free-steaming and immensely powerful. However, this did not preclude Doncaster from fitting five of the class – including the now-preserved No60532 *Blue Peter* – with double blastpipes and chimneys. They swiftly proved their worth with significant improvements in steaming capability and fuel economy. In a further modification, five locomotives were fitted with multiple valve regulators.

At first the A2s were based at depots north and south of the border, ranging from New England (Peterborough) to Edinburgh's Haymarket. In 1949, five were put to work on the Edinburgh-Dundee-Aberdeen route and proved the ideal engines for its stiff gradients and sharp curvature. The A2s also worked to Perth, Glasgow, Carlisle, Newcastle-upon-Tyne and, occasionally, more southerly outposts. In 1963, Nos60525, 60530 and 60535 surprisingly crossed the traditional LNER-LMSR divide and were allocated to a Glasgow depot, Polmadie. They replaced Stanier 'Coronation' Pacifics over the ex-Caledonian Railway route to Carlisle.

The swansong of the A2s, though, came in eastern Scotland with many memorable performances over the Aberdeen road during the early 1960s. However, it was on Stoke bank in Lincolnshire, the scene of Gresley Pacific No4468 *Mallard's* 1938 world speed record, that No60526 *Sugar Palm* attained a speed of 101mph. That record for the A2s was set in 1961. The following year, the first of the 15-strong class was scrapped, with the final trio – Nos60528 *Tudor Minstrel*, No60530 *Sayajirao* and No60532 *Blue Peter* – retired in 1966.

With his Pacifics, Arthur Peppercorn had provided a fitting finale to three glorious decades of LNER express passenger engine development. Since 1992, thanks to the efforts of the North Eastern Locomotive Preservation Group, the main-line performances of the survivor, *Blue Peter*, have merely cemented that opinion.

A1 Pacific No60126 Sir Vincent Raven begins the climb out of Durham, January 1960, with the southbound 'Northumbrian'.

*A2 Pacific No60532 Blue Peter passes Kinnaber
Junction with the 1.30pm Aberdeen-Glasgow on 30 July
1966. Blue Peter was privately preserved, becoming
something of a celebrity courtesy of the eponymous
children's television programme. It is currently based on
the North Yorkshire Moors Railway.*

THE BRIEF RULE OF 'BRITANNIA'

The 'Britannia' Pacific heralded a new era in British locomotive practice, one intended to acknowledge the post-war realities of running a railway.

The Standard Class 7 Pacifics succeeded in registering both a 'first' and a 'last'. They were the first of the British Railways Standard classes to enter service, and the last express passenger steam locomotives to be built in Britain, at least in any quantity. Memories of the 'Britannias', as they quickly became known, are as diverse as opinions of their worth. Engine crews on the Eastern Region, accustomed to only underpowered 4-6-0s on East Anglian express services, welcomed their arrival.

In contrast, their reception on the Western Region bordered on the hostile. As the advance guard of the Standard classes, this 4-6-2 had to

Trailing a pure white exhaust, 'Britannia' Pacific No70017 Arrow passes over Dillicar water troughs, on the West Coast Main Line south of Tebay, with a Manchester to Glasgow train. Built at Crewe in June 1951, No70017 became one of 15 'Britannias' allocated to the Western Region, being based at Old Oak Common and then Cardiff Canton (the sole WR shed to appreciate the qualities of the class!).

bridge long-standing cultural divides. Designed at Derby but built at Crewe, the prototype, No70000 *Britannia*, was unveiled in January 1951. Its name set a trend for the class. Many honoured historical and cultural icons such as poets and playwrights, who rubbed smoke deflectors with an assortment of figures from Hotspur and Hereward the Wake to Earl Haig. Fifteen earmarked for the Western Region, however, re-used names from the roll of long-departed Great Western engines. If the gesture was intended to endear the 'Britannias' to their new owners, it failed. The final six, delivered between August and September 1954, carried the names of

Scottish firths: Clyde, Dornoch, Forth, Moray, Solway and Tay. Appropriately, five of this group spent much of their working lives based at Polmadie depot in Glasgow. From here they were chiefly employed on Manchester and Liverpool expresses, and remained the only 'Britannias' allocated to the Scottish Region.

The first of the six regions to experience what the 'Britannias' had to offer was the Eastern. It urgently needed more powerful locomotives for the ex-Great Eastern lines, particularly that between London to Norwich. Divided between the depots at Stratford (London) and Norwich, the 'Pacifics' had an immediate and dramatic impact on punctuality. As a consequence, new timetables showed improvements in both frequency of service and journey times. At one time, no less than 22 Class 7 4-6-2s were on Norwich's books. As with the remainder of the class, they benefited from rocking grates, self-cleaning

MAKING SAVINGS

The doyen of the Standard Pacifics, No70000 *Britannia*, was an apparent candidate for preservation following the locomotive's premature withdrawal from Newton Heath depot, in Manchester, in May 1966. It had sustained a damaged bufferbeam in a collision at Birmingham New Street but, more seriously, had a wasted smokebox and flaws in its copper firebox.

Once No70013 *Oliver Cromwell* had been selected for the National Collection, *Britannia* — now much vandalised — was removed to a site at Redhill in Surrey for inspection by potential buyers, including scrap merchants. Thankfully, by 1969, the East Anglian Preservation Society had raised enough money to buy the engine and

its life in preservation began. Restoration to working order occupied seven years and No70000 was recommissioned by the head of the BR Standard design team, Robert Riddles, on 20 May 1978. At the ceremony, Riddles was asked how *Britannia* came by its name. Was it a moment of patriotic inspiration? Not exactly, came the reply, it was simply that the figure of Britannia was incorporated in the coat-of-arms of the London & North Western Railway, Riddles' first employers.

Britannia remains in private hands and is again undergoing an overhaul to return it to running order. The National Collection's *Oliver Cromwell* has for many years been in the care of Bressingham Steam Museum, at Diss, in Norfolk.

smokeboxes, self-emptying ashpans and springs laminated with carbon steel. The majority also boasted roller bearings on the coupled axleboxes.

The pride felt in this first product of Britain's nationalised railway was evident in the fifth of the 'Britannias', No70004 *William Shakespeare*. The locomotive was turned out in exhibition finish — all chromium-plating and burnished brass and copper — for the 1951 Festival of Britain on London's South Bank. This celebrity status continued when it was allocated to Stewarts Lane running shed in Battersea primarily to work the prestige 'Golden Arrow' boat train. Its new owners maintained it in immaculate condition, as they did classmate No70014 *Iron Duke* which for a time shared the 'Golden Arrow' duty. The Southern Region briefly took delivery of a third 'Britannia', No70009 *Alfred the Great*, and placed it at another London shed, Nine Elms. Here, too, it was given top billing and regularly hauled the 'Bournemouth Belle' Pullman.

This was in contrast to the welcome accorded the 'Britannias' on the Western Region. Around 15 spent time there but only one depot managed to get the best out of them, Cardiff Canton succeeding where Plymouth Laira and London's Old Oak Common failed. Blame for this has been attributed partly to drivers' difficulty in adapting to left-hand drive (all Great Western express engines placed the driver's controls to the right of the footplate). There was also the matter of the regulator, which was deemed unresponsive in comparison with the Swindon model. Nevertheless, Cardiff's 'Britannias' became star performers on the 'Red Dragon' and 'Capitals United' expresses. Among other famous named trains regularly rostered for 'Britannia' haulage was the 'Irish Mail', which employed engines

based at Holyhead. These were part of the London Midland contingent that started at just 12 locomotives but, by 1967, embraced all 55 of the class.

Displaced by diesels from express workings, the 'Britannias' were relegated to semi-fast, parcels and freight workings. The progress of electrification south of Crewe eventually limited their sphere of operation to north-west England. Some workings still took them into Scotland and over the Pennines to Leeds and Bradford, and they frequently appeared on football specials. This was especially true when Carlisle United played since all but seven 'Britannias' ended their days at Carlisle's Kingmoor depot (only five of the class were not based there at one time or another). Their twilight years saw the Class 7 Pacifics much in demand for enthusiast railtours.

As late as January 1967, 42 'Britannias' remained in service but by the December of that year that figure had been reduced to 14. The impending closure of Carlisle Kingmoor in January 1968 spelled the end for all but one of those, No70013 *Oliver Cromwell*.

In February 1967, *Oliver Cromwell* had become the last steam locomotive overhauled at Crewe Works and was in prime condition to work a succession of 'end-of-steam' specials. It was a task it performed to the last, hauling BR's valedictory 'Fifteen Guinea Special' between Manchester Victoria, Blackburn and Carlisle on Sunday, 11 August 1968.

A HEAVY FREIGHT CHAMPION

Among the twelve Standard classes, the 9F heavy freight locomotive was the most numerous and, operationally, had the greatest impact. Sadly, it was denied the time to justify the investment.

The 9F was unique among the Standard classes. Where the other eleven designs fell into existing categories — express passenger 4/6/2, mixed traffic 4/6/0 and 2/6/0, as well as 2/6/4 and 2/6/2 passenger tank — the 9F broke fresh ground. For a start, the class '9' power category was new to Britain. Second, the design shared very few components with its companions (elsewhere boilers, for example, were interchangeable). Third, and most significantly, those most closely involved with the 9Fs — footplate crews, running shed foremen, regional operating officers — generally considered them the finest heavy freight engines built in Britain.

Had the view of some senior managers prevailed, however, they would never have been built. A post-nationalisation assessment of the British Railways fleet identified the most pressing need to be for mixed traffic engines. Heavy freight appeared well catered for by the influx of over 700 surplus War Department 2/8/0s. Moreover, every railway company — the Southern apart — had its quota of eight-coupled tender engines. BR had over 2,200 2/8/0s on its books.

There were those, however, who looked beyond the bare statistics. The motive power officer of the Eastern Region argued that a powerful, fast freight engine could work round trips, such as Peterborough to London and Annesley to Woodford Halse, within the footplate crew's eight-hour shift. Apart from higher average speeds, time would be saved on maintenance by the proposed fitting of rocker grates and hopper ashpans — it would add up to substantial savings. Unfortunately, he and his counterparts on other regions had to wait until 1954 for the 9Fs to arrive and prove the point.

In the draft plan for the BR Standard types, the heavy freight class was to have been a 2/8/2 but, encouraged by the success of his ten-coupled design for the War Department, Robert Riddles advocated a 2/10/0 configuration. His opponents argued that having to site the firebox above the rear wheelset (they believed 5ft 3in was the

A STAR IS BORN

The 9F 2-10-0 was a fitting conclusion to 150 years of steam locomotive construction in Britain. Although numerically the final member of the class was No92250 (outshopped from Crewe in December 1958) the last of the estimated 60,000 engines produced for Britain's railways was No92220, built at Swindon. At its completion, a competition was held among Western Region staff to select a suitable name. The choice of *Evening Star* was particularly appropriate: it had originated with a Great Western broad gauge locomotive of 1839 and perpetuated a long-standing GWR tradition of 'astronomical' names. The new nameplates, accompanied by commemorative plaques, were unveiled by K.W.C. Grand of the British Transport Commission on 18 March 1960. While the livery for all other 9Fs was just plain black, *Evening Star* was outshopped in lined green, complete with copper-capped chimney. Withdrawn in 1965, *Evening Star* became part of the National Collection and, following a spell of railtour work in the 1980s, is housed at the National Railway Museum, York.

Against the backdrop of Wild Boar Fell, 9F 2-10-0 No92249 crosses Ais Gill viaduct on 1 June 1966 at the head of a southbound train loaded with anhydrite bound for the ICI plant at Widnes, Lancashire. This was a regular working, usually entrusted to a 9F, from Long Meg sidings near Lazonby, which served local quarries. The sidings took their name from a nearby Neolithic stone circle, Long Meg and her Daughters. No92249 was the penultimate 9F built, its working life lasting under nine years, withdrawal coming in May 1968.

minimum acceptable coupled wheel diameter) would limit both its size and, consequently, the diameter of the boiler barrel. As a result, steam production would be compromised. Riddles countered that, given a well-designed 'front end' (cylinders, valves, steampipes and exhaust blast-pipe) and free-flowing steam passages, a driving wheel diameter of just five feet was perfectly feasible. Moreover, the trailing wheels of a 2-8-2 would not deliver the increased adhesion required in a locomotive intended to haul heavy bulk loads.

Nevertheless, the detail of the 9F 2-10-0 posed some problems for Riddles' drawing office team. For example, when working iron ore and steel traffic in South Wales, the locomotives would have to negotiate tight curves. With a 21ft 8in coupled wheelbase, and no sideplay permissible in the coupled axles, this could have proved problematic. The solution was to omit the flanges from the centre pair of driving wheels, allowing

the 9F to round curves of 400ft radius (reduced to 300ft at very slow speeds). This modification, along with a low axleloading of 15 tons 10 cwt, left the class subject to few restrictions.

This flexibility was promptly demonstrated when the first 9Fs were drafted into South Wales to take over iron ore workings from Newport docks to the steelworks at Ebbw Vale. It would not be the last time these engines proved to be BR's 'trouble-shooters'. In north-east England, they were handed another iron ore working: the arduous haul from Tyne Dock to the steelworks at Consett, County Durham. The 9F proved the master of gradients as demanding as 1 in 35, hauling up to ten trains daily, each weighing over 780 tons. They were equally at home on another tough duty: the heavy anhydrite trains from Long Meg quarries, near Appleby in Cumbria, to the ICI chemical plant at Widnes, Cheshire.

The Western Region, where the response to the BR Standard 'Britannia' Pacifics had been

Harnessed to a Type BR1G 5,000 gallon inset tender, 9F 2-10-0 No92004 trundles into Tebay at the head of a southbound goods on 17 June 1963.

lukewarm, welcomed the 9Fs, as did the Eastern, North Eastern and London Midland Regions. None were initially allocated to the Scottish Region (although inter-regional workings took them north of the border) and the Southern had no immediate requirement for them. This changed in 1961 when the Esso oil refinery at Fawley, on Southampton Water, began generating 100,000-gallon trains for its depot at Bromford Bridge, near Birmingham. Six 9Fs were allocated to Eastleigh to work these 1,200-ton trains, which were routed over the now-closed Winchester-Newbury-Didcot line. There were predictions that the engines would have to be worked so hard on the heavy grades that sparks would fly – literally – and ignite their volatile cargo. Although petrol did seep occasionally from the elderly four-wheel tankers, hot cinders from over-worked 9Fs never ignited it.

There was surprise, however, when first the Western Region and then the Eastern began to use 9Fs on summer passenger work (the absence of steam-heating precluded their use at other times). The small diameter driving wheels proved no obstacle to fast running and reports of speeds between 80 and 90 miles per hour were not unusual on passenger duties. Several astonishing runs were logged as 9Fs replaced failed diesels on East Coast and South Wales expresses. It was a brief fling, however. Worried about the possible effect of sustained fast running on cylinders and running gear, operating departments put the brake on high-speed running. The 9Fs' greatest impact on passenger services came on the Somerset and Dorset route. In taking 12-coach trains over the Mendip Hills unaided, they eliminated the uneconomic double-heading that had beset the line. Sadly, the adoption of the 9F came too late to deter BR from closing this line.

During their lifetime, the 9Fs were subject to a handful of experiments and modifications, the most successful of which was the fitting of double chimneys. In contrast, the building of ten engines with the Italian-designed Crosti boiler (an attempt to reduce coal consumption) was ill-conceived.

One of the 9Fs fitted with air pumps for automatic operation of hopper wagon doors, No92060 is pictured on the working for which it was built – a Tyne Dock to Consett iron ore train – on 1 May 1966.

Mixed results were obtained from incorporating a Giesl ejector in No92250, and from installing American-designed Berkley mechanical stokers in Nos92165-67.

The Modernisation Plan of 1955 had set a timetable for the phasing out of steam traction. Nevertheless, over 200 locomotives were built in the wake of a decision that in a decade or less would render them obsolete (construction of the 9Fs ceased only in 1960). Just four years later, the first examples were scrapped despite having at least two decades' work left in them. Conditions in the 1950s and 1960s demanded simple-to-maintain and easy-to-drive engines that were not fussy about the quality of coal fed into their fireboxes. In those respects, the 9F was the ideal locomotive for its time. Lamentably, with the last withdrawals coming in June 1968, that time was all too short.

THE MAKERS AND THE BREAKERS

For over a century, the majority of Britain's steam locomotives were built by its railway companies, in workshops from Scotland to the south coast of England. Then the makers became the breakers.

Outside contractors supplied the first engines to run on Britain's fledgling railways at the beginning of the nineteenth century. The world's first great locomotive construction concern, Robert Stephenson & Company, built machines for numerous railways both in Britain and abroad. It was soon facing competition from the likes of Sharp Stewart, Fletcher Jennings, Stohert & Slaughter and other manufacturing companies.

By the 1840s, however, several major railways had established locomotive workshops where both repairs and construction could be undertaken. The skills and machinery needed differed little. The Grand Junction Railway chose a site in Cheshire where its line from Birmingham to the north joined those from Chester and Manchester.

Sporting its trademark GW copper-capped chimney, 5101 class Prairie tank No4115 is in the last stages of an overhaul at Swindon Works, a photograph taken in British Railways days. Over 140 years of locomotive repair and construction ended at Swindon in 1986.

This rural settlement went on to become the largest locomotive works in the British Isles, its wayside station the hub of railways in north-west England. The station was called Crewe.

The Great Western Railway lighted upon a small town in Wiltshire located at the point where its branch to Gloucester and Cheltenham diverged from the London to Bristol line. This was Swindon, where the first of over 6,000 engines rolled out of the erecting shop in 1846.

In the East Midlands, three railway companies converged on Derby and each built workshops. When, in 1844, these companies merged to form the Midland Railway, the workshops were combined to form another of the great locomotive engineering centres. Derby Works delivered the first of 2,941 steam locomotives in 1851.

The Great Northern Railway followed the precedent of placing a construction and repair facility at a major junction. 'The Plant', as it became known, opened in 1853 in the South Yorkshire town of Doncaster, meeting point of the GNR line from London and Peterborough with those to York, Leeds and Sheffield. Some 76 miles to the north, Darlington evolved to become the principal works of the North Eastern Railway. Across the Pennines, the Lancashire & Yorkshire Railway located its works at Horwich, near

One of the first BR Standard Class 4MT 4-6-0s nears completion in the Swindon erecting shop on 27 September 1951. The locomotive appears to lack just a front bogie. All 80 of this class were constructed at Swindon between May 1951 and January 1956. In the background, 6800 'Grange' class 4-6-0 No6837 Forthampton Grange undergoes overhaul. No6837 would be around for a further 14 years, being withdrawn from Worcester in November 1965.

Bolton. By 1912, its erecting shop could accommodate 100 engines and 30 tenders. The boiler and machine shops were built on a similar scale and supplied by steel, brass and iron foundries. Horwich even generated electricity to power cranes, motors and lighting.

Only a handful of locomotive works were set up in major cities. Glasgow boasted two: the Edinburgh & Glasgow Railway (subsequently North British Railway) plant at Cowlairs, and the Caledonian Railway's establishment at St Rollox. There were three in London, the largest being the Eastern Counties Railway's (later Great Eastern Railway's) works at Stratford. The London, Chatham & Dover Railway had its shops at Longhedge, Battersea, while the North London

Railway's works at Bow was one of the country's smallest, covering only ten acres (in contrast, Swindon Works occupied 140 acres). The Manchester, Sheffield & Lincolnshire Railway built its workshops at Gorton, in Manchester, and the Shrewsbury & Birmingham opted for Wolverhampton. The most southerly plant was at Brighton and belonged to the London Brighton & South Coast Railway; the most northerly was built by the Great North of Scotland Railway, at Inverurie, sixteen miles north-west of Aberdeen.

The network of Britain's locomotive works was completed in 1909, with the opening of the London & South Western's plant at Eastleigh, north of Southampton. After the 1923 Grouping, the 'big four' companies concentrated work at

The Midland Railway's works at Derby began building locomotives in 1851. On 6 July 1926, a Midland design, the 4F 0-6-0, remained under construction (these are the frames and cylinders of No4250). The last of 3,952 steam and diesel engines was outshopped in 1967.

A rarity undergoing overhaul at Eastleigh on 20 September 1931. No2326 was the sole representative of the ex-LB&SCR Class J2 4-6-2 tank.. Designed by Earle Marsh, it was built at Brighton in 1912, and named Bessborough. Remarkably for a 'one-off', it lasted in service almost 40 years.

Steel or copper stays — hundreds of them — hold apart the inner and outer wrappers of a firebox. As the space between acts as a water jacket, wastage through corrosion inevitably occurs. A firebox, seen upside-down with the grate section to the top, undergoes restaying at Derby.

their major plants and downgraded, or in some cases, closed works inherited from smaller concerns. Some were relegated to undertaking only 'light' repairs, which included overhauling valve gear, renewing firebox stays, reboring cylinders and fitting axleboxes. 'Heavy' repairs such as boiler renewals, retubing, new axles and cylinders, and the fitting of fresh wheel tyres, required locomotives to await their turn at Ashford, Crewe, Darlington, Derby, Doncaster, Eastleigh, Gorton, Horwich, Swindon or one of the other major locomotive workshops.

During the 1950s, the major workshops were occupied construction of the twelve British Railways Standard classes, with Crewe contributing the largest number. Substantial orders for diesel and electric locomotives and multiple units followed. Overall, however, locomotive numbers were declining and there was insufficient work to occupy all the thirty or so locations.

Smaller plants, such as Kilmarnock and Bow, were the first to be closed and, in 1962, the British Transport Commission announced a drastic closure programme. The BTC estimated that, with the elimination of steam traction, the amount of workshop activity would drop by one-third over a five-year period. It proposed closing 12 of the 29 main workshops over three years, with a reduction in the total workforce from 56,000 to 38,000. A hostile reaction from trade unions led to some rethinking on the plan, but it failed to prevent some ten plants disappearing by the end of the 1960s. Ashford, Brighton, Cowlairs, Darlington, Gorton and Horwich were included in the list of closures.

For many of the remaining workshops, the construction and repair lines of the 1950s were transformed into scraplines. Enormous numbers of steam locomotives were disposed of at, among other locations, Swindon, Darlington, Eastleigh and Doncaster, where 207 were cut up during 1963. Crewe, where once two new locomotives were being built each week, was now cutting up 20 engines a month.

BUILT AT CREWE

Around 7,300 locomotives built over a period of 115 years made Crewe the most productive of British workshops. In addition, it could fashion everything from sheet steel to bars of soap.

'This grand manufactory will be the finest and most extensive railway workshop in the world.' That was the prediction of John Moss, Chairman of the Grand Junction Railway, when his company announced its plans for the Cheshire hamlet of Crewe. The site had its disadvantages. There were no sources of coal or iron nearby, and no local workforce, but it was an established railway junction. Just as importantly, there was plenty of space, which was

Finishing touches in the Crewe paint shop for one of the first of the streamlined 'Princess Coronation' class Pacifics. The initial batch of five locomotives was built between June and July 1937 and wore the blue 'Coronation Scot' livery with silver 'speed whiskers'. Each locomotive (with tender) cost the LMSR £11,641.

not the case at the GJR's existing works at Edge Hill, Liverpool. Moss appointed Joseph Locke to supervise the building of the new plant and, by 1843, it was in production. The first Crewe-built locomotive, No32 *Tamerlane*, was outshopped that December.

Development of the works continued over many years and it diversified into producing just about everything the GJR's successor, the London & North Western Railway needed to run its trains. Along with locomotives and rolling stock, Crewe supplied rails and much of the signalling equipment. There was a plant making lubricating grease, and one turning out bars of soap, both made from the residue left by washing thousands of dirty cleaning cloths after they had been used in the engine sheds. The L&NWR took pride in being self-sufficient.

Like many Victorian employers, Crewe Works took a paternal approach to its employees. For their physical well-being it built good housing, and for their spiritual welfare, a church. The company promoted self-improvement by establishing a Mechanics' Institute. Opened in 1845, its library, reading room and evening classes were open to all in the town (very few of who were not connected in some way with the railway works).

During the 1850s and 1860s, the works grew to such an extent that an 18-inches gauge railway system was constructed to carry raw materials and parts from one part of the site to another. The line extended into Crewe Station and remained in use until the 1920s.

A notable landmark was reached in 1866, with the delivery of the 1,000th Crewe-built locomotive, DX 0-6-0 No1513. A total of 943 of these engines came from Crewe, making the DX the most numerous British locomotive class. The occasion was marked with proper ceremony and the pride felt was summed up in the illuminated address presented to erecting shop foreman George Dingley by his loyal workforce:

'The position which Crewe Works has attained in the front rank of British workshops is due to the skill and perseverance with which such men

LOOK ON MY WORKS

While on one of the guided tours that Crewe Works' management seemed happy to entertain, the urge to see the lines of new and overhauled engines was all-consuming. As a result, many visitors failed to appreciate how much went on in the numerous buildings scattered across the 137-acre site. There was a steel foundry where two electric arc furnaces produced castings. In the welding shop, arc welding of locomotive assemblies took place, with most of the plates turned out by oxy-acetylene cutting machines.

There seemed to be a shop for every component that went to make up a steam locomotive: tender shop, spring shop, tube shop, copper shop, wheel shop and a brass finishing shop that undertook all the specialist non-ferrous work. The heavy machine shop took care of the machining and assembly of bogies and dealt with cylinder renewals.

Maintenance of the works' plant was entrusted to the millwrights and chain shop, and to the joiners who also produced all the wooden fittings, including footplate food boxes. Lamps, oilcans and the like would be fabricated in the tin and sheet metal shop. The boiler shop, with firebox and smokebox riveting underway, was the noisiest place imaginable.

as yourself have carried out the ideas of our respected superintendent Mr John Ramsbottom.' These were the workers who, in 1878, succeeded in building an 0-6-0 goods engine from scratch in just 25 hours 30 minutes.

In the decade from 1868 to 1878, Crewe developed yet further. More workshops and a new carriage works were erected, the in-house steel making facility modernised and a new paint shop built. It was here, in 1887, that the 3,000th Crewe locomotive received its L&NWR livery of lined 'blackberry black', as the shade was known. In 1910, the Works completed its first superheated

engine, 'George the Fifth' class 4-4-0 No2663. The following year, another of the class, No5000 *Coronation*, announced Crewe's most recent production landmark in its number.

However, there was no escaping the conclusion that by 1910 Crewe was underperfoming in its prime role of building and repairing locomotives. Straightforward overhauls were taking, on average, 40 days to complete. Apart from being uneconomic for the Works itself, the situation compelled the L&NWR to maintain a much larger fleet than it needed simply to cover for the

inordinate amount of time engines were spending 'off the road'. Moves to address the problem were curtailed by the outbreak of war in 1914. Locomotive construction ceased as foundries, forges, plate fabrication plants and heavy lifting gear were adapted to armaments manufacture. As with other major railway works, Crewe became part of the war effort.

It took an outsider to restore Crewe's pre-eminence. In merging with the Lancashire & Yorkshire Railway in 1922, the L&NWR gained the considerable skills of George Hughes, its Chief Mechanical Engineer. At the L&YR's Horwich Works, Hughes had established one of the most efficient plants in the country and was now expected to repeat the achievement at Crewe. Hughes's first action was to build a new, well-equipped erecting shop and he followed that by reorganising working practices. In the past, gangs of fitters had each been allocated one locomotive to overhaul and repair. They saw the job

through from stripping down to test steaming. Hughes replaced this with a 'belt' process. Lines of engines were strung out along the 'belts' (as they were called) and each works gang was given a set task to perform on each one. They had to complete the work in an allotted time before the locomotive was winched on to the next stage. The time taken to complete the twelve stages of a general overhaul was cut from the pre-war figure of 40 days to twelve.

George Hughes bequeathed to his successor, William Stanier, the locomotive works he would need to undertake the massive task of restocking the LMSR fleet. At the peak of the new building programme, in the mid-1930s, the company claimed that two new engines were leaving Crewe each week. However, during World War II Crewe's resources were again put to military use. Among other armaments, the works produced Covenanter tanks. By 1944, the workforce had increased from 6,500 in 1939 to 7,500, which included 1,000 women.

Crewe Works played a key role throughout the British Railways steam era. It handed over its 7,000th locomotive, 2MT class 2-6-2T No41272, in 1950 and in 1951 unveiled the first of the BR Standard designs, No70000 *Britannia*. Crewe built the majority of the 9F 2-10-0s, beginning with the very first, No92000. Fittingly, it was the hugely successful 9F that brought 115 years of steam locomotive construction to an end. When No92250 left the paintshop in December 1958, it was, according to records, the 7,331st Crewe-built engine. Some railway historians believe it to have been number 7,357. Either way, it's an awful lot of locomotives. Around 60 Crewe-built steam and diesel locomotives have been preserved, ranging from 2-2-2 No49 *Columbine* of 1845 to 9F 2-10-0 No 92245 of 1958 and Class 52 C-C diesel hydraulic NoD1062 *Western Courier* of 1963.

FED AND WATERED

...not by God's almighty hand, but by a host of ways of fuelling locomotives with coal and water. Some were complex; others would have been recognised by the crew of Stephenson's 'Rocket'.

Obtaining good quality fuel has always been a prime concern for those operating steam locomotives; keeping it in good condition has been another. Not all coal is suitable, and some locomotives could be choosy about the fuel shovelled into their fireboxes.

'Yorkshire hards', the kind of coal mined around the Doncaster area, fuelled the record-breaking exploits of the LNER's Gresley Pacifics. 'Midland hards', coming from collieries in Nottinghamshire and Warwickshire, was another good burner. The Great Western hesitated to use anything other than Welsh steam coal.

Wherever the colliery, its output was graded for railway use. Ideally, the finest quality coal was set aside for the front-rank locomotives but it did not always work out so tidily. If the opportunity arose, any driver or fireman would fill the tender of his elderly six-coupled goods engine with first-grade coal. Even on mundane goods work, the better stuff made a difference.

At major depots, coal was graded and stored in bunkers. At others, it was formed into 'coal stacks'. Good quality coal deteriorated little with exterior storage, but the elements could play havoc with inferior fuel. Coal that weathered badly gradually mutated into a mess at the bottom of the stack before eventually finding its way into someone's tender.

Checking fuel quality was the job of coal inspectors. They took samples for testing and tackled the suppliers if they were below standard. However, the coal shortage in the immediate post-war years left them with little choice other than to take what was on offer. A little arithmetic demonstrates how much of Britain's coal output was being devoured by its railways. There were over 20,000 engines burning an average of three tons each day. Hard-worked locomotives could easily consume up to nine tons.

How these engines received their fuel supply varied widely. At its most basic, it was a matter of shovelling the coal into the tender or bunker, either from trucks or from raised wooden coal stages. Some small depots relied on a crane. Tubs of coal were hoisted on the jib and their hinged doors released at the right moment.

An advance on this was the elevated coal stage. Loaded wagons were propelled by a shunting engine into a covered area some 13 feet above yard level. There the coal was emptied into wheeled tubs that were pushed to the front of the coal stage, tilted and emptied into the tender or

A begrimed ex-L&YR Class '21' 0-4-0 saddle-tank, No51217, takes water at Bristol Barrow Road shed, September 1960. Between 1891 and 1910, 57 of these diminutive shunters were built at Horwich to the design of John Aspinall. Originally employed in the docks and industrial areas of Liverpool, Fleetwood, Salford and Goole, in BR days they were more widely dispersed. BR withdrew No51217 in November 1961, but two 'Pugs', as they were nicknamed, have been preserved.

bunker of the locomotive standing underneath. The procedure continues in use at Didcot Railway Centre in Oxfordshire, which has a typical Great Western coaling stage.

At motive power depots of any consequence, mechanical coaling plants were the only realistic answer to the task of fuelling large numbers of engines each day. By 1939, any shed on the LMSR or LNER with an allocation of more than 40 engines was equipped with one. By contrast, none were employed on the GWR, which feared mechanical handling would reduce its friable Welsh coal to dust. These mechanical plants — known as 'cenotaphs' from their resemblance to the war memorial in London's Whitehall — were massive affairs. Wagons were raised electrically to a height of around 60 feet and then tipped through 130 degrees or so to discharge their contents into a bunker. From here it gushed into the locomotive tender, the driver regulating the flow.

As with coal, there were diverse means of delivering water. It was not unusual for a locomotive to consume upwards of 10,000 gallons a day, which is why supplies were made available at many locations other than at depots. There were water cranes on station platforms and troughs were installed on many main lines. The simplest water cranes were standpipes, while others, known as parachute columns, were surmounted by cylindrical water tanks. Both employed leather pipes, or 'bags', which were manoeuvred into the tank filler hole and the water turned on. At the depots, large tanks maintained a constant head of water to the cranes sited alongside the locomotive preparation pits. Ideally, these tanks would be roofed over to keep out sulphur-laden engine smoke and other undesirable elements.

However, there was always a problem of sludge build-up. This was especially problematic in the treatment plants. Additionally, the tanks, like any iron structure, were vulnerable to corrosion.

All this effort, duff coal and dodgy water to contend with, and so far not a wheel turned in revenue-earning service. It was when those wheels had turned that the hard work really began.

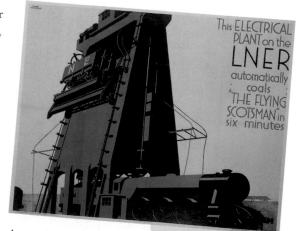

203

DIRTY WORK AFOOT

It wasn't the 'romance of steam' that left its mark on running shed staffs, more ash, clinker, soot and sludge.

Stanier 'Jubilee' class 4-6-0 No5557 New Brunswick stands on the turntable inside the roundhouse at Bristol Barrow Road on 5 July 1947. This was the Midland Railway's depot in Bristol, remaining under London Midland Region control until 1958, when it was transferred to the Western Region. When closed in 1965, Barrow Road had an allocation of 41 engines.

To the poets among railway photographers and painters they were 'cathedrals of steam'. Doubtless the *chiaroscuro* effects created by shafts of sunlight streaming through holes in the roofs would have inspired Rembrandt. In truth, however, steam locomotive running sheds could be hellish places to those performing the dirtiest jobs in what was always a dirty business: the fire-droppers, tube-blowers and ashpit labourers.

Burning coal leaves a residue of three products, none especially useful or easy to dispose of. There is the ash that, at certain temperatures, is prone to fuse into awkwardly shaped lumps known as clinker. That is followed by carbon – in other words, soot – that collects in the boiler fire-tubes and superheater elements, progressively inhibiting heat transmission as it builds up. Finally, comes the char that collects in the smoke-box every time the locomotive is used. Neglect to deal with any of them and the engine simply will not perform.

In the main, dropping the fire and clearing the ash was the lot of the fireman. Like any domestic fire, but on a larger scale, ash passed through the firebars and collected in the ashpan below. On older locomotives, this had to be emptied entirely manually. The ash, much of it still red-hot, either fell into an ashpit or was deposited on the trackside. The introduction of lever-operated hopper ashpans made the fireman's task easier, but that was only half the job. Someone still had to deal with the piles of ash.

In primitive sheds it fell to unfortunate souls known as 'ashpit labourers' to heave the ash out of the pit and then load it into adjacent wagons. At major depots, the task was made more bearable by motorised conveyor or belt devices. These carried the ash to an ash plant where it could be emptied into the wagons. Alternatively, the ash was shovelled into small four-wheel tubs running on a narrow-gauge track beside the ashpits. However, although it could be hosed down from water hydrants installed either in the pits or alongside them, inevitably the ash still hung in the air. It could be tasted in the mouth, and irritated the eyes.

The final stab at ash disposal was the most effective but was never extended beyond some front-rank depots. The 'wet ashpit' was where ashpans were emptied through grids into water, he sludge removed at intervals by a crane. There were still drawbacks: the drainage often seized up, leaving a foul-smelling effluent around the pits.

Locomotives had their fires 'dropped' at regular intervals to allow sludge and scale to be washed out of the boiler and for a boiler and firebox inspection to take place. The boilersmith – seen here emerging from the firehole – would enter the firebox to check the the stays, firebox tubeplate, brick arch and firebars. He would also enter the smokebox to examine the blastpipe, main steampipe, smokebox tubeplate and superheater header (if fitted).

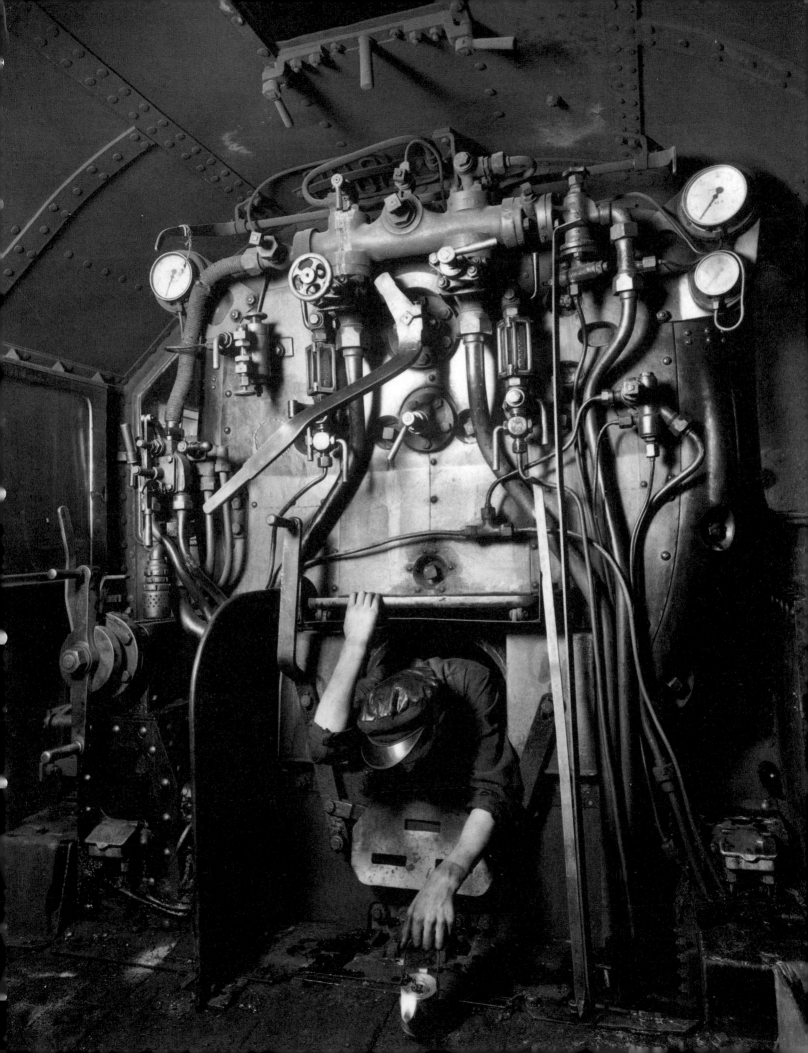

A4 Pacifics undergo cleaning at 'Top Shed', as London's King's Cross was known. Note the burnished buffers of Nos4490 Empire of India and 4492 Dominion of New Zealand.

Undoubtedly clinker qualified as enemy number one and a little more science was applied in getting rid it. Clinker was amazingly hard stuff and clogged the spaces between the firebars at the base of the locomotive's firebox. At worst, it may have combined with small pieces of coal to produce pockets where the unevenly intensified draught was so fierce that it ignited the firebars themselves. Once clinker was allowed to build up and block the air passages in the grate, combustion was inevitably impaired and with it an engine's ability to steam. A brutal, but effective means of releasing a severe build-up of clinker was to yank some of the firebars to one side to create a larger opening for it to drop through. This was permissible if the engine was being allowed to go 'cold' for maintenance work, but there was always a risk of dropping a firebar or

two. Make that mistake when it was hot and due back in steam, and the culprit could expect his parentage to be questioned by the boilersmith landed with the job of reassembling the grate!

Along with hopper ashpans, newer engines were also fitted with rocker grates. The rocking action of the grate section was intended to fracture the clinker and deposit it into the ashpan. Sadly, all too often the clinker triumphed, blocking the grate and ultimately affecting the steam pressure. Freeing it up was invariably an extremely laborious business.

Nevertheless, hopper ashpans and rocking grates were laudable attempts at improving the crude process of 'disposal', as it was termed, as were self-cleaning smokeboxes. Some types of coal deposited more char in the smokebox than others; the way the locomotive was fired also had

an effect. Again, it was the lot of the fireman to get rid of the detritus. To avoid a faceful of smoke and fumes when releasing the smokebox door, a useful ruse was first to close the firehole doors and then apply the locomotive's 'blower' to force lingering gases through the chimney. The fireman would still open the door with care, however, to avoid smouldering char cascading on to his boots.

In self-cleaning smokeboxes (indicated on British Railways' locomotives by the letters 'SC' on the smokebox door), an arrangement of mesh screens and plates was used to box in the blast-pipe and chimney cowl in the hope that the char would be ejected as part of the exhaust. Unfortunately, with some classes of locomotive, even if the device worked, it had to be removed because it compromised steaming capability.

If ash, clinker and char disposal were simply tedious and unpleasant tasks, the filthiest job of all had to be that of the tube-sweepers who removed the soot. Mercifully, it was a process that only had to be performed at intervals, but it was a vital one. At its most basic, it required the individual cleaning of each boiler tube with a selection of rods and brushes, and there were over 200 tubes on most engines. Compressed air blowers were available at many depots and these could be valuable in dislodging the soot, which was occasionally blasted into the face of the user.

The LMSR, which had a more enlightened approach to the miseries of day-to-day maintenance than other companies, was the first to fit tube blowers to its newer locomotives. An intense jet of steam was used to loosen the soot and shoot it through the blastpipe and out the chimney. However, there were no mechanical aids that could entirely replace the need for dirty manual labour. It was hardly surprising that, in the post-war climate, fewer and fewer people wanted the job of clearing up the mess left by steam locomotives. Railway chiefs were left with a stark choice: either modernise and 'humanise' the day-to-day chores of locomotive maintenance, or ditch steam to make way for something else. We know which option they took.

ON COMMON GROUND

The building of the giant motive power depot at Old Oak Common in west London was another bold idea of George Jackson Churchward. Rather than undertake piecemeal extensions of the existing, but inadequate facilities at Westbourne Park, Churchward found a large 'green field' site some three miles from Paddington. Here, he built the largest locomotive running shed on the Great Western Railway. The main building measured 444ft by 360ft and housed four turntables, each 65ft in diameter. Radiating from each turntable were 28 roads, giving a total of 112 engine pits.

Other features of the shed included an exceptionally well-glazed roof and electric lighting, a novelty for the early 1900s. In addition to the running shed, Old Oak Common boasted a well-equipped lifting and repair shop, with twelve inspection pits and an external traverser.

Also the largest of its kind on the GWR was the elevated coal stage where locomotive tenders and bunkers were filled from tip-up trucks. Since these trucks were hand-filled, the fuel could be vetted for quality with the best coal reserved for the top-link passenger engines.

Old Oak Common opened on 17 March 1906 and closed to steam 59 years later on 22 March 1965. Just five years earlier it was home to 160 engines. No less than 34 of the 'Castle' class 4-6-0s wore the depot's 81A shedplate, as did 16 'Kings'. They were joined by 22 'Halls' and 'Modified Halls', five Churchward 4700 class 2-8-0s and two Collett 2251 class 0-6-0s. By 1960, it had also become home to 11 of BR's 9F 2-10-0s.

Old Oak Common remains an important maintenance facility. English Welsh & Scottish Railway (EWS) has a diesel depot on the site of the steam shed and continues to use the ex-GWR repair shop. First Great Western has a High Speed Train (HST) maintenance facility nearby and that has recently been joined by a depot for the Heathrow Express electric multiple units.

Above: Pannier tanks stand under smoke vents inside the huge roundhouse at Old Oak Common. On 11 May 1963, 5700 class condensing tank No9706 slumbers alongside 9400 class No9495.

WHISTLE WHILE YOU WORK

It was only a trill emanating from the cooling fan, but it was a sound peculiar to the English Electric Type 4 diesel-electrics. It ensured they would always be remembered as the 'Whistlers'.

The English Electric Type 4 hit the headlines in 1958 when the first of the class, D200, left London's Liverpool Street with the first diesel-hauled express to Norwich. A large headboard on the front of the locomotive proclaimed the significance of the event. Schedules on the ex-Great Eastern main line again could be accelerated in much the same way as occurred seven years earlier when the 'Britannia' Pacifics were introduced.

Following NoD200's debut, the ten pilot engines, NosD200-209, performed well enough in Eastern Region service to merit further orders. With a top speed of 90mph, the 2,000hp Type 4 became British Railways' first express passenger diesel to go into production. The soundness of the design meant that few changes were needed and 200 (D200-399) were delivered up to 1962.

English Electric Type 4 NoD380 awaits departure from Euston with a Liverpool express one afternoon in August 1963. These 2,000hp diesels were an interim replacement for steam on the West Coast Main Line prior to the completion of electrification south of Crewe. Reclassified Class 40 by BR, this example became No40180.

It was, though, a design with antecedents, all based around English Electric's 16SVT Mark II engine. This power plant – then rated at 1,600hp – had been used in the LMSR's two 1947 Derby-built prototype diesels, Nos10000 and 10001. Uprated to 1,750hp, it then powered two British Railways 1Co-Co1 locomotives, Nos10201 and 10202, built at BR's Ashford Works in 1951 to a blueprint drawn up by the old Southern Railway. A third example of the Southern design, No10203, was delivered in 1954 with the English Electric engine further uprated to 2,000hp. Both engine and No10203's 1Co-Co1 wheelbase (in which the outer guiding axles are unpowered) were adopted for the Type 4. It came in at nearly 70 feet long and weighed 132 tons.

A distinctive feature of the Type 4 was its nose compartment, which performed two functions. First, it housed the traction motor 'blower' for the adjacent bogie. Second, it was a way of overcoming the trance-like effect of 'sleeper flicker' that could distract drivers of flat-fronted diesel and electric locomotives. The extended nose led the driver's line-of-sight forward of the track. (Experience later showed that the problem could be overcome equally successfully with careful cab design.)

As most coaching stock was still steam-heated, the EE Type 4 was equipped with a steam-heating boiler. It could replenish its boiler water supply from the water troughs which remained in place on some main lines even though the steam locomotives for which they had been installed were fast disappearing.

Initially, some questioned the power offered by the EE Type 4. They argued that 2,000hp was on

the low side compared to what, for example, a Stanier 'Coronation' Pacific could produce, and consideration was given to uprating the engine to 2,400hp. However, the idea was rejected since that power was constantly available (which is the case with all diesels, but not with steam traction).

The second batch of Type 4s was drafted on to the West Coast Main Line but only as an interim replacement for steam before electrification. Acknowledging the London Midland Region's links with the port of Liverpool and the ship-building city of Glasgow, NosD210-35 were named after famous ocean liners. With a 20-ton axleloading guaranteeing a fairly wide route avail-ability, later batches were allocated to the North Eastern and Scottish Regions. Here, as elsewhere, the Type 4s gave excellent service. They were robust and reliable, with consistently high avail-ability. This was especially noteworthy as, before

the building of dedicated maintenance depots, diesels had to co-exist in steam running sheds. Such conditions were alien to keeping complex items such as traction motors in efficient order and some diesel classes suffered as a direct conse-quence of this.

The introduction of higher-power diesels such as the 'Deltics', Brush Type 4 and Class 50 – another English Electric product – saw the 'Whistlers' downgraded from top link duties. They found fresh employment on Crewe-Holyhead and York-Newcastle (by way of the north-east coast) and Glasgow-Aberdeen services. Their appearances at the head of freight trains also increased greatly. After almost three decades' service, in 1987 the last of the EE Type 4s (by now Class 40s) was withdrawn. Seven have been preserved, including the prototype D200, which is now part of the National Collection.

The southbound 'Royal Scot', with Type 4 1Co-Co1 diesel-electric NoD301 in charge, passes Lamington, in the Clyde Valley, April 1961. Eventually, the Type 4s were displaced from west coast express passenger duties, both by electrification and by the introduction of the more powerful Classes 47 and 50 diesels.

GETTING SHIPSHAPE

*An improbable example of European cooperation brought about the building of
the Western Region's 'Warship' class diesel-hydraulics.*

On its exit from Bristol,
the eastbound 'Bristolian'
accelerates past
Stapleton Road Junction
and begins the climb to
Filton Junction. From June
1959, with 'Warship'
diesel-hydraulics in
charge, the train was
allowed just 100
minutes for the 118.3
miles to London.

As the home of Dr Rudolf Diesel (if not
the birthplace, which was Paris), it was
West Germany that led the way – at
least in Europe – in developing diesel traction.
While Deutsches Bundesbahn (DB) engineers
concentrated on improving the hydraulic system
developed by Dr Rudolf Diesel, their French and
American counterparts had adopted electric
transmission for diesel locomotives. When BR's
Western Region approached DB for help in
establishing its diesel fleet, it became the only BR
region to place its faith in hydraulic transmission.
This, consciously or otherwise, perpetuated the
tradition of isolation beloved of its predecessor,
the Great Western Railway.

Initially, that faith had been tested by the indifferent performance of the first five main-line
hydraulics, a quintet of A1A-A1A locomotives
built by the North British Locomotive Company.
Nevertheless, the WR persisted in its quest and,

Sporting a yellow warning panel, Type 4 'Warship' B-B diesel-hydraulic NoD835 Pegasus heads west through Dawlish with a train of LMR stock on 4 August 1962. It was one of a batch of 33 built by the North British Locomotive Company of Glasgow between 1960 and 1961.

looking to Germany, lighted upon the 2,100hp V200 class B-B diesel hydraulic. Built by Krauss-Maffei of Munich, the V200 was a standard Deutsches Bundesbahn design with – and this was the chief advantage of diesel-hydraulics – an impressively high power-to-weight ratio (26 horsepower per ton of engine weight). The Western Region would have invested in one for trials had its dimensions not been 10-inches outside the British loading gauge, in width as well as height.

Undeterred, the WR obtained a licence from Krauss-Maffei to build a variant of the V200 in Britain. The task of translating the German notes into English and metric measurements into imperial fell to the drawing office staff at Swindon works. They also had to rework the design, with assistance from Krauss-Maffei, so that it conformed to the BR loading gauge. It was decided that the transmissions and bogies (apart from wheel diameter) should be identical to those of the V200 but other components were rescaled in Britain. The maximum speed was fixed at 90mph.

The first of the Swindon-built locomotives, D800, appeared in 1958. Its two 12-cylinder Bristol Siddeley-Maybach V-type engines generated 2,270hp and this power was conveyed to all eight axles through a pair of Mekydro hydraulic transmissions.

By August 1959, nine of the class were in service on express workings out of Paddington. They had suffered their share of failures, but by far the greater percentage of those were attributable to electrical and wiring problems rather than the engines and transmissions. Once the teething problems had been overcome, the diesels recorded some impressive statistics. On average, they were covering 380 miles per day compared to the 153 miles of the 'Castle' class 4-6-0s they were earmarked to replace. Admittedly, the diesels were new and were being given assignments that would fully exploit their continuous availability, but the comparison was nonetheless striking.

Construction continued until 1961, by which time the class totalled 71. Swindon Works built 38 (the last 35 uprated to 2,400hp) while North British contributed the remainder. The latter differed in having NBL/MAN (Maschinenfabrik Augsburg, Nurnberg) Anglo-German engines and Voith transmissions. A solitary locomotive, D830, was equipped with two 12-cylinder Paxman engines of 1,200hp each. With two exceptions, the class was named after famous Royal Navy warships.

Displaced from the Western Region by Type 4 diesel electrics and High Speed Trains, the 'Warships' enjoyed an 'Indian summer' on the Southern Region where they proved ideal for the lightly loaded Waterloo-Salisbury-Exeter services. However, in the British Railways scheme of things they were decidedly non-standard and, like their fellow diesel-hydraulic classes, obvious targets for early withdrawal. Two, though, have survived: D821 *Greyhound* and D832 *Onslaught*.

INFLAMING OPINION

An incident involving one of the 'Warships' raised some concern in the House of Commons. On 23 June 1963, at the head of the 1.30pm Paddington-Plymouth, NoD861 *Vigilant* caught fire near Exeter. The fire, which was caused by a spray of oil from a broken fuel pipe coming into contact with a hot exhaust pipe seriously damaged the locomotive and prompted one Western Region driver to refuse to undertake any single-manned duties on main-line diesels. He argued that, if there was a similar fire to that on D861, it might prove beyond the capability of a single crew member to prevent damage to the train and injury to the passengers. It was a contingency the Western's management was forced to consider, especially as soon afterwards a prominent Member of Parliament openly announced his sympathy for the driver's view.

PEAK PERFORMERS

The honour of becoming number 'D1' in the stocklist went to a British Railways-built diesel locomotive. This lofty status was reflected in its name, Scafell Pike, *a peak that was itself 3,206 feet high!*

During the late 1950s, British Railways' major main line diesel engine suppliers – Bristol Siddeley, English Electric and Sulzer – refined their designs to deliver higher outputs without a proportionate increase in size and weight. One class of diesel to benefit from this work was the 'Peak' class, a Type 4 1Co-Co1 diesel electric built in British Railways' workshops at Crewe and Derby. The name derived from the first ten locomotives in the class, which were named after the highest mountains of England and Wales. The sequence began with Scafell Pike in the Lake District, at 3,206ft England's highest. In later years, many in the class carried regimental names from withdrawn 'Royal Scot' 4-6-0s.

The single 12 cylinder Sulzer engine in these first ten examples produced 2,300hp but was uprated to 2,500hp for all subsequent construction. (Later the output was increased still further to 2,750hp, when the engine became the heart of the 'Brush 4' Co-Co.) This small increase in output actually boosted performance significantly, particularly as the Sulzer engine had to move a hefty 138 tons of locomotive as well as its train. The additional power was secured mainly by using intercooling and pressure charging. Both are ways of increasing the density, and therefore the quantity, of the air injected into the engine's cylinders. This then allows the proportion of fuel in the combustible mixture to be raised and the power output enhanced.

The 'Peaks' first proved their worth on the Midland main line out of London's St Pancras. They worked through to Derby, Nottingham, Sheffield and Leeds, and to Manchester before the closure of the line through the Peak District. Their duties also took them from Leeds to Edinburgh, over the Settle Carlisle route. Their extra power was welcomed especially on the revitalised Newcastle Leeds Manchester Liverpool expresses where the new schedules demanded locomotives with a high power capacity. On the well patronised ten coach trains, the incumbent motive power, 2,000hp English Electric Type 4s,

BR/Sulzer Type 4 diesel-electric NoD7 Ingleborough passes Greenholme on the climb to Shap summit with a Perth-London train on 30 July 1960. As one of the first ten 'Peaks', all of which were built at Derby, D7 had its Sulzer engine rated at 2,300hp. For subsequent production, the power plant was uprated — through intercooling — to 2,500hp. D1-D10 became BR Class 44.

had permitted little in the way of acceleration, particularly over the difficult section between Leeds and Manchester.

One great advantage of diesel locomotives is their ability to run much greater mileages than steam locomotives between servicing stops. They are limited only by the capacity of their fuel storage tanks. In the early years of British Railways dieselisation, however, this capability was woefully under used. Opportunities for inter-regional working were limited by the lack of standardisation in the locomotive fleet, which meant that crews were unfamiliar with many of different classes being used.

However, by the end of 1961, classes such as the 'Peaks' had reached sufficient numbers (193 in its case) to allow crews of all regions to acquaint themselves with them. This allowed some interesting examples of inter-regional collaboration. The cross-country route from Bristol to Newcastle by way of Birmingham, Derby, Sheffield and Leeds was one. A 'Peak' would travel through the night at the head of the 7.25pm sleeping-car express from Bristol, arriving at Newcastle at 4.33am. It then began its southbound journey on the 6.25am goods from Newcastle's Heaton yard to York, returning to Bristol on the 12.52pm express from York.

The prodigious tractive effort of the 'Peaks' (up to 70,000lb in later versions) made them first-rate heavy freight haulers and this increasingly became their role as they were displaced from passenger work by the newer Brush Type 4s. Nevertheless, they remained on cross-country and other passenger services well into the 1980s. One 'Peak' met a spectacular end when it was destroyed in a stage-managed crash. The collision between a train and a road vehicle was intended to show the resilience of the flasks used to transport nuclear waste from power stations.

Though no longer serving British Railways, ten 'Peaks' live on in preservation, including two of the original series, D4 (44004) *Great Gable* and D8 (44008) *Penyghent*.

Type 4 1Co-Co1 diesel-electric NoD146 approaches Barrow Road, Bristol, with the northbound 'The Devonian' from Paignton to Bradford Forster Square on 11 July 1969. Built in Derby between 1961 and 1963 this group earned its own classification from BR, becoming Class 46.

EMPERORS OF THE EAST COAST

It was the sound — the ground-shaking rhythm of 36 pistons working in harmony — as much as the sight that excited the senses. The 'Deltics' proved that diesels didn't have to be dull!

Sporting the 'winged thistle' headboard, 'Deltic' NoD9019 Royal Highland Fusilier cruises through Manors Station, Newcastle, with the southbound 'Flying Scotsman' on 1 August 1964. Built by English Electric at its Vulcan Foundry works in 1961, Royal Highland Fusilier is one of six preserved production 'Deltics'.

Imagine standing on a station somewhere on the West Coast Main Line in the mid-1950s. An express hastens through with a Stanier Pacific or 'Royal Scot' at its head; a freight rumbles by behind an antique 0-8-0 or Fowler 0-6-0. It's all very familiar. Then, from a distance, comes a throbbing sound belonging to no steam-powered machine. In a blur of blue and yellow stripes, the locomotive roars by, trailing a rake of maroon coaches. You just make out the carriage indicator boards: 'The Red Rose — Euston-Liverpool'. All that lingers is a pungent haze from the exhausts of two Napier 'Deltic' diesel engines and their distinctive sound retreating down the track.

The engine manufacturers, Napier & Sons, were part of the English Electric group. In the late 1940s, they designed a high-power diesel engine for the Admiralty. Intended for Royal Navy patrol boats, the engine had a distinctive shape — that of an inverted triangle. It also resembled the Greek letter delta, and from that derived its name: 'Deltic'. English Electric saw another application for the Napier engine and, in 1951, began construction of a prototype main-line diesel locomotive. It took four years, and cost £250,000, but in 1955 the 'Deltic' was ready to begin trials on British Railways. Delivering 3,300 horsepower from its twin 18-cylinder two-stroke engines, this Co-Co diesel-electric was the most powerful single-unit diesel locomotive in the world.

The prototype Deltic was based on the London Midland Region and mainly used on heavy London-Liverpool expresses. At the time, not only were diesels still a rarity, but the livery — blue with yellow chevron stripes — was a vivid departure from the BR standard colours of green and black. The performances of this locomotive were as striking as its looks and, after successful trials on the heavy grades of the Settle to Carlisle line, it passed to the Eastern Region.

At first, British Railways' diesel programme did not foresee a need for something in the 'Deltic' power class. Moreover, high-performance, twin-engined machines were both costly to build and maintain. However, the prototype had left its mark on the Eastern Region's management. It saw the 'Deltic', with its capacity for sustained high-speed running, as a way of accelerating services on the East Coast Main Line. It concluded, too,

that no other diesels could satisfactorily replace its fleet of ex-LNER Pacifics.

An order was placed with English Electric for 22 production 'Deltics' at £200,000 each and delivery took place over a 12-month period from March 1961. A new timetable based on 'Deltic' haulage was introduced in summer 1962. Three prestige services – 'The Elizabethan', 'The Talisman' and 'The Flying Scotsman' – were given six-hour timings between Kings Cross and Edinburgh while other trains to Yorkshire and the north-east were accelerated. Subsequent upgrading of the track along the east coast allowed the 'Deltics' to realise fully their potential. Happily running flat out for long periods, they maintained speeds in the high nineties and frequently exceeded 100mph. It allowed more time to be clipped from the schedules: one train, for example, was allowed just 91 minutes for the 138.5 miles from Retford to Kings Cross, requiring an average speed of 91.32mph.

The prototype 'Deltic' was retired after around 400,000 miles service and, in 1963, went on display at the Science Museum, London. It was later moved to the National Railway Museum in York. The production 'Deltics' went on to record far greater mileages, most passing the two million mark. A two-tone green livery suited them well and they quickly gained names. Famous regiments shared the honours with the LNER's ever popular source of inspiration, champion racehorses. Like the best racehorses, they garnered something of a cult following, especially as their retirement approached. Most ended their days based at York, relegated to working secondary services. Six have been preserved.

During its trials on the Eastern Region, a 'Deltic' prototype descends through Harringay, London, with the 1.38pm from Doncaster to King's Cross on 27 March 1959. The locomotive is now in the National Railway Museum, York.

The second of the production 'Deltics', D9001 St Paddy, rests at King's Cross after bringing in the 11.00am from Newcastle on 25 January 1969. British Railways allowed the east coast operators to order 22 'Deltics' after the main line electrification proposed in the Modernisation Plan was abandoned. They worked the principal expresses until replaced by High Speed Trains in 1978.

A DIESEL BY DESIGN

The 'box-on-wheels' notion of the diesel was challenged by the 'Westerns', locomotives which combined style with substance.

In one significant respect, the last of the Western Region's diesel hydraulic designs was also a 'first'. The 'Westerns', as they were named, benefited greatly from the expertise of a consultant industrial designer appointed by the British Transport Commission Design Panel – a body that had been set up too late to have any great influence on the earlier diesel designs. The happy outcome of full cooperation between the industrial designer and the engineers was that the 'Western' was one of the first main line diesels where, subject to technical constraints, the fullest attention was paid to the styling. The striking, almost rakish

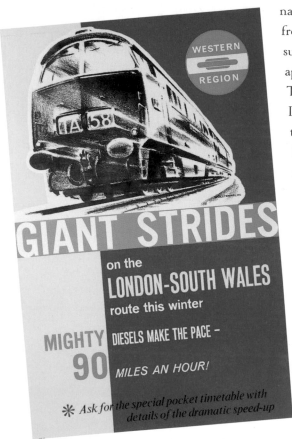

machine that emerged from Swindon Works was a refreshing antidote to the severity of many of its forebears. Moreover, it was achieved without resorting to any phoney streamlining.

The 'Westerns' were conceived after it became apparent that the 'Warship' diesel-hydraulics, which had entered traffic in 1958, were underpowered for some of the work expected of them. Design work began in 1959 and, like their predecessors, the 'Westerns' were almost entirely enclosed in a 'skirt' down to rail level. It was, though, cut away to expose the six-wheel bogies.

Thanks in part to the design of this stressed-skin outer shell, the weight of the locomotive was kept down to 108 tons. The maximum axleloading came in at 18.25 tons.

Power was derived from two Bristol-Siddeley-Maybach MD655 engines, a revised version of that used in the Swindon-built 'Warships'. Each of these power plants produced 1,350hp from its 12 cylinders, which were arranged in a 'V' formation. Voith transmissions transferred that power to the bogies, where the six axles gave a high tractive effort for the comparatively low axleloading. This made the 'Westerns' ideal for hauling heavy passenger and freight trains over the testing grades of the South Devon banks and on the undulating main line through Cornwall. The locomotives had a maximum speed of 90mph and a fuel capacity of 850 gallons.

The late delivery of some parts, including the German-made transmissions, delayed the locomotives' entry into service. It was not until January 1962 that the prototypes, NoD1000 *Western Enterprise* and NoD1001 (later named *Western Pathfinder*) began trials. The production run was set at 74, with construction shared between two BR workshops. Under-capacity limited Swindon to 30, NosD1000-29, while Crewe delivered the remainder, NosD1030-73, which were the only diesel-hydraulics ever to be built there.

When first delivered the 'Westerns', as expected, were rostered for the principal West of England expresses but additionally appeared on the Paddington-Birmingham-Wolverhampton-Shrewsbury run. They initially performed up to expectation but then their reliability dramatically declined. A problem arose with the bogies at speeds of over 80mph, when the transmission shaft roller bearings had a habit of seizing. All the locomotives were withdrawn temporarily for checks to be made and, for a time, the 'Westerns' had something of a bad name in the WR's running department.

These question marks against the 'Westerns' simply emphasised an already-evident drawback of the diesel-hydraulics: maintenance costs were noticeably higher compared to the equivalent diesel-electric classes. True, the two small engines employed in the hydraulic designs were lighter and easier to remove for servicing but that hardly compensated for the day-to-day problems faced by maintenance crews.

The 'Westerns' were displaced by diesel-electrics on mainline service because they could not be used with the new air-conditioned or electrically heated rolling stock. Many ended their days working stone trains originating from quarries in the Westbury area. Their high starting

TOWARDS A BRIGHTER FUTURE

Alongside their external styling, the first two 'Westerns' attracted notice with their liveries. NoD1000 was painted in a shade described as 'desert sand' while NoD1001 wore a rich maroon. Both were a refreshing change from the monotony of BR standard green that had been applied to all other diesel classes. The argument that lighter colours would not wear well and would show the dirt was losing ground as steam traction was eliminated. Operating conditions were now relatively clean and the new diesel depots included locomotive washing facilities. However, the fitting of cast number- and nameplates to the 'Western' diesels, with raised numerals and letters harked back to a Great Western tradition. As the name suggests, all these names had a 'Western' prefix, such as *Western Glory*, *Western Envoy* and *Western Champion*.

tractive effort of 72,000lb was useful in moving these heavy loads. All were withdrawn by 1978, but seven have been preserved.

The experimental maroon and 'desert sand' liveries of the first 'Westerns' eventually — and inevitably — lost out to uniform BR blue and yellow, as seen here on D1026 Western Centurion, seen leaving Bristol Temple Meads with a Paignton service in August 1967. D1026 was one of the 30 'Westerns' built at Swindon between 1962 and 1964.

A BRUSH WITH SUCCESS

If Britain's railways have a diesel equivalent to the mixed traffic steam locomotive, it is the 'Brush 4'. Equally at home on passenger and freight, this 'maid-of-all-work' has served every rail region since its introduction in 1962.

These were the diesel-electric locomotives that should have been built at the very outset of British Railways' dieselisation programme in the mid-1950s. That way, some expensive and embarrassing flops may have been avoided. The 'Brush 4', as it has always been known, was the most modern of the early BR diesel classes and compared to its predecessors, it was a radical design. The engine and ancillary equipment were housed in a lightweight, stressed-skin body shell. That way, the heavy chassis needed to underpin other diesel designs could be exchanged for two swing-bolster three-axle bogies and the weight kept down to 117 tons. All six axles were powered.

The power plant originated with the Swiss Sulzer company. It was an uprated version of the LD engine already employed in the 1Co-Co1 'Peak' diesel-electrics introduced in 1959. Brush Traction of Loughborough, in Leicestershire, supplied the electrical gear, such as the traction motors, and undertook the assembly of what become one of the most enduring and reliable classes of diesel locomotives.

The first 20 'Brush 4s' went to the Eastern Region where they quickly showed their worth, proving capable substitutes for failed 'Deltics' on east coast expresses. More orders followed with construction shared by Brush and BR's works at Crewe. By 1967, 542 were in service, the largest number of any British diesel class, apart from the Class 08 shunter. Over the years, the 'Brush 4' went to every region except the Southern, although they regularly appeared on SR metals.

Following their success on the Eastern, batches of 'Brush 4s' were allocated to the Western and London Midland Regions where they displayed the power to handle most types of passenger and

freight services. After trials on the WR demonstrated that the class was capable of sustained speeds of over 100mph, the original stipulated maximum speed of 90mph was raised to 95mph.

In the 40 years the 'Brush 4' (now Class 47) has been in service, it has undergone several modifications that have successfully extended its working life. These included downrating the engines to 2,580hp, so overcoming minor problems encountered when working the heaviest (around 1,500 tons) freight trains. Examples were also modified for specific duties, such as those equipped for push-pull operation on express services between Glasgow and Edinburgh. Others allocated to 'merry-go-round' (pit-to-power station) coal trains were fitted with an automatic slow-speed 'creep' control. This allowed the locomotives to haul their trains through unloading plants at power stations, discharging their hopper wagons while travelling at just half-a-mile an hour.

Substantial numbers remain in service, including a batch re-engined specifically to work on container trains (and re-classified as Class 57). Their new General Motors power plants allow the Class 57s to work Freightliner services at speeds up to 75mph. Two Class 47s, Nos47798 *Prince William* and 47799 *Prince Henry*, have been set aside to work the royal train.

A diverted Glasgow-Birmingham express passes Ais Gill, on the Settle and Carlisle line, on 1 August 1965 behind 'Brush 4' NoD1633. The original two-tone green livery, seen here, suited these engines well. Today, they sport all manner of colours, from lined black to grey, red, pink(!) and the dark green carried by the 12 locomotives rebuilt by Brush specifically for fast container trains. These have been reclassified and renumbered in the Class 57 series.

Sunshine and snow greet Brush Type 4 Co-Co diesel-electric NoD1622 as it passes Kingmoor yard, Carlisle, with a Glasgow to London service, April 1966. The 500-plus 'Brush 4s' (BR Class 47) were undoubtedly the most successful of the early main-line diesels and some 200 remain in service.

DELIVERING *8* THE GOODS

*The coal for the fire, milk for the fridge,
food for the table and the raw materials for
Britain's industries were all carried by train.*

BY THE WAGON-LOAD

*For over a century the 'mixed' freight, with its jangling assortment of wagons,
delivered the goods to communities throughout Britain.*

In the days of gritty black-and-white movies about working-class life, you could be certain of the accompaniment to at least one nocturnal scene. It would be the sound of wagons being shunted in some nearby goods yard. Somehow that symphony of off-key clanging, like the peal of cracked church bells, stood for the sound of a city by night.

In the days before road traffic, when steam engines were the sole form of mechanised land transport, railways were the only practical way of carrying goods over distances. However, it was a conditional monopoly since, under the Railway and Canal Traffic Act of 1854, they had become 'common carriers'. This obliged them to accept any article – animal, vegetable and mineral – presented for carriage, barring potentially lethal payloads such as explosives.

The consequence of this was that, at the hundreds of goods yards around Britain, you could see an extraordinary variety of cargoes being loaded and unloaded. Vans containing fruit, vegetables, dairy produce and flowers might share sidings and a loading dock with wagons full of bricks, timber, stone or machinery.

The extensive goods yard at Copley Hill, Leeds, was typical of those once found in industrial locations all over Britain. Equally typical was the yard shunting locomotive (or locomotives). Here, the role is undertaken by LMSR 3F 0-6-0 tank No47571, one of a class of 422 built between 1924 and 1931.

Carrying the competition. English Electric Type 4 diesel-electric NoD214 passes Falshill summit, on the Edinburgh-Carlisle 'Waverley' route, on its way to Birmingham with a trainload of trucks and trailers from the vehicle plant at Bathgate, in Lothian.

It was a time when many of Britain's most famous brands reached the shops by train, from Colman's mustard to Bass beer, Saxa salt, Huntley & Palmer's biscuits, Cadbury's chocolate, Wedgwood pottery, Kidderminster carpets and Yorkshire woollens. In some cases, the railway itself was a spur to commercial success. The growth of the malt whisky industry in the Scottish Highlands followed the opening of the

A traffic long vanished from Britain's railways. At a rural siding in Wrenbury, Shropshire, cows clamber into the once-familiar cattle wagon. The Liverpool & Manchester Railway was carrying livestock as early as 1831. The last cattle trains ran in 1975.

An eastbound milk train approaches Aller Junction, near Newton Abbot, Devon, behind 'Castle' class 4-6-0 No7004 Eastnor Castle. Opposite: Stanier 5MT 4-6-0 No44852 gazes upon the grandeur of Ingleborough as it stands in the up loop at Blea Moor sidings with a southbound freight on 2 August 1967.

A wartime plea from all of the 'big four' companies as labour and materials shortages delay wagon repairs.

Great North of Scotland Railway. The GNSR delivered coal and barley to the distilleries and took the casks of whisky to the blending houses.

Another liquid that came to depend on rail transport was milk. Trains enlarged the area from which fresh milk could be delivered to cities such as London, where several 'milk docks' were built. One was at Kensington, which received daily loads from Great Western territory – the West Country, Wales and the shire counties. Similarly, the fishing industry, in Scotland, Humberside, East Anglia and Cornwall, relied on fast freights to deliver its catches to towns and cities.

Two types of freight train evolved, the specialist express and the general, or mixed goods, which was far from 'express'. The express goods was reserved for loads such as perishable foodstuffs, animals and newspapers. In contrast, the 'mixed' goods was made up of wagonloads of whatever needed to be carried and was usually restricted in its speed.

What limited that speed was the wagons themselves. The typical British four-wheel truck or van lacked any power brakes, whether vacuum- or air-operated. It relied solely on a handbrake, which was 'pinned' down by a pole-wielding shunter, or by the guard. However, the leisurely nature of many freight operations could only partly be blamed on braking inadequacies.

The daily pickup goods was a feature of many lines until well into the 1960s. It would potter between stations – this at a time when the majority of them had a goods yard of some kind – and undertake some shunting. It might collect a single-load truck or two, or a van loaded with 'sundries' – many small consignments gathered together in one vehicle. Its 'pickups' completed, the train would head for the nearest marshalling yard where its assortment of wagons would be placed into trains bound for their final destination. However, it was not always straightforward. In the larger yards, such was the volume of traffic being processed that wagons would be marooned for days. It was not uncommon for wagons to be 'lost' in the system; there were, after all well over one million of them. By the early 1900s, however, control offices had been introduced to bring some measure of co-ordination and centralised management to freight operations.

By 1913, Britain's railways were carrying 367 million tons of freight a year. To cope with this volume an increasing number of vacuum-brake fitted wagons were entering service, which was just as well as, after World War I, the threat from road transport began to be felt. Between the wars, a number of new express goods services were promoted, with average speeds of up to 50mph.

THE IRON ROAD

One of the toughest, yet most efficient freight workings on British Railways was the daily haul of imported iron ore to feed the furnaces of the Consett steelworks in County Durham. The journey was only 23 miles but each mile was hard-won. From the banks of the River Tyne to Consett, the line rose 900 feet. For around nine miles, locomotive crews faced gradients ranging from 1 in 49 to 1 in 70.

Until 1953, the only means of unloading ore from the ships was in tubs. They were filled by hand, hoisted by cranes and then tipped into hopper wagons. Given that the steelworks could consume 3,000 tons a day, it was an unrelenting task.

When the steelworks expanded, it was clear that the existing system would be unable to cope. British Railways, the Tyne Improvement Commission and the Consett Iron Company collaborated on a mechanisation scheme. Five electrically powered cranes were installed on a new quay at Tyne Dock. They were able to offload 300 tons of ore each hour on to conveyors. These took the ore to huge storage bunkers that spanned the railway sidings. British Railways supplied new bogie hopper wagons of 56 tons capacity that were loaded from these bunkers. Ore cascaded into eight-strong trains of hoppers 14 times a day.

A feature of these hoppers was that their sidedoors, which disgorged the ore at Consett, were air-operated, Four small compressed air engines were fitted to each wagon, operated by opening an air valve on the locomotive footplate. This required the rostered locomotives, five ex-LNER 01 class 2-8-0s and five Q7 class 0-8-0s, to be each fitted with a brace of Westinghouse air pumps. The 2-8-0s hauled the ore trains, while the 0-8-0s supplied rear-end assistance.

In late 1955, Tyne Dock shed took delivery of the first of seven new BR Standard 9F 2-10-0s. These were similarly fitted with Westinghouse pumps to work the ore trains and their extra power allowed a ninth hopper to be added to the trains. This total amounted to 450 tons of ore and adding the weight of the wagons made a load of 750 tons. To see a 9F getting to grips with this haul on the 1 in 40 start from Tyne Dock, exhaust roaring into the sky, was awe-inspiring. Two hours later it pulled into Consett, unloaded, and returned to the riverside ready for more.

Above: BR 9F 2-10-0 No92066 offers energetic rear-end assistance to a Tyne Dock-Consett iron ore train as it tackles the 1 in 35 climb at Stanley.

DELIVERING THE GOODS

A clerk checks the varied contents of his parcels van, which include some milk churns. It is easy to forget that Britain's railways were once legally obliged to carry all goods traffic, with the exception of items that were either dangerous, or of dubious legality.

Faster services, allied to the elimination of bottle-necks at major marshalling yards, meant that by the mid-1930s, over 70 per cent of wagonload goods traffic was reaching its destination the day after despatch. There was also an increasing use of containers, standard-size steel boxes that could be swiftly transferred from road to rail and vice-versa. Despite these innovations, World War II was to be the last time Britain's railways carried 300 million tons of freight in a year.

British Railways' freight business faced challenges on three fronts. First, the system itself was exhausted by war, with locomotives and rolling stock run into the ground, and it was 1951 before fast freight services were restored to pre-war levels. Second, road freight could now compete on speed, reliability and cost, and was much more flexible. Finally, the heavy industries that for over

a century had generated so much rail traffic, such as coal and steel, began to decline.

There was some success in attracting new customers: car manufacturers and frozen food producers were among those attracted to rail, and container services became popular. Freightliner trains were introduced in 1965 and, by the end of 1966, had carried 27,000 containers. However, despite efforts to reverse its fortunes, the traditional wagonload freight service had become a serious loss-maker.

A National Freight Train Plan, published in 1966-67, concluded that railways were equipped best for transporting bulk loads from terminal to terminal. These were trains of chemicals, gases, petroleum products, fertiliser, cement, stone, china clay, ores and other industrial minerals and the traditional staples of coal, iron and steel. The

Once one of the most important bulk loads carried by rail, cement traffic has declined in recent years due to road competition. Here, a Class 40 diesel-electric takes the curve near Chinley with a long rake of purpose-built pressure-discharge cement tankers bound for Manchester.

report maintained that a limited but reliable range of services would justify investment in new, purpose-built freight vehicles. This plan rescinded the obligations of railways to be common carriers and led to their withdrawal from wagon-load freight. This had far-reaching consequences. Many marshalling yards, some built relatively recently, became virtually redundant.

Freight depots closed and many customers had no option but to switch to the roads. One stark statistic sums up the decline of rail freight. At nationalisation in 1948, British Railways had 1,216,690 goods wagons (600,000 privately owned). By 1988, that figure was 48,353.

CARLISLE UNITED

In common with many other locations, freight working in the Carlisle area was bedevilled by the legacy of past rivalries. Each of the seven railway companies that originally projected routes into the border city built its own goods yard; in some cases, more than one. As late as 1962, nine of those yards were still in use. Consequently, 'trip' working – moving loads from one yard to another – was not only complicated but a big operational expense. Many of the yards were inconveniently laid out and inefficient in their freight operation, which only compounded the problem. Anglo-Scottish through traffic regularly required three trip workings and consumed the best part of an eight-hour shift to negotiate the Carlisle area.

A new central yard at Carlisle was crucial to the London Midland Region's 1959 Freight Plan. Anglo-Scottish freight services had to be accelerated to stay competitive. A site was secured some two-and-a-half miles north of the city and, in October 1959, the process of removing over a million tons of earth from the site began. At the time, Kingmoor yard was probably the biggest single civil engineering scheme undertaken as part of British Railways' modernisation programme.

The 480 acre site was overlaid with 72 miles of track and 381 sets of points and crossings. The basic arrangement was for two virtually identical yards, one for northbound traffic, one for southbound. The whole yard stretched for 2.5miles alongside the West Coast Main Line and could deal with 5,000 wagons each day. It was estimated that opening of Kingmoor yard in 1962 would reduce the number of daily trip workings from around 36 to two, a saving of 7,300 engine hours each week. Yearly operational savings for BR's London Midland Region would be over £350,000. Sadly for BR's freight managers, this kind of cost-cutting and rationalisation were the exception rather than the rule.

GETTING THE COAL IN

'A 165,000,000 ton customer,' was how a 1950s publication described British Railways' relationship with the coal industry. It's a relationship that goes back more than 200 years.

In the early 1950s, of the 200 million tons of coal mined in Britain each year, 165 million tons was carried by rail. It filled thousands of wagons that, in turn, occupied hundreds of miles of sidings in marshalling yards and coal depots the length of the country. From there, it went to power stations, gasworks, factories, ports and local supply merchants. Since domestic central heating was in its infancy, most people depended on coal fires. Every high street had its coal merchant and their lorries made regular deliveries to homes and businesses in the area.

Britain also exported a vast quantity of coal: approaching 50 million tons each year during the 1930s, a figure that had dropped to 10 million tons by the mid-1960s. Among the coal industry's biggest customers were the railways themselves. In 1948 alone, it supplied fuel for over 20,000 steam locomotives.

A bond between railways and coal mining has existed since the 18th century and many of the earliest railways were built to serve mines in northern England. Coal-carrying was the function of the first railway to be authorised by an Act of Parliament, the Middleton Railway in Leeds, which gained Westminster's approval in 1758. As with many other lines, the Middleton conveyed coal to a canal or river for onward shipment to towns and cities. The prime role of the first public railway to use steam traction, the Stockton & Darlington, was to ferry coal from the Bishop Auckland area to the River Tees.

In north-east England, as in southern Scotland and South Wales, extensive railway systems were developed during the nineteenth century solely to tap the vast coal deposits. Some of the finest steam coal in the world lay beneath the valleys of South Wales, all of which were situated close to the Bristol Channel and the ports of Cardiff, Barry and Newport. A dense pattern of lines came to serve the mining valleys, in some cases in competition. One railway hugged the eastern side of the valley, the other the western. Several of the major coal-carrying railways of South Wales were

locally run outfits, but larger companies such as the Great Western, London & North Western and Midland were intent on taking a share of the spoils, sometimes in alliance with local concerns. While the valley lines ran north-south — following the Taff, Rhondda and Rhymney, for example — the Great Western and L&NWR drove east to west. In doing so, they faced formidable physical obstacles and overcoming them was costly, but the prize justified the price.

The L&NWR and Midland tracks were carried along high viaducts and through tunnels burrowed into the mountain ridges. For the engines and crews of the Great Western, the biggest challenge was presented by the gradients of the Severn Tunnel. A stud of powerful tank locomotives was maintained at Severn Tunnel Junction depot to assist trains through the tunnel, piloting them as far as Stoke Gifford yard, to the north of Bristol. In these trains of 80 wagons and more, the GWR conveyed vast quantities of coal to London.

However, it was not the only major railway to cater for the capital's fuel needs. The first railway to bring coal to London on a large scale was the Great Northern. The GNR set itself up both as carrier and merchant, buying the coal at Yorkshire pitheads, shipping it to London and selling direct to the public. In this way, it was able to cut the price of domestic coal dramatically.

Like the GNR, the Midland became a major coal carrier. There was sufficient output to keep both railways working to their line capacity, but

Norton Hill, between Midsomer Norton and Radstock, was one of several collieries within the North Somerset coalfield. Mining began in the mid-1600s and reached its peak with the steam age. Coal traffic ceased in 1973.

BLYTH SPIRIT

As in South Wales, coal hauls in Northumberland and Durham were generally of the short, pit-to-port variety. A characteristic way of unloading coal in this area was the staith, a high wooden gallery built on the quayside. Trains of hopper wagons were propelled on to the staiths and, one by one, pushed over a point where their hopper doors were opened. Coal was discharged into chutes leading into the holds of the colliers tied up alongside.

At Blyth, on the Northumberland coast, the maximum train load that was allowed on to the staiths was 18 hoppers, weighing around 550 tons. Propelled by a single small tank engine (the staiths' wooden construction preclude anything heavier), sound and fury filled the air as the locomotive blasted its way up on to the staith!

*For decades, most of
Britain's coal was carried
in wagons such as this:
four-wheeled, wooden-
bodied and, with only a
handbrake to restrain
them, slow-moving.*

the Midland had to take bold action to keep its coal trains on the move. The most clogged area was between Normanton, in South Yorkshire, and Nottingham. To ease the congestion, the Midland laid a new line along the Erewash Valley, from Trent Junction to Clay Cross south of

Chesterfield, which by-passed both Derby and Nottingham. At the southern end of the line it built enormous marshalling yards at Toton that dealt almost exclusively with coal traffic.

Until nationalisation, colliery companies owned and maintained their wagon fleets. Every working day, hundreds of these wagons arrived at Toton from a host of collieries for sorting into 'block loads' for London and elsewhere. Groups of wagons for various coal merchants were marshalled together. Yards at Peterborough performed a similar role in marshalling southbound coal trains on the East Coast Main Line.

However, this relatively efficient large-scale handling at the start of the journey was not matched at the final destination. For many decades, domestic coal was delivered to thousands of private sidings and coal yards for manual transfer to road vehicles, both motor and horse-powered. It was not until the 1950s that large mechanised and centralised coal handling plants were set up, resulting in the closure of most of the smaller depots.

By the 1960s, although domestic coal consumption was falling, there was a growing demand from new coal-fired power stations. Delivering

NAVAL ACTION

To take coal out of South Wales, the London & North Western Railway built a line across the heads of the valleys, from Merthyr, Dowlais, Nantybwch and Brynmawr down to Abergavenny. It was a route of formidable gradients: 1 in 38 and 1 in 40 over long stretches.

During World War I, this section marked the start of one of the longest regular hauls of coal undertaken. The warships of the Royal Navy were then coal-fired and the Admiralty's preferred fuel was South Wales steam coal. It was hauled from South Wales to north-east Scotland

to refuel the ships then based on Scapa Flow.

After the gradients of South Wales, the trains had a relatively easy run through the Welsh Marches to Cheshire and on into Lancashire before facing the haul up Shap and then Beattock banks. Then came the pull over the Grampians to the highest railway summit in Britain, at Druimuachdar Pass, before arrival at the port of Thurso. The trains were known as 'Jellicoe Specials' after the Commander-in-Chief of the Grand Fleet (later Admiral of the Fleet) Earl Jellicoe.

coal to these stations has become a type of shuttle working using trains of modern, all-steel hopper wagons. These are loaded at the pithead or coal terminal, unloaded automatically at the power station, then returned for reloading. Two or three trains per day call at some of the bigger power stations. In essence, the 'merry-go-round', or MGR, operation, as it has become known, is not very dissimilar from the 'coalface-to-canal' workings established by the Middleton Railway 250 years ago.

Class J27 0-6-0 No65879 coasts along the Silksworth colliery branch on Wearside with a rake of loaded coal hoppers, 31 August 1967.
Below: Coal from Kent: Maunsell N class mixed traffic 2-6-0 No31408 brings a northbound train through St Mary Cray.

A FORGOTTEN FIELD

Little survives as a reminder that one of Kent's chief commodities was coal from collieries in the east of the county. The quantity produced was relatively small – two million tons each year during the most productive era, the 1930s – but 90 per cent of that travelled by train. The four principal collieries were at Chislet, east of Canterbury; Snowdown, between Canterbury and Dover; and at Betteshanger, north of Deal, on the coastal line between Ramsgate and Dover. The fourth colliery, at Tilmanstone, north-east of Dover, was – from a railway point of view – the most interesting. From 1913, it was served by the East Kent Light Railway. This was one of the routes engineered by that enthusiastic promoter of light railways, Colonel Dolman F. Stephens. Along with coal, the EKLR carried passengers and general goods traffic, and retained its independence until 1948.

The bulk of Kent coal was burnt in the county, and in Surrey. The paper and cement industries were major users, followed by power stations, gasworks and the railways. The opening, in 1963, of Richborough power station near Ramsgate was a boost for the, by then, declining fortunes of the coalfield. Nevertheless, Chislet colliery closed in 1969 and its companions followed over the ensuing two decades.

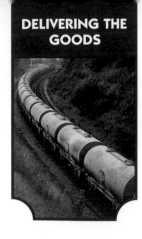

MAIL BY RAIL

Railways and the Royal Mail have worked hand-in-hand since the earliest days of train travel.

Mail was first carried by train in November 1830, between the north-western cities of Manchester and Liverpool on the world's first intercity railway. Liverpudlians received tidings from their Mancunian cousins in half the time it took the horse-drawn mail coach.

In 1838, using a converted horsebox, the London & Birmingham Railway operated the first Travelling Post Office. That same year, the carriage of mail by train was authorised by Act of Parliament. It was the beginning of a partnership that, at its peak, saw 80 per cent of the letters posted in the British Isles conveyed by train.

Since the earliest days, there were two key routes for the Royal Mail, both starting at London's Euston Station. The destinations were Holyhead, for the sea crossing to Ireland, and Scotland, by way of Lancaster and Carlisle. Interchange points were established along the way, with Crewe at the hub of the network. This was the junction for Manchester, Liverpool and the Potteries; Shrewsbury, Hereford, Cardiff and mid-Wales; and Chester, the North Wales coast and Holyhead. Only insomniacs, and those who had missed their last train home, probably witnessed the scene of intense activity that was Crewe station after 11.30pm.

This focus on the West Coast route meant that the London & North Western Railway the pre-eminent mail carrier among 19th century railway companies. Its 'Irish Mail', inaugurated on 31 July 1848, was the world's first 'named train'.

Elsewhere, the Great Western Railway began operating postal specials between Paddington and Bristol on 1 February 1855. The most celebrated GWR postal service became that between Plymouth and London, the 'Ocean Mails Express'. This carried post off-loaded from trans-Atlantic liners calling at Plymouth and was the source of fierce competition with the London & South Western Railway. The L&SWR also wanted this lucrative and prestigious traffic and, for a time, had the advantage of a shorter route to London, by way of Salisbury. The GWR could only counter with speed, one result of which was the first recorded instance of a locomotive, *City of Truro*, attaining 100mph (see chapter 7).

Although railways had a virtual monopoly in carrying the post, at least until the introduction

At the head of a down mail train on 5 August 1967, a BR Standard 'Britannia' Pacific takes water from Dillicar troughs south of Tebay.

of the first air services in the 1920s, the Post Office was a hard taskmaster. It had the right to veto timetable changes that might affect the time-keeping of postal specials and even stipulated minimum average speeds for some trains. The 'Irish Mail', for example, was expected to average 42mph between Euston and Holyhead, and this led the L&NWR to introduce one of the unique features of the steam age — the water trough. To allow the locomotive hauling the 'Irish Mail' to cover the 84 miles between Chester and Holyhead without stopping to take on water, the first

troughs in Britain were installed at Aber. The L&NWR also pioneered another time-saving device, the lineside exchange apparatus where mail pouches were dropped off and collected at speed (see below). By 1911, there were 245 such installations on Britain's main lines but by 1967 the figure had dropped to 34. The last use of the system on British Railways was at Penrith, in Cumbria, on 4 October 1971. However, Didcot Railway Centre in Oxfordshire has a working lineside TPO apparatus and mailbag exchanges are a feature of most 'steamdays' there.

A postal van, complete with mailbag pickup equipment, is the first vehicle in this King's Cross-bound train. Photographed at Hadley Wood, Hertfordshire, during the Great Northern era, the locomotive is one of Henry Ivatt's 'small Atlantics', No950. Built at Doncaster in April 1900, it was retired – as LNER No3950 – in December 1937.

The 'Irish Mail' has arrived at Holyhead and dockers transfer mail on to the SS Scotia, bound for Dun Laoghaire.

ONE NIGHT IN TAMWORTH

In the early 1960s, mailbag transfers between the low-level platforms of the West Coast Main Line and those on the high-level serving the Bristol-Birmingham-Derby route were the principal reason for the rebuilding of Tamworth Station in Staffordshire. Tamworth had been a transfer point since 1847 and, by 1962, was handling up to 2,000 mailbags nightly.

The Post Office had 20 employees based there and each night seven TPO services called. The busiest hours were from 10.45pm to 1.45am during which period the 'West Coast Postal' was scheduled to stop for just nine minutes, from 10.45pm until 10.54pm. It was followed by the Bristol-Newcastle at 10.51pm, the Newcastle-Bristol a little later at 1.09am and the Aberdeen-London postal at 1.23am. Mail was interchanged between these trains, and with Post Office road vehicles from Birmingham, Stafford, Leicester, Lichfield and Coventry.

The southbound 'West Coast Postal' (or, to give it its correct title, 'Up Special TPO') heads through Craigenhill, near Glasgow, behind Type 4 diesel NoD343 on May 30, 1963. In October that year, the 'Up Special', hauled by a similar locomotive, became the target of the notorious 'Great Train Robbery'.

'THIS IS THE NIGHT MAIL...'

'...crossing the border, bringing the cheque and the postal order. Letters for the rich, letters for the poor, the shop at the corner, the girl next door.' How well W.H. Auden's verse captured the fascination of the mail train, and the legendary 'West Coast Postal' in particular, in the famous 1936 documentary. Not that the 'Postal' was known by that name to either railway or Post Office. The official title of the 8.30pm from London Euston to Glasgow and Aberdeen was the 'Down Special TPO' (the equivalent southbound train was the 'Up Special TPO'). The service was inaugurated jointly by the L&NWR and Caledonian Railway on 1 July 1885.

The 'West Coast Postal' was not the sole example of a Travelling Post Office (the GWR, for example ran one between Penzance and Paddington), but it was certainly the most celebrated. Its romance was only enhanced by the Central Office of Information film that used Auden's words, together with Benjamin Britten's music, to such memorable effect.

The 'West Coast Postal' left Euston each evening. Apart from the locomotive crew, the only railway worker on the train was the guard and he was completely barred from entering any of the postal sorting vans. There, the post office clerks would have begun sorting the mail an hour before departure.

Inside each van, the mailbags were emptied on to sorting tables. Working at lightning speed, the clerks sorted letters into bundles and placed them in pigeon-holes, all marked with the names of towns and cities served by the 'Postal'. Along the other side of the van, a row of pegs held mailbags into which the bundles were placed.

Two methods were employed to deliver the mailbags to their destinations. At major junctions, such as Rugby, Tamworth, Crewe and Carlisle, the 'Postal' would stop. In readiness, on the exterior of the mail coaches, postmen would have chalked the names of the towns that had bags on board. Mail for North Wales, for example, was offloaded at Crewe and taken on by a connecting service.

The 'Postal' also had its 'feeder' services. Mail from the West of England was collected at Bristol, taken forward to Birmingham New Street and then on to Crewe. On the way, the train halted at Cheltenham to collect bags from Swindon and as far south as Southampton.

Elsewhere, though, valuable time was saved by using a lineside exchange apparatus. Here, mail could be both dropped and collected at speed. A net thrust out from the side of one of the vans grabbed 'incoming' mail hanging on a lineside post. 'Outgoing' mailbags were hooked on to a steel arm that was swung out from the side of the van at the right moment. They would then be scooped into a waiting 'catching net'.

Undertaking this procedure at 60mph was quite a feat. Since it generally happened in darkness, the exact location of the train had to be judged. Extend the dropping arm at the wrong moment and it might hit a bridge or signal post. The postal clerks became skilled at knwoing their whereabouts by external sounds, or by counting the bridges from the last station. To counter the violence of the action, the mailbags were placed in tough leather pouches. These crashed into the sorting van and slithered across the floor, entering with such force that an alarm bell was rung to warn the occupants to stand clear.

INDUSTRIOUS TYPES

Largely unseen by the public, remarkably diverse railway systems served the needs of Britain's industries.

Industry grew side-by-side with railways, with the first lines laid to serve quarries, mines and ironworks. By 1900, that relationship had expanded to include factories, docks, brickworks, chemical plants, cement works, steelworks, breweries, even sugar beet processing plants – anywhere where raw materials and finished products needed to be moved around. Extensive railway systems were also built by water companies and sewage works, by gas-works and coking plants, and by power stations. Some industrial railways enjoyed great longevity, while others were temporary constructions laid to serve a specific purpose – a major construction project, for example – and were then removed.

The gauges of these railways varied widely. Of necessity, lines linked to the national system had to be of standard gauge but others adopted narrow gauge, which was cheaper to build. The slate quarry railways of Wales, for example, were all narrow gauge.

On many of the earliest industrial lines wagons were hauled by horses, towed by cables or moved by force of gravity. Later, locomotives were either bought new or redundant locomotives acquired from public railways. A number of companies specialised in building locomotives for industrial customers. Among the first were E.B. Wilson & Co. and George England & Co. who began catering for this market in the 1850s.

Most industrial locomotives were four- or six-coupled tank locomotives, either of the saddle tank or side tank variety. There were variations, though, since some industrial users had particular requirements. Crane engines were in demand in shipyards and ironworks and, during the 1950s, the Pallion shipyard in Sunderland employed seven of them. Kilmarnock-based Andrew Barclay developed a 'fireless' locomotive for locations where smoke and sparks would pose a hazard – chemical works and paper mills, for example. The locomotive did not generate its own steam but had a reservoir that was filled periodically off-site with steam from a stationary boiler.

Many industrial railways had a fascination all their own: the Waterside colliery system in Ayrshire was one, as were the coal-carrying lines in County Durham and South Wales and the ironstone railways of Oxfordshire, Northamptonshire and Lincolnshire. A remarkable system served the vast gasworks at Beckton, in east London, while in the heart of the Scottish Highlands, the aluminium smelter at Kinlochleven was furnished with a railway between 1924 and 1929.

Although petrol-driven locomotives began to appear on narrow-gauge lines from the 1920s,

Hunslet 0-6-0 saddletank No3840 of 1956 at Pontardulais, north of Swansea.

THE SHIPPING LINE

One of the longest and busiest of industrial railways was that serving the Manchester Ship Canal. One of the great civil engineering works of the 19th century, the canal was opened by Queen Victoria in May 1894. Sea-going vessels on the River Mersey joined the Ship Canal at Eastham, near Ellesmere Port, and sailed inland to the docks at Manchester. The raw materials brought in and the finished goods taken out contributed greatly to Manchester becoming the commercial centre of north-west England.

Complementing the canal was its railway system, which extended westwards from Manchester as far as Ellesmere Port. There were 33 route miles and, adding in all the sidings and yards, around 200 track miles. In the late 1950s, operating the canal railway called for 69 tank locomotives and a fleet of over 2,500 wagons. The volume of traffic handled annually amounted to around 7 million tons. On its way westwards, the railway served a variety of industries, among them a soap works, a margarine factory, paper mills and flour mills. There were also junctions with British Railways' lines at 12 points between Manchester and Ellesmere Port.

The canal railway's locomotives were maintained at seven sheds, the largest of which – Mode Wheel Road, near Salford – was home to 30 engines. With 26 examples, the predominant design was an 0-6-0 inside cylinder tank built by Hudswell Clarke. Fitted with flangeless centre driving wheels so they could negotiate the many sharp curves on the system, these strong machines could handle trains of 30 to 45 wagons without difficulty.

steam traction remained predominant. Some larger industrial railways had workshop facilities that would do justice to a main-line railway, the Philadelphia works of the Lambton, Hetton and Joicey Colliery Company in County Durham being a case in point.

The last steam locomotive built in Britain for British industrial use was an 0-6-0 saddletank constructed by Hunslet of Leeds in 1964, the last of 484 engines produced to this design. It was bought by the National Coal Board and employed at the Manvers Main coal preparation plant at Rotherham in South Yorkshire.

As late as 1975, there were over 40 such locations around Britain where steam locomotives were still at work. It was not until the 1980s that the remaining industrial railways put the last of the breed out to pasture.

9 RAILWAYS AT WAR

Railways were responsible for evacuating children and also making weapons, and transporting the troops who would use them.

WAR ON THE LINE

As in 1914, Britain's railways went to war entrusted with the task of conveying troops, munitions, fuel and equipment, as well as workers to their factories and offices. This time, however, they faced dangers themselves.

On 1 September 1939, two days before war was declared, the government took control of Britain's railways. From that day, they were called upon to tackle the biggest and most arduous job in their history, and in conditions of unprecedented danger. The railways themselves became a major target, sustaining over 10,000 air attacks between 1939 and 1944. One

Railway workers assess the damage at London's St Pancras after a night of bombing during 1940. Usually, the clear-up was accomplished remarkably quickly.

2.5 mile stretch of line near London was bombed on 92 occasions over a nine month period. The courage and commitment shown by railway workers during air raids was matched by the resourcefulness with which engineers set about repairing shattered tracks, bridges and stations. When damage was reported – particularly to track and signalling – teams were rushed to the scene to begin repairs, often while the air raids carried on around.

This was seen at its best in the wake of the attack on Coventry on 14 November 1940. Of 600 incidents of damage reported, 122 were on railway property. Forty high-explosive devices landed on one 3.5 mile stretch of track alone. Two days later, on the evening of 16 November, the lines to both Birmingham and Leamington Spa had reopened to traffic. Other lines were more severely damaged and took longer to repair but, by the end of the month, rail services in the West Midlands had returned to normal.

In addition to roles also undertaken in World War I such as carrying troops and supplies, this second war with Germany presented the railways with a new task. The evacuation of huge numbers of people – principally children – from cities and other endangered areas was unprecedented. Between 1 and 4 September, the Great Western alone ran 164 trains carrying 112,994 evacuees from the London area. The GWR additionally evacuated a total of 57,985 people from the West Midlands, Liverpool and Birkenhead.

The Southern Railway ran over 200 evacuation specials from London, while a further 50 trains from the Medway area – considered vulnerable because of its naval and merchant shipping installations – carried 35,000 people.

From the London area alone, 4,349 trains evacuated 1,428,425 inhabitants during this initial evacuation period in 1939. There were similar evacuations from other industrial areas as far north as Glasgow. Later, as the invasion threat grew, a scheme was prepared for the evacuation of the entire civil population from areas around the east and south coasts.

At Newhaven Harbour, two weeks after D-Day – 6 June 1944 – British troops leave their train to embark for France and play a part in the Allied invasion. Below: One of the most famous wartime posters, aimed at discouraging unnecessary travel at a time when the railways' capacity was being stretched to its limit. The simple but effective image was created by Bert Thomas.

IS YOUR JOURNEY REALLY NECESSARY?

RAILWAY EXECUTIVE COMMITTEE

In a bid to repel the threatened invasion, twelve armoured trains carrying anti-aircraft guns were deployed along the south and east coasts, and in Scotland in June 1940. Three of these trains were manned by soldiers from the Polish army. The following year, 116 special trains were run over a 27-day period to station troops at potential invasion sites.

Railways also served the factories making vital supplies, not only conveying the raw materials and the finished products, but the people that made them. During 1944, nearly 7,000 trains were run every week to carry workers to government factories alone.

Given this amount of extra traffic, it was not surprising that a government poster asked: 'Is your journey really necessary?' By 11 September 1939, most express services had been drastically curtailed and decelerated. The authorities imposed limits on the number of passenger trains, but public demand continued at a high level. Overcrowded trains were commonplace, with locomotives worked to the limit of their capacity. Moreover, everyone faced the added difficulty of operating under 'black-out' conditions.

Station buildings and platforms were unlit, carriage blinds had to be pulled down (for a time no carriage lighting whatsoever was allowed) and, on tender engines, a tarpaulin screen covered the footplate to hide the glare from the fire. Nevertheless, during 1942, main line passenger travel totalled 30,000 million miles, an increase of 50 per cent on pre-war figures.

As in World War I, railway workshops joined the war effort. The Covenanter tank, for example, was drafted in the Derby drawing office and built at Crewe. The ex-Lancashire & Yorkshire Railway plant at Horwich, near Bolton, built the Matilda tank, which had been designed at another Lancashire locomotive works, Vulcan Foundry at Newton-le-Willows. In total, Crewe and Horwich contributed 642 tanks. Elsewhere, guns and gun mountings were produced at Doncaster and Swindon. The latter, along with Eastleigh Works, also made shells, ball-bearings, bridge sections and landing craft. In addition, railway workshops undertook the manufacture of aircraft fuselages and wings, gliders, mobile kitchens, and the conversion of rolling stock into ambulance trains.

When the time came to hit back at the enemy, railways were first involved in delivering the materials and equipment to build over 150 new airfields in East Anglia and southern England. Trains then brought in the personnel, followed by the fuel and munitions. Mounting a 1,000

THE HEROES OF SOHAM

British and American airfields in East Anglia relied on the railways to deliver fuel and ammunition. On the night of 2 June 1944, War Department 2-8-0 No7337 was undertaking just such a duty. Driver, Benjamin Gilbert, and fireman, James Nightall, had charge of a volatile cargo of explosives but all appeared well as they set out from Ely, turning south-east along the Newmarket line.

Approaching the town of Soham, the train slowed and driver Gilbert leaned out to collect the single-line token. To his horror, the first wagon was on fire.

Gilbert and his fireman immediately realised what might happen but, disregarding their safety, brought the train to halt and uncoupled the locomotive and burning wagon from the rest of the train. They then took both forward to the signal box with the intention of getting the 'line clear' from the signalman that would allow them to head into open country. At that moment, the wagon exploded, killing the signalman and fireman Nightall as well as severely injuring driver Gilbert. However, their courageous action had prevented the rest of ammunition train from exploding, which would undoubtedly have devastated Soham. Both Gilbert and Nightall were later awarded the George Cross.

It took almost 40 years for the railways to acknowledge their bravery. On 28 September 1981, in a ceremony at March, in Cambridgeshire, two Class 47 diesels were named after them. Incredibly, enough of 2-8-0 No7337 survived for it to be returned to the North British Locomotive Company in Glasgow where it was overhauled and returned to traffic.

US-built six-coupled shunters – or switchers, to use their American name – wait to play their part in the war effort. Official British War Department numbers are stencilled on to the cabsides.

Guns undergo reconditioning in the Southern Railway's works at Eastleigh, Hampshire. Adapting the tools, facilities and engineering expertise of such workshops to wartime needs proved vital. Inevitably, however, locomotive maintenance did suffer.

A poster by Leslie Carr emphasising the railways' priorities in wartime, and showing the reason for delays to passenger services. Even a Pullman express must give way to an armaments train.

All Clear for the Guns ON BRITISH RAILWAYS

Far right: We'll meet again. Soldiers say their farewells.

bomber raid called for 28 fuel trains and eight trainloads of bombs.

Along with committing resources to the war, the railways saw many of their staff join the armed forces, 110,000 in all. The consequence of this was that women found themselves in new roles. Before the war, Britain's railways employed 26,000 women, mostly in clerical work, and they now took on many different new roles, including heavy engineering.

Women could be found working as guards, ticket inspectors, crane o p e r a t o r s, painters and parcel handlers. They even got to drive trains, as well, albeit electric ones. In the workshops, women were responsible for electric and oxy acetylene welding, as well as operating lathes, grinders and power hammers.

They undertook the examination, cleaning, oiling and greasing of carriages and wagons, and worked in signalling or on track upkeep. One depot that made concrete sleepers was staffed entirely by women.

Britain's railways came under greatest pressure during the D Day invasion and the build up to it. From 26 March 1944 until D Day itself, 6 June, they succeeded in amassing the astonishing statistic of running 24,459 special trains. The week before D Day saw 3,636 extra trains scheduled. In the four weeks after D Day, the demand became even greater with the need to maintain reinforcements and supplies, provide ambulance trains and transport for prisoners of war, as well as undertaking routine tasks such as delivering the forces' mail. Over 18,000 special trains were run up to early July. Much was asked of Britain's railways during World War II, and at times they buckled under the strain, and the damage caused by the German Luftwaffe. Somehow, the trains always got through. As the German Chief of Staff, General Erich von Ludendorff, forewarned at the end of the World War I: 'There comes a time when locomotives are more important then guns.'

Ministry of Supply 'Austerity' 2-10-0s are unloaded at Calais on 9 May 1945, ready to help restore rail services in Continental Europe. No73755 made its way to The Netherlands and was based at Utrecht, working until May 1951

Far right: With a gas mask slung over every shoulder, evacuees wait to board a train.

OVER HERE

United States troops began arriving in Britain from May 1942 and by December they were being joined by American-built locomotives. Classified S160, a total of 2,120 2-8-0s were built by the three principal American builders, the American Locomotive Company (ALCO), Lima, and Baldwin, and shipped to Europe. In Britain, some 800 S160s put in useful work before being sent overseas after the D-Day invasion of June 1944. They saw use throughout Europe, in North Africa and South-East Asia, and in China, India and the former Soviet Union.

A number of people derided the S160s for being only good enough for five years' work, conveniently forgetting that Britain's War Department 2-8-0s were built as 'disposable' engines. In reality, the American design was intended to work for five years without recourse to works overhaul. The S160 coped well with its duties despite the unpredictable quality of fuel available. Like its British counterparts, many S160s remained in service for much longer, a point borne out by the fact that examples were still at work in Greece during the 1970s.

HOMES FROM HOME

Procedures and timetables were in place for civilian evacuation, and children had been rehearsed in what would take place. There had even been a 'pilot' evacuation at the time of the Munich Crisis in 1938. Nevertheless, nothing could prepare families for the pain of separation. This was made even more distressing because railway staff were forbidden to disclose train destinations. This emotive restriction was an early example of the harrowing consequences of 'total war'.

The first two days of the evacuation were set aside for children. Mothers with children and the infirm followed in the ensuing days. Lines of children marched from schools to assembly points to join the buses that would take them to the terminus stations or, in the case of the GWR, Ealing Broadway in west London. With its easy access from the Underground platforms to the main line, this was preferred to Paddington as a transfer point. A journalist there described the scene: 'Children collected from every nook and cranny of London...poured out of the Underground trains in a never-ending stream to change on to the West of England expresses.'

On departure a telegram was sent to the destination station advising the number of children on board each train. Each child had a cardboard box containing a gas mask slung round his or her neck and wore a nametag. At the journey's end, volunteers met incoming trains and shepherded the children on to the buses and coaches that took them to school and village halls for the process of 'billeting'. Far away from home, probably for the first time, they were foisted on to strangers, and not always willing ones at that. For some families, this prospect was unacceptable. They rejected the safety (not always guaranteed in some of the areas selected, it has to be said) of evacuation to stay together and take their chances.

THE TRAINMAKERS

Britain was trainmaker to its empire and much of the rest of the world, until it paid the price for a poor home record.

By 1900, a vast locomotive building industry had developed near towns such as Crewe, Darlington, Derby, Doncaster and Swindon, where railway-owned workshops met most of the needs of main-line companies. Independent locomotive builders had to find other outlets, one of which was supplying the burgeoning industrial sector: iron- and steelworks, factories, power stations and public utilities. The other was the overseas market, principally Africa, the Middle East, South-East Asia, India, Ceylon (Sri Lanka), Australia, New Zealand and South America – in other words, wherever British engineers had built railways.

Britain's independent engine builders gathered in five main areas: north-east England, the West Riding of Yorkshire, Sheffield, Manchester, Staffordshire, Bristol and southern Scotland.

Europe's largest locomotive builder was the Glasgow-based North British Locomotive Company. Formed in 1903 by the amalgamation of three long-established firms – Neilson, Dübs and Sharp Stewart (which had moved from Manchester in 1888) – NBL delivered 11,500 engines over six decades. It was one of the handful of independents that also added substantially to the British locomotive stock. NBL built 'Jubilees' and 'Royal Scots' for the LMSR, Pacifics, 2-8-0s and 4-6-0s for the LNER, 'King Arthurs' for the Southern Railway, pannier tanks for the GWR, and War Department 2-8-0s and 2-10-0s. The company made a valiant attempt to

Beyer Garratt articulated locomotives, constructed by Beyer Peacock at its plant at Gorton, Manchester, are loaded on to a ship sometime in the 1930s. The cranes are carrying engine units, while a boiler section sits on the quayside. Large numbers of British-built Garratt locomotives were exported and worked throughout Asia, Africa, Australasia and South America. Some are still in action in South Africa and Zimbabwe.

grab a share of the diesel market but was forced into liquidation in the spring of 1962.

The north-east was the traditional home of locomotive building. Several firms followed the example of Robert Stephenson and set up business in the area. After 1900 Stephenson's moved to Darlington and, in 1938, merged with Hawthorn Leslie to form Robert Stephenson & Hawthorns Ltd, later part of English Electric.

Manchester boasted two companies: Beyer Peacock and Nasmyth Wilson. The former earned a world-wide reputation for its Garratt articulated locomotives, some of which are still be at work in Africa. Near Liverpool, Newton-le-Willows was home to another major locomotive factory: Vulcan Foundry. It, too, became part of the English Electric empire.

The West Riding of Yorkshire could claim the greatest number of locomotive builders, with Leeds home to no fewer than six firms. The most successful, and longest-lived, was the Hunslet Engine Company, which started in 1864. Along with creating Britain's most numerous class of industrial locomotive – the six-coupled 'Austerity' saddletank – Hunslet's was an early convert to petrol and diesel locomotive production.

Based in Sheffield, the Yorkshire Engine Company also tried gamely to break into the diesel market before closing in the 1960s. Nearby, Markham's of Chesterfield was one of the country's 'cottage' locomotive builders, producing just 19 engines between 1888 and 1914. In contrast, between 1864 and 1880, Fox Walker & Company of Bristol built nearly 400. That year, Thomas Peckett opened his Atlas Works to adapt Fox Walker designs, and survived into the 1960s by building diesels. Meanwhile, Edwin Walker, co-founder of Fox Walker, set up a new firm in Bristol, the Avonside Engine Company, which closed in 1933.

The Midlands boasted three famous names. W.G. Bagnall of Stafford opened in 1875, surviving until the 1960s. It is said that, during the Depression of the 1930s, Bagnall's built engines at a loss purely to provide work for its employees.

A boiler undergoes testing at the North British Locomotive Company's works in Glasgow. The safety valves have lifted at the stipulated pressure. Established in 1903, North British became not only Britain's largest locomotive manufacturer, but Europe's. Sadly, it failed to make a lasting impact in the diesel field and surrendered its markets to American and German competitors.

Kerr Stuart of Stoke-on-Trent was founded in 1892 and closed in 1929, while Brush of Loughborough, an early and successful producer of diesel engines, is still going strong. In Shropshire, the Sentinel Waggon Works of Shrewsbury forged an independent path with its designs for vertical-boiler, chain-driven geared locomotives and railmotors. Up to 1958, over 600 Sentinel shunting engines were constructed for both home and overseas markets.

Despite increasing competition from their leading rivals in the United States and Germany, Britain's engine builders sustained a healthy export business up to the 1960s. However, as more and more countries switched from steam to diesel traction, American companies such as General Motors were able to play their trump card. GM's Electro-Motive Division had been building main-line diesels for US railroads since the 1930s and used that experience to its advantage. The Americans also reaped the benefits of standardisation and mass production. Popular US diesel designs could be ordered more-or-less 'off the shelf'. In Britain, companies such as English Electric, Brush Traction, North British and Metropolitan Vickers had to wait until the late 1950s for orders from British Railways and, with them, a stage on which to showcase their products. For some, the chance came too late.

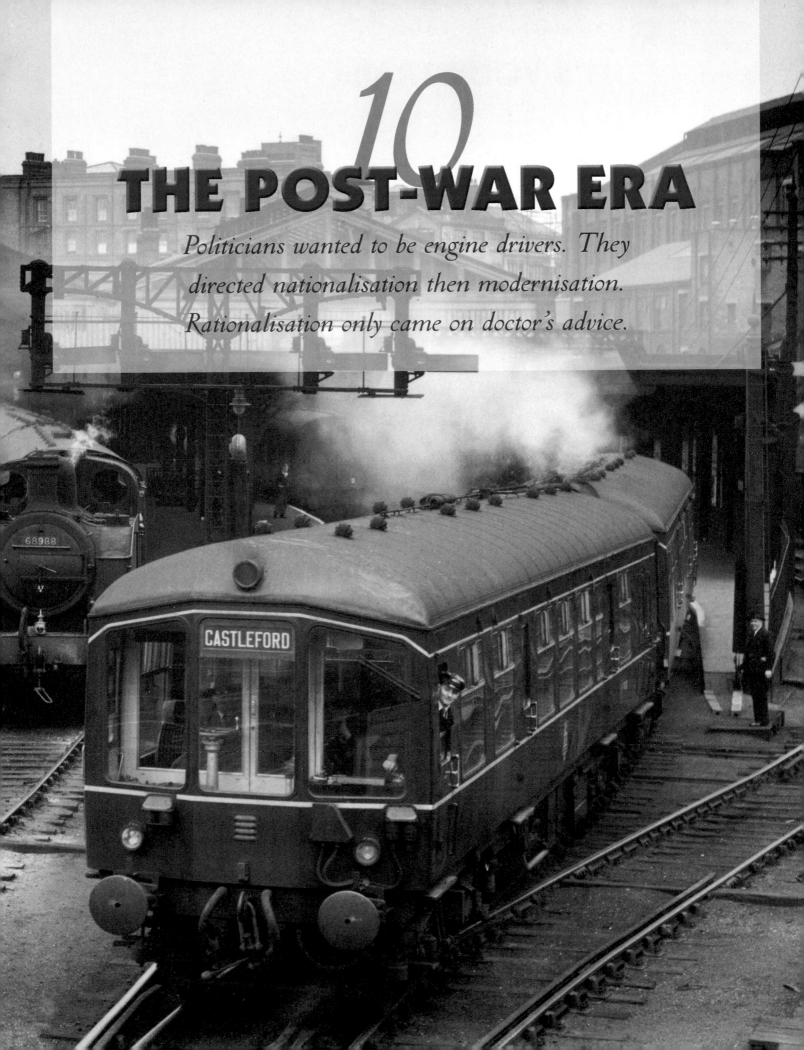

10
THE POST-WAR ERA

Politicians wanted to be engine drivers. They
directed nationalisation then modernisation.
Rationalisation only came on doctor's advice.

IT'S YOUR TRAIN

Or, more exactly, your trains. Overnight, Britain's railways became public property as well as public transport. But not everybody was celebrating.

The British Railways lion-and-wheel emblem is applied to a locomotive tender. While the design was being finalised, time was also spent deciding locomotive liveries, especially for express passenger classes. Blue was the colour of choice before dark green, lined with black-and-orange, was settled on as the national standard.

At midnight on 31 December 1947, drivers of night trains sounded their whistles enthusiastically. They were not just welcoming a new year, but a new era. From that point, Britain's railways became state-owned. Nationalisation had been inevitable since the election of a Labour government three years earlier, but not everyone welcomed the change. There was strong opposition from the boards of the four main railways, who refused to co-operate in setting up the new structure.

The 1947 Transport Act did more than authorise the nationalisation of the railways. It set up a new umbrella organisation, the British Transport Commission, with overall responsibility for public road transport, canals, docks and London Transport, as well as British Railways. The intention was for the BTC to develop an integrated transport system, an idea that never fails to attract support and, equally, has never been successfully implemented.

The Railway Executive formed to run the rail network on behalf of the BTC concluded that the new British Railways should consist of six regions. While the former Great Western and Southern Railway territories mutated with few changes into the Western and Southern Regions, it was decided that the old LMSR and LNER were too large. Both ceded their lines north of the border to form the Scottish Region, while the LNER was split into the Eastern and North Eastern Regions, with the boundary drawn north of Doncaster and Sheffield.

As for investment, the message to a system still recovering from the war amounted to "make do and mend". Unlike the railways of, for example, France and The Netherlands, which were ripped apart by war and had to be rebuilt, Britain's railways could be repaired. The French and the Dutch seized the opportunity and invested heavily in electrification. In Britain, only the completion of postponed pre-war electrification projects were authorised, the most important of which was the trans-Pennine Woodhead route from Manchester to Sheffield.

Without investment, the Railway Executive had no option but to persist with steam traction, where its inheritance was, at best, diverse. There were over 20,300 engines distributed among more than 400 classes. Many of these, especially the goods engines, shunters and passenger tanks, were products of the 19th century. Wartime exertions and neglect had exhausted thousands of engines while others were underpowered for the work required of them. Fortunately, construction of certain of the more modern designs developed by the 'big four' regional railways prior to nationalisation was allowed to continue. In total, 1,538 locomotives using these designs were built under British Railways auspices up to 1951, the majority of which were mixed traffic 4-6-0s and 2-6-0s.

This gave the Railway Executive's technical team time to evolve a range of British Railways 'standard' locomotive classes. The process began in 1948 with a series of exchange trials to compare performances of current designs. Despite generating considerable interest and debate, the results were disappointingly inconclusive. Moreover, some classes were never in the running. Outstanding as the Southern's 'West Country' class Pacific proved, post-war conditions were not sympathetic to complex 3-cylinder engines with 'air-smoothed' casings and exotic chain-driven valve gear. Only the LMSR designs of Stanier and Ivatt met the prevailing strictures and they would become the models for the new generation of British steam locomotives. There was no time – and nor was it the time anymore – for bold experimentation.

Last of the line. FW Hawksworth's 2-cylinder 'Counties' represented the final development of the Great Western passenger 4-6-0. No1015 County of Gloucester, captured on Dainton bank with a Goodrington-Plymouth service, was one of the 30-strong class built between 1945 and 1947. It spent its life based at Laira (Plymouth) and was retired in November 1962.

TAKING STOCK

It is interesting to compare British Railways' stock at nationalisation with that of 40 years later. A figure of 20,352 locomotives in 1948 had been reduced to 2,376 by 1988. A fleet of 55,666 carriages had diminished to 14,312, while perhaps most tellingly the number of freight wagons had shrunk from 1,216,690 to 48,353.

By 31 December 1948, British Rail had cut its locomotive fleet to 20,211 of which 2,527 were passenger tender engines and 1,347 classified as passenger tanks. There were 3,317 mixed traffic and 6,956 freight tender engines, and a further 6,015 tank engines categorised as mixed traffic or freight types. Intriguingly, 49 engines qualified as 'miscellaneous'.

Unsurprisingly, among the tender engines, the largest number (4,210) consisted of archetypal British 0-6-0s.

The second most numerous type was the 4-6-0 with 2,575, followed by the 2-8-0 with 1,983. There were just 342 Pacifics (the ex-LNER A1s and A2s and ex-Southern 'Battle of Britains', 'Merchant Navies' and 'West Countries' were still being built), but the venerable 4-4-0 numbered a remarkable 1,504.

Among tank types, the 0-6-0 again predominated with 3,010 examples. It was followed by the 0-6-2 with 1,190 representatives. The 2-6-2 and 2-6-4 tanks numbered 785 and 638 respectively, while 562 0-4-4 tanks were still active, many of which must have been approaching pensionable age.

Alongside these figures for steam traction, BR could muster just 67 diesel-electric locomotives (65 of them shunters) and 17 electric locomotives.

PUTTING NAMES TO TRAINS

The post-war railway scene was brightened by the reintroduction of a number of famous trains, and the appearance of some new names on locomotive headboards.

BR Standard 'Britannia' Pacific No70025 Venus leaves Bath Spa with the westbound 'Bristolian' from Paddington. The 'Bristolian' was created by the GWR in 1935, and was revived by BR in 1951.

Though at first reluctant to revive the 'named' trains of the pre-war era, the nationalised British Railways swiftly had a change of heart. Not only did many of the famous expresses make a comeback, a host of new ones entered the timetables. Some, notably the streamliners of the late 1930s, were gone forever, but the reappearance of the 'Flying Scotsman', 'Cornish Riviera Express', 'Bournemouth Belle' and 'Royal Scot' rekindled some of the pre-war prestige and glamour. There was even a return for the most venerable of named trains, the 'Irish Mail' between Euston and Holyhead.

The 'Irish Mail' fell into one category of named train, the straightforwardly descriptive. Another group took the geographical approach: the 'Cambrian Coast Express'; the 'Merseyside Express'; the 'Thames-Clyde Express'. A third category consisted of more imaginative and evocative names, those with historical or other connections. As early as 1849, the name 'Flying Dutchman' was applied informally to the Great Western's principal express service between Paddington and Exeter. This was not in recognition of Wagner's eponymous opera, first produced six years earlier, but a tribute to a recent winner of the St Leger and the Derby (named after the horse, not the jockey).

Similarly, the ten o'clock departure from Kings Cross to Edinburgh officially became the 'Flying Scotsman' only in 1923 but had been known by that name for at least 50 years. During the 1920s and 1930s, competition among the 'big four' companies was defined by their much-publicised prestige trains, described as 'star turns'. In contrast, the post-1948 regions of British Railways were expected to co-operate rather than compete, but a measure of that pre-war rivalry remained.

The Eastern and Western Regions in particular seem to have relished putting names to trains. Besides restoring the 'Bristolian' and 'Cornish Riviera Express' to their pre-war schedules, between 1950 and 1957, the Western added nine new titles to the timetable. Two made their debuts in 1950, the stirringly named 'Red Dragon' linking London and Cardiff and the less inspiring 'Inter City' between Paddington, Birmingham and Wolverhampton. South Wales gained three more titled services to-and-from London: the 'Pembroke Coast Express' to Pembroke Dock (1953); the 'South Wales Pullman' to Swansea (1955); and a second Cardiff train, the 'Capitals United' (1956).

The sea-faring traditions of the port of Bristol were recognised by the 'Merchant Venturer', which took to the rails in 1951. Plymouth's connections with the Pilgrim Fathers were commemorated in the 'Mayflower', a replacement in 1957 for the venerable 'Flying Dutchman'. That year also saw the 'Royal Duchy' added to the roster of Paddington-Penzance services and a newcomer on the Cotswolds route to Worcester and Hereford, the 'Cathedrals Express'.

LNER Class A1 Pacific No60118 Archibald Sturrock *dashes through Sandal, south of Wakefield, with the King's Cross-bound 'Yorkshire Pullman'. The LNER instigated this London-Leeds-Bradford train in September 1935 and, after wartime suspension, reinstated it in November 1946.*

Following the reintroduction of the non-stop 'Flying Scotsman' to Edinburgh in 1948, travellers from Kings Cross were similarly regaled with a raft of new east coast expresses. If Newcastle-upon-Tyne was their destination, the Eastern Region offered the 'Tees Tyne Pullman', the 'Tynesider' and the 'Northumbrian'. Around the same period, 1948-50, Leeds was first served by the 'White Rose' and the 'West Riding', the latter recalling the spirit of one of the 1930s streamliners, if not the substance.

The novels of Sir Walter Scott were recalled in three new Anglo-Scottish services, the 'Heart of Midlothian', the 'Fair Maid' and the 'Talisman'. The first two connected Kings Cross with Perth, while the last travelled to Edinburgh. The most famous post-war east coast express, however, began life in 1949 as the bland 'Capitals Limited'. After the coronation of Queen Elizabeth II in June 1953 it was renamed the 'Elizabethan' and made its first trip between London and Edinburgh on the 29th of that month. In the 1954 timetable, the 'Elizabethan' offered the fastest ever non-stop service between the capitals. Loaded to 425 tons, and scheduled to leave Kings Cross at 9.30m, it covered the 392.7 miles in 6.5 hours, an average speed of 60.4mph. The

'Elizabethan' was always the preserve of the Gresley A4 4-6-2s based at King's Cross and Haymarket (Edinburgh). The immaculate green Pacific and its maroon coaches made a proud sight and there were many thrilling runs during the train's eight-year reign as the 'non-stop'.

The intention was for 'Deltic' diesel-electrics, the first production example of which had been delivered to the Eastern Region in March 1961, to take over the 'Elizabethan' schedule but this proved unworkable. It was left to the Haymarket and Kings Cross crews and their engines to ensure a fitting finale for the express and they did not disappoint. Pride of place belonged to the now-preserved No60009 *Union of South Africa* which undertook 14 consecutive journeys between 31 August and 9 September. On that last date, 'No9' worked the last non-stop to Edinburgh, while the London-bound train was entrusted to the most famous A4 of all, the record-breaking No60022 *Mallard*.

It was not solely on the east coast that the Eastern Region spiced up its schedules with titled trains. The ex-Great Central route out of Marylebone gloried in the 'Master Cutler' that, as the name suggests, served the steel city of Sheffield. The more prosaically named 'South Yorkshireman' went on to Bradford Exchange.

The ex-Great Eastern lines out of Liverpool Street received a boost with the introduction of two expresses to Norwich, Cromer and Sheringham. The 'Norfolkman' first appeared in the timetable in 1948 and was followed two years later by the 'Broadsman'. The appeal of both services was subsequently enhanced by the arrival of new BR Standard 'Britannia' Pacifics, which enabled a dramatic improvement in schedules on the Norwich run. 'Britannias' were also entrusted

Sporting a hybrid Southern/BR livery 'Merchant Navy' class Pacific No35005 Canadian Pacific approaches Battledown Flyover, near Basingstoke, with the westbound 'Atlantic Coast Express'.

with the summer-only 'Easterling', which ran non-stop from Liverpool Street to Beccles. There it was divided, with one portion going on to Great Yarmouth and the other to Lowestoft. The 'Fenman', which began operation between Liverpool Street, Kings Lynn and Hunstanton in 1949, was the pride of the Cambridge line. It was usually headed by a B1 class 4-6-0.

The London Midland Region added six titled trains between 1950 and 1957, as well as reintroducing its quota of pre-war favourites. The Midland route out of St Pancras gained a companion Anglo-Scottish service to the 'Thames-Clyde Express', the Edinburgh-bound 'Waverley'. At Euston, it became a case of all the 'Ms'. The 'Manxman' and the 'Merseyside Express' for Liverpool, the 'Midlander' for Birmingham and Wolverhampton, and the 'Mancunian' for Manchester. You could also travel to Liverpool

by the 'Shamrock' and the 'Red Rose' and, from 1954, the 'Emerald Isle Express' connected with the Irish ferries at Holyhead. Finally, in 1957, the 'Royal Scot' and 'Midday Scot' gained a partner on the Glasgow run, the 'Caledonian' which, like its predecessor, the 'Coronation Scot', enjoyed the power of Stanier's 'Princess Coronation' Pacifics.

On the Southern, the Pullman 'Belles', to Brighton, Bournemouth and Devon, were restored to the timetable after World War II, as was the 'Atlantic Coast Express' from Waterloo to Plymouth, Padstow and Ilfracombe. Discounting boat train specials run to Southampton Docks to connect with sailings such as 'The Cunarder', only three new named trains were introduced by the Southern Region. The 'Thanet Belle' (subsequently the 'Kentish Belle') began service between Victoria and the Kent coast in 1948, the Waterloo-Bournemouth-Weymouth route gained the 'Royal Wessex', and by 1953 the 'Man of Kent' ran from Charing Cross to Sandwich.

By now, it will have become evident that the majority of titled trains began and ended their journeys in London. There were exceptions, of course, such as the 'Devonian' that conveyed holidaymakers from Bradford to Torquay and Paignton. The 'Cornishman' performed the same role between Wolverhampton and Penzance. The 'North Briton' ran between Leeds and Glasgow. Heading north from Glasgow, the 'North Briton', 'Saint Mungo' and 'Granite City' all served Aberdeen, while the 'Fife Coast Express' went to the home of golf, St Andrews.

There was no doubt, however, that 'The 'Pines Express' was the most famous, and photographed of the cross-country named trains. This began running between Liverpool, Manchester and Bournemouth in 1927. Until September 1962, it was routed over the spectacular Somerset and Dorset line from Bath to Broadstone Junction, then one of the most fascinating stretches of railway in Britain. The 'Pines' was the 'star turn' on the S&D and it was fitting that the locomotive in charge on its last run was also the last of its line, 9F 2-10-0 No92220 *Evening Star*.

LAST OF THE LINE

The mandate was to deliver sound and serviceable locomotives that would replace life-expired machines inherited by British Railways. Britain's last main-line steam locomotives were an appropriate response to post-war conditions, but did they also point to a missed opportunity?

Opposite, top: Finishing the mould for the Britannia nameplates for the smoke deflectors of the first of British Railways Standard locomotives, 7P6F Pacific No70000. The engine was officially named at a ceremony at Marylebone Station, London, on 30 January 1951.

Following the decision to persist with steam traction after nationalisation in 1948, the Railway Executive set up a team to design a range of modern, versatile locomotive classes. They were to embody the best features of pre-nationalisation designs but be more economical and have wider route availability (their usefulness was not to be compromised by loading gauge constraints). The new designs were expected to undertake a wide range of duties and achieve high mileages between overhauls. Simplicity, efficiency and ease of maintenance were the key elements and, among existing types, some came closer than others to meeting those requirements. These were the locomotives produced under Sir William Stanier and his successors for the London Midland & Scottish Railway.

In certain respects, the most modern locomotives being built in the late 1940s were the 2-6-0 tender engines and 2-6-2 tanks designed by George Ivatt for the LMSR. With ease of maintenance paramount, they employed a straightforward arrangement of two cylinders and outside Walschaerts valve gear. Rocker grates, hopper ashpans and self-cleaning smokeboxes made ash disposal and fire-cleaning less laborious. Coal bunkers were inset to improve the crew's view when running tender-first.

The Ivatt designs became the basis for three of British Railways' Standard classes and in the case of the Class 2MT 2-6-0 and 2-6-2 tank only minor alterations were made. Apart from some modest experiments with valve gear, boilers and exhaust systems, there was little innovation within

Right: No72009 Clan Stewart was the last of the Standard Class 6 Pacifics, only ten of which were built, at Crewe, between 1951 and 1952. Clan Stewart is captured here at Harthope, on a Crewe-Perth-Aberdeen service Opposite: The maverick — Class 8 Pacific No71000 Duke of Gloucester passes Kenton with the northbound 'Midday Scot' on 11 March 1957.

the twelve BR Standard classes. Admittedly, novelty was not part of the design brief, but the very fact that twelve were thought necessary suggests a reluctance to break with convention. At least two designs – the Class 6 Pacific and Class 3 2-6-0 – were superfluous. Consequently just ten Class 6 and twenty Class 3 engines were built. It is arguable that a single design of 2-8-2s, for example, would have done the work of several classes.

Other Standard classes – the 'Britannia' Pacifics, 4-6-0 types, 2-6-4 tanks and 4MT and 2MT 2-6-0s – were well received. However, the most successful class, and – with 251 examples – the most numerous, was the 9F 2-10-0. Finally, here was a British heavy freight locomotive with the power and adhesion weight to handle the heaviest hauls easily and economically.

In planning the Standard designs, Riddles and his colleagues anticipated that they would remain in service well into the 1970s, by which point the major trunk routes would have been electrified. Over 20 years, the investment in the locomotives would have been repaid. Instead, many had working lives of less than ten years. The last of the 9Fs, for example, entered service in 1960, five years after the decision to phase out steam traction was taken. In 1962, the first of the 999 BR Standards was put to the torch. It was a criminal waste.

THE LOST MASTERPIECE

In a way, the solitary BR Standard Class 8 Pacific, No71000 *Duke of Gloucester*, was built by accident. Robert Riddles had proposed an express passenger design in this power class but was turned down on cost grounds. Then, in 1952, the horrific destruction of No46202 *Princess Anne* in the Harrow and Wealdstone disaster left a gap in the Pacific fleet. Riddles gained permission to fill it by building a prototype for his stillborn Standard Class 8.

To generate the desired power output, Riddles opted for a 3-cylinder layout that employed a Caprotti rotary cam poppet valve gear to solve the problem of getting effective steam distribution to the inside cylinder. The intention was to marry the Caprotti gear to the Kylchap exhaust system, unquestionably the finest device of its kind. To the dismay of the design team, however, an orthodox double chimney and blastpipe were installed. The argument that this set-up would prove incapable of dealing with the fierce exhaust generated by the Caprotti gear was rejected.

The fitting of this chimney was the first, and most damaging, of a number of miscalculations that would compromise the performance of No71000 *Duke of Gloucester*. Regarded as erratic, unpredictable and difficult to fire, it was no surprise that its working life was limited to eight years, 1954-62, all spent based at Crewe North shed.

Upon withdrawal, No71000 was at first retained for the National Collection. It was then decided that only the cylinder assembly and valve gear were of interest. The rest was sent for scrap, and if ever a locomotive looked beyond restoration, this was it. However, the Duke of Gloucester Locomotive Trust undertook the daunting task and rebuilding was completed in the autumn of 1986. The opportunity was taken to right the errors that had blighted the locomotive, including the fitting of a Kylchap exhaust. Since returning to the main line in 1990, No71000 has produced a series of spectacular runs that have astonished those who recall the perplexing performer of BR days.

Since 1990, further refinements have removed any remaining doubt that a full complement of Standard Class 8 Pacifics would have numbered not only among the finest British express passenger locomotives, but the world's.

ACCORDING TO PLAN

The modernisation of British Railways was to be an orderly affair, conducted over 15 years, and with a smooth transition from steam to diesel and electric traction. At least, that was the plan.

In 1955, seven years after nationalisation, the overdue modernisation of Britain's railways was given the go-ahead by the government. A sum of £1,240 million was to be invested over a 15 year period, much of it on new motive power and rolling stock. Diesel and electric traction were the keys to revolutionising the speed and frequency of train services. There was also provision for extensive track renewals and resignalling. Stations and depots would be renovated or rebuilt, while the freight business would be reorganised, with new wagons and new or modernised marshalling yards.

One objective was to make railways a more attractive proposition for both passengers and freight customers, and recover traffic lost to the roads; the other aim was to reduce operating costs. One thorny subject that the authors of the 'Modernisation and Re-equipment of British Railways' managed to avoid was that of line and station closures. If it was not in their remit, it surely should have been. To imagine that new trains and new signals alone could breathe fresh life into moribund parts of the system was to be either blinkered or naive.

Overall, the picture painted was hopelessly optimistic. Fundamental obstacles, such as archaic operating practices, were glossed over. No account was taken of the limited practical experience with diesel traction. British companies were building diesel locomotives for overseas markets but few, if any, could be adapted to British Rail's

The new order meets the old at Carlisle in July 1967. Brush Type 4 No D1874 (left) awaits departure with a Glasgow-Liverpool train, while English Electric Type 3 1,750hp Co-Co diesel-electric No D6737 stands on one of the centre roads.
The contrast with a smoke-blackened 'Britannia' Pacific, No 70051 Firth of Forth, is dramatic.

requirements. There were suitable and proven diesel designs available that could have been introduced more-or-less immediately; they just happened to be American. Although buying American designs made practical and economic sense, politically the idea was a non-starter.

The plan proposed building an initial batch of 174 main line diesel locomotives ranging in power from 800 to 2,300 brake horsepower. These were to be evaluated thoroughly before any large orders were placed, with performance and maintenance records assessed and compared. This was only prudent, since Britain's railways were about to trigger a change without precedent in its scale and complexity. It was new territory for everyone: those building the diesels, whether in private industry or British Railways' workshops, and those operating them.

Regrettably, this commendable, not to say vital, process was overtaken by events and the evaluations left incomplete. Two pronouncements appear to have alarmed the BTC's managers. The first revealed BR's financial situation to be much worse than anticipated. Freight traffic had not picked up as hoped for, principally because of the national economic situation. The second was a warning from the National Coal Board that the quality and supply of locomotive coal could no longer be guaranteed. This provoked the BTC

into accelerating the withdrawal of steam and launching into a hasty programme of dieselisation.

Orders were placed for the mass production of several diesel types, in some cases before prototypes were completed. It was inviting trouble and it duly arrived. Design inadequacies were compounded by a lack of purpose-built maintenance depots and trained staff, and by a failure to appreciate fully the high tolerances and scrupulously clean conditions needed to produce diesel engine components.

By 1961 well over 1,000 main line diesels were in service and a further 800 were on order. They

A driver takes the controls of a new diesel locomotive. That symbol of the steam age, the greasetop cap, is yet to be relinquished despite the cleanliness of his new working environment.

Though begun in the 1930s, the electrification of the Liverpool Street to Shenfield suburban line was delayed by war and not completed until after nationalisation. Approaching Ingatestone from the west is one of the original 3-car multiple units, May 1971.

were distributed across no less than 19 classes, at least four of which were next-to-useless. So much for the promised standardisation.

The situation was complicated further by a divergence in diesel types used. Most regions adopted diesel-electrics, but the BTC allowed the Western Region to construct diesel-hydraulic locomotives, licenced from German companies and five diesel-hydraulic classes entered WR service. Although they promised a better power-to-weight ratio than the diesel-electrics, their advantage was offset by higher construction and maintenance costs. This was compounded by the fact that diesel hydraulic engines were not as powerful as their diesel electric counterparts, so in order to generate over 2,000bhp, the power output required by express passenger classes, a diesel hydraulic locomotive had to be fitted with two engines and two transmissions. The hydraulics also suffered more than their share of failures.

Already enjoying advantages of cost and wider availability, diesel-electrics also closed the power-weight gap, depriving the hydraulics of their key selling point. Nevertheless, it took until the 1970s for the WR finally to bid farewell to its 'Warships', 'Westerns' and 'Hymeks'.

Early on in the dieselisation process, it became uncomfortably apparent that the classes under construction in the 2,000-2,500bhp power range were incapable of making dramatic reductions in journey times, at least with normal 14 or 15 coach train loadings. There were improvements in speed and reliability, but the promised average express speed of 75mph proved unattainable. Only in 1961 did BR acquire diesel locomotives – the English Electric 'Deltics' – of sufficient power to accomplish that aim. Sadly, their impact was limited as only 22 'Deltics' were built.

It took a decade to remedy the consequences of the rush into dieselisation. Unsuccessful designs were discarded or downgraded to minor duties. Finally, production was standardised on a single diesel-electric design in each of four power bands, which ended the chaos considerably.

Electrification, the other principal element of the 1955 Modernisation Plan, also suffered its share of compromises and failures. Again, reality intruded on the vision of the future – a network of electrified routes radiating from London. Electrification was scheduled for the lines from Euston to Birmingham, Manchester and Liverpool, from Kings Cross to Doncaster, Leeds and, possibly, York. Lines out of Liverpool Street would be electrified as far as Ipswich and Bishops Stortford, and third-rail electrification would be extended to all Southern Region main lines east

of Portsmouth and Reading. (It would have been impracticable to convert the existing SR dc electrified lines to the overhead ac system that was adopted elsewhere.)

Electric traction scored over diesel in several respects, especially where services were intensive and lines in constant use. It was cheaper, cleaner and more reliable. The sole drawback was the high initial cost, since more was involved than simply erecting the masts, suspending the wires and switching on at the mains. Electrification usually included resignalling, track renewals, improved telecommunications and – if a public perception of a 'new' railway was to be formed – station rebuilding and complete refurbishment.

These 'extras' prompted Parliamentary concern about the huge increase in the cost of the flagship electrification on the West Coast Main Line. No sooner had the first section between Manchester Piccadilly and Crewe been commissioned in September 1960, than further work was suspended while the financial situation was examined. The WCML project was allowed to continue, but other main line projects, such as the east coast electrification, were shelved.

It was no shock that the 1955 plan came in for reappraisals. The revised plan of 1959 was much tougher and it was this exercise that elected to hasten the demise of steam traction. As a result the motive power make-up of British Railways altered radically in the period 1958-63. In 1958, the roll-call read: 16,108 steam locomotives, 108 main line diesels and 2,417 diesel multiple unit (dmu) cars. By 1963, the steam fleet had been cut by over 9,000 to 7,050, while 2,051 main line diesels were in service alongside 4,145 dmu cars. However, this transformation was nothing compared to what was to follow. And what followed was another plan, its author a high-flyer in industry named Dr Richard Beeching.

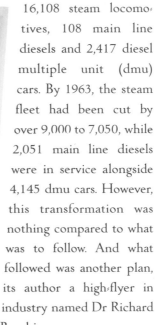

EASE THE STRAIN – GO BY TRAIN

Train services and fares from BRITISH RAILWAYS stations offices and agencies

THE DOCTOR'S PRESCRIPTION

That prescription was surgery — drastic, and quick. Yet Dr Beeching's diagnosis of British Railways' ills should have surprised no one, least of all the patient.

Dr Richard Beeching (1913-85) steps on to the platform to catch a train from his local station, a convenience subsequently denied many of his fellow citizens by the closures ushered in by the so-called 'Beeching Plan'.

With British Railways' losses mounting, the government, in the shape of Transport Minister Ernest Marples, questioned the chances of the 1955 Modernisation Plan bringing about the anticipated reversal of fortunes. A committee was appointed to examine the future role of railways and how they were to be administered and financed. A key recommendation was the setting up of a new controlling body, the British Railways Board (BRB). Shortly after, a member of the committee, the eminent physicist and then technical director of Imperial Chemical Industries (ICI), Dr Richard Beeching, was appointed the BRB's first chairman. In that role, Beeching infamously wrote his name into railway history; whether as hero or villain continues to divide opinion.

Under Beeching, the BRB took a searching look at the system. About half the rail network carried 95 per cent of its traffic. Of the 7,000 stations, half generated 98 per cent of the total passenger traffic. With buses able to serve rural areas more efficiently, and the rapid increase in car ownership, it was impossible to justify retaining all the other 3,500 stations, and the loss-making lines they served.

It is often overlooked (especially by those who like to cast him as the villain of the piece) that Beeching produced two reports. The first was the notorious 'Reshaping of British Railways', which proposed the closure of 2,363 stations and the withdrawal of all train services from about 5,000 route miles. The uproar that followed its publication utterly overshadowed Beeching's second report, 'The Development of Major Trunk Routes', which proposed substantial investment to produce a modern 'core' rail network.

The reports' findings confirmed government misgivings that the targets outlined in the 1955 Modernisation Plan could be achieved by equipping alone. They recommended that this would have to go hand-in-hand with changes in operating methods and the pruning of loss-making services. It was also felt unlikely that projected increases in some passenger revenues would offset the heavy losses being made by the freight sector. Beeching presented his political masters with the stark proposal that British Railways should be treated as two entities: one that could become commercially viable, and one that warranted public subsidy because it was a social necessity. It was down to the politicians to decide which services qualified as 'necessary'. Since the go-ahead was given for Beeching's closure programme, the answer was not many.

Closures of loss-making rail services were not unknown before 1964. Some, suspended during World War I, were never revived. Others vanished in the 1930s and the process gathered pace during the 1950s. However, the wielding of the 'Beeching axe', as it was termed, was savage. Branch lines were decimated; cross-country lines – and even some main lines – disappeared. Areas of Scotland, Wales and the West Country became 'railway deserts'. Services were withdrawn from some major towns, Mansfield in Nottinghamshire being a prime example. However, not all the closure plans were implemented. If they had been there would now be no train services north of Inverness, for example.

Among the leading casualties were the ex-Great Central main line between Sheffield, Nottingham, Leicester and London Marylebone, the Somerset and Dorset route between Bath and Bournemouth, and the ex-L&SWR route across north Cornwall to Bude and Padstow. It was goodbye to other picturesque lines: the ex-North British 'Waverley' route from Carlisle to Edinburgh and the Midland main line through the Peak District from Buxton to Manchester among them. Following the closure of so many local stations, stopping passenger trains ceased on many routes. The direct savings arising from closures, as estimated in 1963, were between £34 and £41 million a year. Major changes were made on the freight side, too. Beeching had become convinced that railways were most effective as bulk carriers, with most freight conveyed as trainloads rather than wagonloads.

For all the opprobrium heaped upon him, Dr Richard Beeching offered vision, drive and managerial acumen. He began the process of creating an efficient railway system attuned to both social and economic needs, but ultimately did not get

the opportunity to see it through. In 1965, Beeching found himself at odds with the new Labour government and resigned. He did, however, go on to be made a life peer. Some of his conclusions concerning the railways do, however, still ring true:

'I see railways as a national asset, owned by the nation and therefore to be used in the best interest of the nation as a whole. The quality and cost of the service should satisfy BR's customers and the conditions of service and pay should satisfy BR's staff. Both should be achieved without imposing an intolerable burden on the country as a whole.'

Above: A derelict former GWR station, one of over 2,000 closed as a consequence of Dr Beeching's plan for the 'reshaping' of British Railways.

Below: A June 1960 scene with rebuilt 'Patriot' class 4-6-0 No45534 E. Tootal Broadhurst heading the northbound 'Welshman' alongside a newly-opened and, ironically, almost empty stretch of motorway.

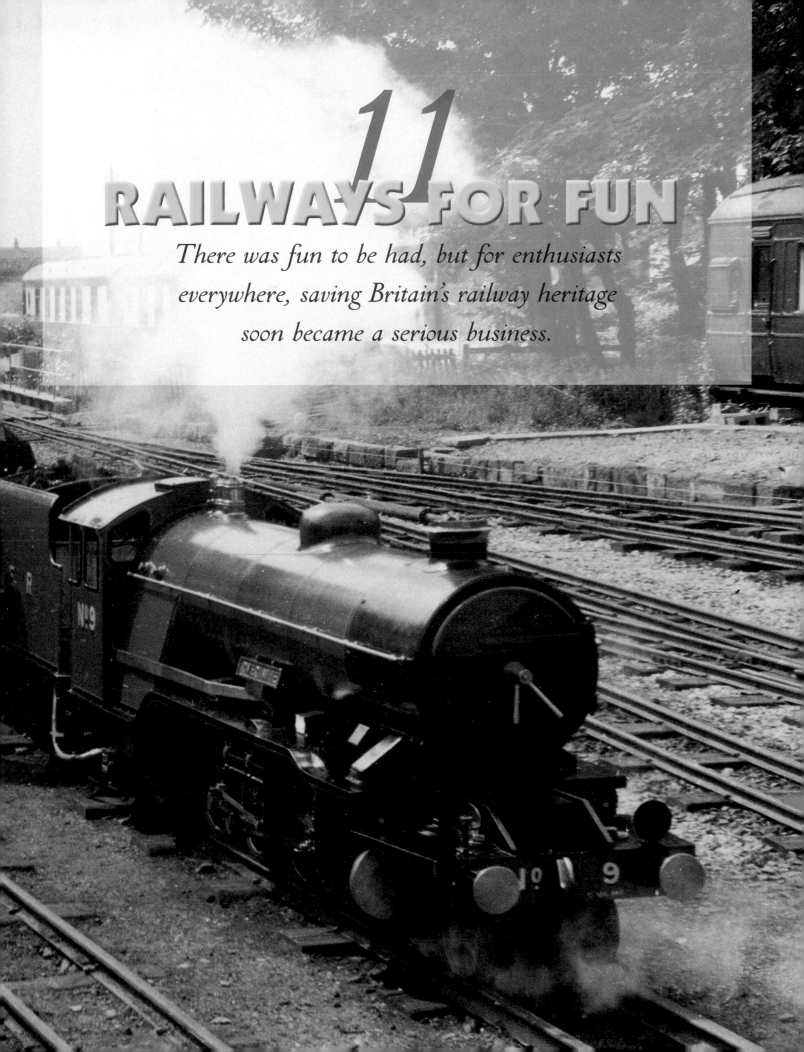

11
RAILWAYS FOR FUN

*There was fun to be had, but for enthusiasts
everywhere, saving Britain's railway heritage
soon became a serious business.*

THE PRESERVATION PHENOMENA

It began with a narrow-gauge line in Wales and spread to every part of the country. What persuaded so many people that it would be fun to run a railway?

For enthusiasts, the closure of so many branch lines and country railways, accompanied by the demise of steam traction, in the post-nationalisation years was hard to take. Many people, however, were spurred into action and the 1960s and 1970s witnessed the growth of a new phenomenon: railway preservation.

Perhaps 'new' is not strictly accurate. For decades, historic locomotives had entered museums upon retirement. What was original, though, was the notion of saving not just engines and rolling stock, but entire stretches of railway. Right across Britain, enthusiasts and local people combined to take over closed lines and revive train services, most of them worked by restored steam locomotives. These lines, though, took on a different character: from formerly being a transport system linking one place with another, after restoration it no longer mattered where the lines went. Now the journey itself was the attraction.

DOLGOCH STATION
ON THE
TALYLLYN RAILWAY
TOWYN MERIONETH WALES

The sylvan setting of Dolgoch Station on the Talyllyn Railway in west Wales, as seen through the eyes of one of Britain's greatest railway painters, Terence Cuneo (1907–1996).

What can now be enjoyed right across Britain, from Cornwall and Kent to the Scottish Highlands began in west Wales in 1950. That year, the Talyllyn Railway Preservation Society was founded with the aim of saving its narrow-gauge line. The Talyllyn was opened in 1866 to carry slate from the quarries above Nant Gwernol to Tywyn on the coast. The slate quarry closed in 1946, but its owner, Sir Henry Haydn

Jones, somehow kept the railway running. At his death, a group of volunteers formed the TRPS and took over the running of the line, which became the world's first railway preservation scheme. The following year, another slate-carrying line, the Festiniog, was saved by enthusiasts, since when several other narrow-gauge railways in Wales have joined the list.

An exception is the 11.75-mile Vale of Rheidol Railway running between Aberystwyth and Devil's Bridge. Opened in 1902 to transport lead, timber and tourists, the VoR amalgamated with the Cambrian Railway and subsequently became part of the Great Western. In 1948, it was nationalised and became part of British Railways – remaining BR's sole steam-worked line after 1968 – until sold in 1989.

The first standard gauge preserved lines, the Bluebell Railway in East Sussex and the Middleton Railway in Leeds, were opened within a couple of months of each other in 1960. Saving the Middleton was particularly important from an historical viewpoint since, in 1758, it became the first railway to be authorised by Act of Parliament. A host more preservation projects opened during the 1960s and 1970s, most occupying sections of an abandoned branch line. In the case of the Keighley & Worth Valley Railway in West Yorkshire the entire line was saved, providing an unsurpassed recreation of the branch line atmosphere.

A few organizations have revived sections of main line. The most notable of these is the Main Line Steam Trust, which has reopened part of the former Great Central route in Leicestershire and has recently reinstated double-tracking along much of its length.

One of the three locomotives employed on the Vale of Rheidol Railway, No8 Llywelyn, storms the final bank before the terminus of Devil's Bridge.

Money is one thing railway preservation will never have enough of; the other is volunteers. However, some railways have grown to the point where paid administrators and engineers are essential. Locations such as the Midland Railway Centre, the East Lancashire Railway, the Swanage Railway and the Birmingham Railway Museum, which originally struggled to restore locomotives and rolling stock under the most basic conditions, now boast first-class workshop facilities.

The pioneers of the 1950s and 1960s could never have imagined where their efforts would eventually lead. Today they would be astonished at the scale of railway preservation in Britain — and utterly perplexed that similar effort is now being put into saving the diesel locomotives they came to despise for usurping the role of steam after nationalisation.

In South Devon, the Dart Valley Railway became the first preservation project to be run by a commercial company. With unconcealed irony, the guest of honour at the reopening in 1969 was Dr Richard Beeching. The North Norfolk Railway became the first to offer shares and its success spurred other locomotive preservation societies and railways to follow suit.

One of the stalwarts of the Bluebell Railway fleet, Stroudley A1X class 0-6-0T No72 Fenchurch, climbs away from Horsted Keynes with a train for Sheffield Park on 1 June 1969. The latest overhaul of this 1872-built engine was completed in 2001, making it probably the oldest working locomotive in Britain.

TRAVEL BACK IN TIME

With its Victorian steam locomotives and vintage electric trams, the Isle of Man has become an island of delights for railway enthusiasts.

The Isle of Man may be only 40 minutes flying time from the mainland, but to travel on its trains and trams is to step back a century and more. The island boasts the longest operational narrow gauge railway in the British Isles and one of the earliest surviving electric tramways. It earns another mention in the history books for the Snaefell Mountain Railway, the world's first electrically powered mountain railway, which is still in operation.

The 3-feet gauge steam railway covers a total of 15.5 miles and runs along a stretch of coastline in the south-east of the island, connecting Douglas with Port Erin. It climbs to give spectacular coastal views before plunging into wooded valleys, calling at six intermediate stations, rattling over no less than 12 level crossings, and pulling into the Swiss-style station at Port Erin.

This stretch of line was the second section of the Isle of Man Railway system to open, in August 1874 (the first railway, which ran from Douglas to Peel, had begun services the previous year). Initially, local people had been hired build the line. Unfortunately, most of these workers were also fishermen who would promptly leave the job and return to their boats when the herring season began! In order to complete the project, the railway's promoters brought over labourers from the mainland

By 1900, the other main town on the island, Ramsey, had a rail connection with Douglas — the Manx Northern Railway — and a branch line

At the head of a morning train for Port Erin, 2-4-0 tank No4 Loch, built by Beyer Peacock of Manchester in 1874, blasts out of Nunney Cutting, Douglas, on a summer morning in July 1969.

TAKING THE TRAM

The Isle of Man was an unlikely pioneer in the use of electric tramways. Trams have always been regarded primarily as a form of urban transport yet, before trams appeared on the streets of London or Birmingham, they were serving Manx towns and villages.

Gradients as steep as 1 in 24 in the north-east of the island ruled out an extension of the steam railway. When it was shown that this was no obstacle to electric traction, plans were approved for a tramway linking Douglas with Groudle, just over two miles away. Power was supplied to the motor coaches by an overhead conductor wire and, like with the steam railway, the three-feet gauge used.

Trams began operating on 7 September 1893 and over 20,000 passengers were carried, at a fare of threepence, during the first 17 days of operation. The following year, the line was extended to Laxey and its construction aroused considerable interest both at home and abroad. In terms of distance (seven miles from Douglas), the gradients tackled and the electrical engineering involved, the Isle of Man was breaking new ground.

Following the opening of a ten-mile extension from Laxey to Ramsey in 1898, a half-hourly service was introduced along the full length of the tramway. Similar to the steam, the tramway suffered from a post-World War II decline in tourism. However, local efforts again ensured not only its survival, but a remarkable revival.

was built to the mining village of Foxdale. The area was rich in lead, silver and zinc and a large six-coupled tank locomotive was imported solely to haul the ore trains to the harbour at Ramsey.

Subsequently, the closure of the Foxdale mines left the MNR in financial trouble and it was taken over by the Isle of Man Railway in 1904. During this period, the station at Douglas was the largest and busiest narrow-gauge terminus in Britain, with over 100 departures each day. By the 1920s, however, the railway's pre-eminence was under threat from bus services. Traffic declined over the ensuing decades and, by the 1960s, the entire system faced closure.

The lines to Peel and Ramsey disappeared, but the line from Douglas to Port Erin clung on until, in 1977, public pressure forced its reopening. The following year the railway was bought by the Isle of Man government and has become one of the island's principal tourist attractions. With some of the world's oldest working locomotives – for example engine No4 Loch, built by Beyer Peacock in Manchester in 1874 – the line is a magnet for steam enthusiasts.

Right: One of the electrically-powered cars of the Snaefell Mountain Railway leaves the summit on its way down to Laxey, 2,000ft below, on 9 July 1969.

AN ELECTRIFYING CLIMB

Snaefell (Scandinavian for 'Snow Mountain') is, at 2,036 feet, the highest point on the Isle of Man. For 107 years, since August 1895, tourists have been able to take an electric tramcar to within 44 feet of the summit.

These 100 horsepower cars – the most powerful in Britain at the time of construction – ascend from the terminus at Laxey and climb 4.5 miles at a ruling gradient of 1 in 12. Amazingly, the Snaefell Mountain Railway took just seven months to build. Moreover, this period included a spell when heavy snow stopped work, as well as a strike by the 100-strong workforce that believed it deserved more than £1 1s 0d for a 60-hour week. It seems, however, that the strike failed and no increase was forthcoming.

AN ENTHUSIASTIC RESPONSE

The steam locomotive has survived all attempts to finish it off. After August 1968, it was supposed to be confined to museums but, almost 35 years later, it is possible to travel behind steam somewhere in Britain most days of the year. It's all down to enthusiasm and, of course, enthusiasts.

Ivatt Atlantics No990 Henry Oakley and No251 prepare to leave King's Cross with the 'Plant Centenarian' special bound for Doncaster on 20 September 1953.

The first railway enthusiasts' railtour in Britain was organised by the Railway Correspondence and Travel Society on 11 September 1938. It employed one of the most historic of Great Northern Railway locomotives, the Patrick Stirling-designed '8-foot Single' No1 (the '8-foot' referring to the diameter of the two driving wheels). The 68-year-old engine hauled a train of ancient six-wheelers from London Kings Cross to Peterborough and back, all for a fare of five shillings.

Railway enthusiasm as a pursuit predated this journey by several decades. The hobby of timing trains while travelling on them dates from at least the 1870s. By the late 1890s, publications such as The Locomotive and Railway Magazine, and commentators like E.L. Ahrons and Charles Rous-Marten were supplying a focus for that

enthusiasm. The interest grew, principally in locomotive design and performance, but extended to rolling stock, civil engineering, timetables, tickets and signalling.

At first, railway companies discouraged any amateur interest in their activities but then acknowledged the public relations value. The Great Western Railway Magazine was started by the company's Temperance Society in 1888 and proved so popular that its publication was taken over by the GWR itself in 1904.

Along with broad-based railway periodicals, a demand grew for magazines devoted to specialist areas such as history and engineering. Many clubs and societies were founded, some catering for the partisan enthusiast who revered one railway company above all others. In terms of local allegiance, Great Western devotees appeared to outnumber the rest!

It was fortunate that such passion for railways, and for the steam locomotive in particular, refused to be quenched by the 'isations' of the 1960s: modernisation, rationalisation and dieselisation. With some much-lamented exceptions, examples of our principal locomotive designs have been preserved. Some of the more famous locomotives were saved by official bodies, but many more owe their survival to the tenacity of groups or individuals. It was this that brought about the rescue of over 200 engines from a South Wales scrapyard.

TRAVELLING MAN

The only person known to have travelled over every section of railway in the British Isles that carried a passenger service, including sections used only occasionally, was Thomas Perkins (1872-1952). He began his mission to explore the entire British railway network in 1893 and completed his achievement in 1932 after travelling over 22,000 miles along all the individual lines and making detailed notes on all his journeys.

HE BOUGHT AN ENGINE

One class of locomotive would have been consigned to the history books had it not been for the audacity of one Captain W.G. (Bill) Smith VRD RNR. After a childhood spent admiring the locomotives of the Great Northern Railway and the LNER, Captain Smith was determined to ensure the survival of at least one of his favourites. However, this was 1959 and the notion of buying a locomotive from British Railways was unheard of. Nevertheless, Bill Smith wrote to BR's Eastern Region and asked if they would sell him an engine. The reply was encouraging and Captain Smith of the Royal Naval Reserve was soon at the King's Cross depot making his selection. At first, the shed pilot, Ivatt J52 class 0-6-0ST No68846, held little attraction alongside the Gresley and Peppercorn Pacifics, despite its excellent condition. However, after gentle persuasion from his companions, Bill Smith settled on the 1899-built saddletank.

On 7 May 1959, Captain Smith became the owner of the first privately preserved locomotive in Britain. The engine was allowed to work on main-line specials for a further three years and, in 1965, took up residence on the Keighley & Worth Valley Railway. It was here that it starred in the first (and arguably the finest) film version of *The Railway Children*. In 1980, Captain Smith decided to donate the locomotive, by now carrying its GNR number of 1247 and apple green livery, to the National Railway Museum.

Ex-Great Northern Railway saddletank No1247, the first locomotive to be bought privately from British Railways.

12
OUT OF STEAM

As British Railways bade farewell to steam,
in Wales a surprise welcome awaited the
preservation movement.

THE DAY THE FIRES WENT OUT

As steam traction was eliminated from one area after another, some unlikely locations became places of pilgrimage. Suddenly, it was all down to one month, and then just one fateful day.

The decision was irreversible but, as late as 1963, it was difficult to really believe that the steam locomotive was doomed. Although it was displaced from many passenger services, it remained at work in most areas. The withdrawal in the ensuing twelve months of around 2,000 engines and the disappearance of legends such as the Stanier 'Coronation' Pacifics dispelled any lingering self-delusion.

Perhaps 1965 was the year of greatest change. On the majority of routes, that summer was the last that steam locomotives were used on regular express passenger services. On 11 June, the final scheduled steam-hauled service from Paddington, the 4.15pm to Banbury, left behind 'Castle' class 4-6-0 No7029 *Clun Castle*. By the end of the year, not only had the 'Castles' gone, but so had all the ex-GWR 4-6-0s as the Western Region declared itself steam-free. Elsewhere, the stock of LNER Pacifics, once numbering over 200, had been reduced to just 17. All bar four – a quartet of Peppercorn A1s at York – were enjoying one last fling in Scotland. However, by the end of July 1966, the era of the east coast Pacific was over.

The last full year of steam working, 1967, saw 1,689 engines listed as still active. Come May, only around 20 locomotives remained at work in Scotland and, by the end of the month, there were just two. Oddly, they were not from modern BR Standard, or even LNER or LMSR classes. Instead there were a pair of ex-North British J36 0-6-0s built in 1897 and 1900.

It was a time of 'lasts'. The final branch line steam workings in Britain took place on 1 and 2 April as BR Standard 4MT 2-6-4T No80152 and LMSR 2MT 2-6-2T No41312 concluded duties on the Brockenhurst-Lymington line in Hampshire. This was the prelude to the demise of steam on the Southern Region, which came in July. It was paradoxical that the region with the greatest electrified mileage should be the setting for Britain's last regular steam-hauled expresses but Bulleid Pacifics, aided by BR Standard 4-6-0s, still ruled the Waterloo to Bournemouth service. Their crews determined to bow out in a blaze of glory, the spring and early summer of 1967 witnessed some remarkable runs by the Bulleids.

Then, on 9 July 1967, 'Merchant Navy' No35030 *Elder Dempster Lines* ran into Waterloo with the 2.07pm from Weymouth and not only brought down the curtain on Southern steam, but all steam working in the capital.

By the autumn of 1967, over 60 per cent of surviving steam locomotives were to be found in Yorkshire, Cheshire and Lancashire, with the majority (around 550) in the red rose county. The

DRUM ROLE

In its twilight years, steam still managed to set one new record. In June 1965, an ex-LMSR Stanier 8F 2-8-0 had charge of what was claimed to be the heaviest single load ever carried on British Railways: a 240 ton boiler drum. It travelled from Staffordshire to a new power station at Egborough, on Humberside, loaded between two special 24-wheel wagons. Three such drums were conveyed, routed by way of Walsall, Lichfield, Burton-on-Trent, Derby and Chesterfield.

The use of rail not only kept these giant loads off the roads, it enabled the manufacturers to reduce the product cost. Had rail transport not been available, the drums would have had to be fabricated in smaller sections on site. This would have required the erection of special buildings in which to undertake the specialised welding, and the final testing.

The very last steam working of 1967 took place on New Year's Eve. A Hogmanay special from Manchester to Glasgow was taken over at Carlisle by 'Britannia' Pacific No70045 *Lord Rowallan* for what proved to be its last outing.

One of the 55-strong 'Britannias', No70013 *Oliver Cromwell*, remained in BR stock on 1 January 1968. It was the only Pacific among the 356 surviving steam locomotives. The majority (150 of each) were Stanier 'Black 5' 4-6-0s and 8F 2-8-0s. The 9F 2-10-0s, which were still under construction a decade earlier, now numbered just 18. There also remained 23 BR Standard 5MT 4-6-0s, 10 of the Standard 4MT 4-6-0s and four LMSR 4MT 2-6-0s.

By July, the number of operational steam sheds had been reduced to three: Carnforth, Lostock Hall near Preston, and Rose Grove, Burnley. Here, the last 'Black 5s' and 8Fs soldiered on to the end. British Railways' last timetabled steam-hauled train was the 9.25pm from Preston to Liverpool on Saturday 3 August.

It was appropriate that it was hauled by what had once been the most numerous type of British passenger engine, a 4-6-0, No45212. It was also historically fitting that its destination was Liverpool, one of the cities that, 138 years earlier had witnessed the birth of main-line steam with the grand opening of the Liverpool & Manchester Railway.

greatest concentrations were around Manchester and Liverpool, with clusters at Burnley, Carlisle, Carnforth, and Preston.

September brought the closure of the depots at North Blyth, Sunderland, Tyne Dock and West Hartlepool and with them the end of steam in the north-east. On 1 October, the steam stock of the Eastern Region stood at just 21 engines and on 4 November the final duty was undertaken by an Eastern region-based locomotive. However, Yorkshire's Royston depot had no ex-LNER engines to perform this last rite and the 3.00pm goods from Carlton North sidings, near Barnsley, to Goole was entrusted to the locomotive Stanier 8F 2-8-0 No48276.

ONE SUNDAY IN AUGUST

Every railway enthusiast over the age of 40 remembers 11 August 1968. We knew the day would eventually come, but when the poster appeared, its message still took time to sink in. 'British Rail runs out of steam!' they announced, without, as far as one could discern, any intentional irony. Beneath this headline, the poster informed: 'Last steam train makes historic special farewell journey on Sunday, August 11.'

This 'farewell journey' would thereafter be known by the fare that was demanded: the 'Fifteen Guinea Special'. It was not an extortionate price, but it was difficult not to feel that British Rail was out to make a bob or two. There were many for whom fifteen guineas (£15 15s 0d) was more than a week's wages.

As the poster explained, 'This will be the very last train to operate on standard gauge track headed by a BR steam locomotive.' (BR continued to operate the narrow gauge Vale of Rheidol railway in Wales with steam traction.) Then came the details. The 'Fifteen Guinea Special' would leave Liverpool Lime Street at 9.10am, getting back at 7.50pm. It would also pick up at Manchester Victoria at 11.06am, returning there at 6.48pm. The important question that the poster did not answer was which locomotive, or locomotives, would be entrusted with this significant piece of railway history.

A clear candidate was the sole remaining express passenger engine on BR's books, Standard Pacific No70013 *Oliver Cromwell*. Other somewhat more famous locomotives were also available, although the likes of *Flying Scotsman* and *King George V* were by now in private hands. Perhaps BR wanted to keep the event 'in house', and if it was looking for a typically British locomotive then the LMSR 5MT 4-6-0, the 'Black 5', certainly fitted the bill. It has been stated that this 842-strong class were BR's most widely used locomotives, a claim difficult to repute.

Three from the surviving 'Black 5s' were chosen to join *Oliver Cromwell*, Nos44781, 44871 and 45110. It was the last of the trio that was chosen to haul the first leg of the 'Fifteen Guinea Special'. It departed on time

In typically run-down condition, BR Standard Class 4MT 4-6-0s Nos75010 and 75060 prepare for the road at Croes Newydd depot, Wrexham, in 1966.

from the crowded platforms at Lime Street, with the 9.10am electric-hauled express to Euston leaving simultaneously. Two photographic stops were made on the way to Manchester, on the route of the world's first inter-city railway, opened in 1830. Particularly poignant was the stop at Rainhill, scene of the 1829 locomotive trials and the epoch-making triumph of George and Robert Stephenson's *Rocket*.

At Manchester, an immaculate *Oliver Cromwell* took over the train for its run to Carlisle, by way of Blackburn, Hellifield and the Settle and Carlisle line. There was another photocall at Ais Gill, at 1,169 feet above sea level the highest main-line railway summit in England. All 470 on board must have imagined that this would be the last opportunity to photograph steam at this spectacular location. Steam was barred from the main line after 11 August, and the axe seemed set to fall on the Settle and Carlisle itself. Ten years on, not only had the S&C survived, but steam was back in the fell country.

The return from Carlisle to Liverpool was handled in tandem by the other 'Black 5s' and retraced the outward journey. At its conclusion, different fates awaited the quartet of engines that had graced the 'Fifteen Guinea Special'. 'Britannia' Pacific No70013 *Oliver Cromwell* had been selected to represent the class in the National Collection. It had also been agreed that it would go on loan to the late Alan Bloom's Bressingham Steam Museum near Diss, in Norfolk. By 1.30pm on 12 August, Oliver Cromwell was back at the depot where its working life had begun in May 1951, in Norwich. Four days later, it was hauled to Diss, placed on a low-loader and taken to Bressingham, where it remains.

Of the three 5MT 4-6-0s, two survive. After a period in store, in 1970 No45110 went to the Severn Valley Railway, its home ever since. Classmate No44871 took the shorter journey to Steamtown, at Carnforth in Lancashire. In recent years, it has been based on the Bo'ness & Kinneil Railway on the southern shore of the Firth of Forth.

A curious end befell the third 'Black 5'. At first, things looked promising for No44781. It cheated scrapping by being selected to appear in the film of Leslie Thomas's book, 'The Virgin Soldiers'. Somehow the Audley End branch was made to resemble a railway in the Malayan jungle. However, once filming was over, it was unceremoniously cut up on set!

JOURNEY'S END

In just ten years, British Railways despatched over 16,000 steam locomotives for scrapping. Remarkably, a surprising number cheated the cutter's torch.

On 19 March 1971, LMSR 'Royal Scot' class 4-6-0 No6100 Royal Scot *nears the end of its journey from Butlin's holiday camp at Skegness to Bressingham Steam Museum, near Diss, in Norfolk. The locomotive — one of only two preserved 'Scots' — has remained at Bressingham for the past 31 years.*

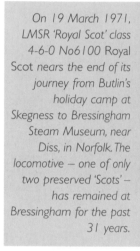

Opposite: Ex-GWR locomotives dominate this view of Woodham Brothers' scrapyard at Barry, South Wales. 5205 class 2-8-0 tank No5227 is in the right foreground, with a 'King' class 4-6-0 on the left.

The scrapping process was not new: British Railways had reduced its steam fleet by around 3,000 since nationalisation. In 1958, however, as the changeover to diesel and electric traction became more of a scramble than a strategy, the carnage began in earnest. It quickly became apparent that BR's workshops alone could not deal with the lines of condemned locomotives and deals were struck with the scrap metal industry. By the summer of 1959, private scrapyards were taking delivery of engines. These first yards were situated mainly in steel-producing areas, such as South Wales. Before long, engines were being broken up in places as far apart as south-west Scotland and the Isle of Sheppey.

Since they were sold off to the highest bidder, locomotives could travel considerable distances to meet their end. The melancholy sight of a string a 'dead' engines being hauled to its fate became depressingly familiar, especially as the evidently healthy locomotive hauling it was unlikely to be making the return trip either.

The pace of withdrawals accelerated during the early 1960s, stretching the scrapyards' capacity. Locomotive 'dumps' appeared in various places and, to clear the backlog, the procedures involved in tendering for, and transporting engines was simplified. This allowed smaller yards to bid for locally based locomotives, but many learned that disposing of 100-plus tons of steam locomotive was no easy matter. Nevertheless, by August 1968, British Railways had succeeded in ridding itself of over 16,000 engines. Ironically, within a few years many of the diesels that supplanted them would themselves be consigned to the same scrapyards. One running shed foreman spoke for many when he commented on the withdrawal of BR Standard engines—some less than a dozen years old—from his depot. They were, he lamented, 'Good for another twenty years.'

ONE FOR THE SCRAPBOOK

Woodham Brothers' scrapyard on Barry Island in South Wales was just one of over 130 such concerns that bought locomotives for scrap. When steam traction ceased officially in August 1968, Woodhams' had 217 engines in the yard. However, as well as disposing of its steam stock, BR was also condemning much of its vast stock of life-expired goods wagons. Cutting up wagons was quicker and easier than torching engines, and this was keeping Dai Woodham's staff busy. The lines of locomotives stood silently alongside awaiting their fate.

What might be termed the 'Barry miracle' began in September 1968. A group of enthusiasts had raised the money to buy ex-LMSR 4F 0-6-0 No43924 for the embryo Keighley & Worth Valley Railway. The exodus had begun and Dai Woodham found himself transformed from scrap merchant to saviour of steam.

Only two more engines departed in 1969, but the following year the pace quickened and eight were saved. Throughout the 1970s and 1980s, societies placed reservations on locomotives in the yard and endeavoured to raise funds to buy them. Inevitably, the engines deteriorated with the passing years. Compounding the effects of exposure to the elements, they were robbed of any components that yielded to a boltcutter: coupling rods, connecting rods, valve gear, buffers, safety valves, even chimneys.

Dai Woodham, although frustrated when rescue efforts stalled or failed, continued to hold off cutting locomotives. He did, though, issue a wake-up call by breaking up two engines in 1980. It had the desired effect. Subsequently, efforts to save the remaining engines were co-ordinated by the Barry Steam Locomotive Action Group. A decade on, in January 1990, the last of 213 locomotives left Woodhams' yard. Of that total, 98 were ex-Great Western locomotives, 41 were from Southern stock (including 28 Bulleid Pacifics), 35 ex-LMSR engines and 38 ex-BR Standards. Because of its distance from ex-LNER territory, only one Eastern Region locomotive found its way to Barry, Thompson B1 4-6-0 No61264.

Back in 1968, the buyers of No43924 had it back in working order within two years. Some restorations have taken the best part of two decades. Apart from a lick of paint, many ex-Barry locomotives remain untouched, parked in sheds and sidings awaiting funding, volunteer labour and their turn in the restoration queue. Remarkably, however, around 100 of these scrapyard survivors have steamed again, such as No5029 *Nunney Castle*, No5051 *Drysllwyn Castle* and No6024 *King Edward 1*.

LOCOSPOTTERS!

Locospotting (never trainspotting) amounted to more than collecting numbers. It could be educational, too, embracing geography, social history and – in totting up a day's tally – arithmetic. There was also tutoring in basic breaking-and-entering!

No one knows when small boys (and they always were boys) began collecting engine numbers. However, it was only after World War II that the pastime became truly organised. In 1942, an employee of the Southern Railway, Ian Allan, published a class-by-class list of his company's locomotive numbers and names. When he followed this with similar pocket books devoted to the engines of the other three main-line railway companies, the 'ABC of British Locomotives' was born. For Ian Allan, it was the starting point of a transport publishing empire. The 'ABCs' were updated on a regular basis and soon a hardback compilation of all four companies' engines appeared, the much-prized 'Combined Volume'. The popularity of the series led to the setting up of the Ian Allan Locospotters' Club (complete with coloured lapel badges displaying which of the BR regions enjoyed your allegiance). The company also began organising railtours to workshops such as Crewe, Derby, Doncaster, Eastleigh and Swindon, and trips behind historic locomotives.

Such was the popularity of locospotting in the 1950s and early 1960s, that the BBC devoted a teatime television programme to the subject titled 'Railway Roundabout'. In Finsbury Park, in north London, a designated 'spotting area' was constructed overlooking the East Coast Main Line. This was opportune since the best vantage point at Kings Cross, the end of Platform 10, could become dangerously overcrowded!

Rewarding as station platforms or the lineside could be, the aim of every locospotter was to penetrate those temples of steam, the engine sheds.

Strictly speaking, to enter these places was to trespass – the signs spelled that out – but that made the triumph all the sweeter. At some depots, gaining access was not a problem. No one seemed to mind as long as you kept your head down and behaved yourself. However, some depots were less-than-welcoming. Although prosecution was unlikely, the police were called on occasion, usually when the numbers of intruders had got out of hand. A stern lecture from a shed foreman could be just as intimidating as a ticking off from the constabulary. In retrospect, their concern was understandable: children fixated on collecting numbers hopping across points, dodging moving engines and jumping over inspection pits was a health-and-safety nightmare. Quite simply, the sight of all those locomotives, numbers ready for the taking, was impossible to resist.

Finding locomotive depots was not always straightforward, especially if looking for a way in other than the official entrance. Since engine sheds exuded an unmistakable aroma, smell was one guide. Sharing knowledge with local 'spotters was another, although there were those who delighted in sending you in the wrong direction (locospotting was competitive).

Then along came Flight Lieutenant Aidan L.F. Fuller, compiler of a comprehensive and reliable guide to all the sheds and workshops in Britain. Fuller even provided walking times, details of useful bus and train services and itineraries for touring major cities. Rightly, in his preface, he emphasised – in capital letters – that his guide did not constitute authority to enter British Railways premises. Doubtless, he did not want to

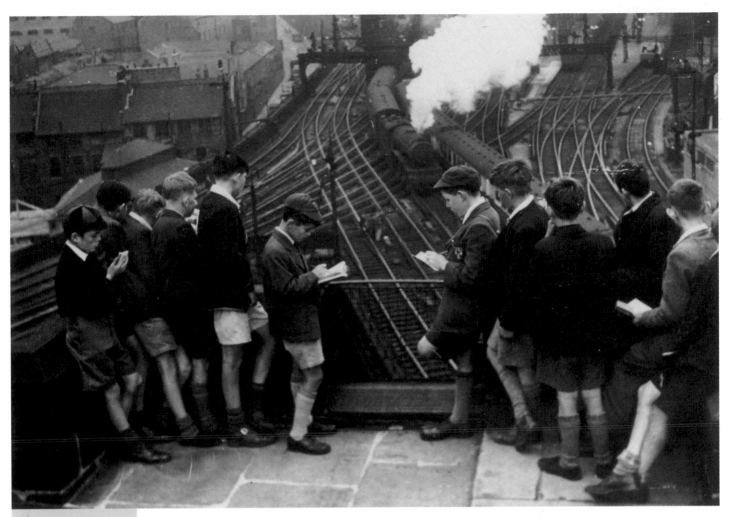

Short-trousered trainspotters in action at Newcastle-upon-Tyne, looking out over the famous diamond crossing at the entrance to Central Station. At weekends and during school holidays similar scenes could be captured at every major station and junction throughout Britain.

be seen as some latter-day Fagin wilfully encouraging boys to commit criminal acts!

There was a legitimate way of visiting depots and works. You could apply for a permit in person or, more likely, your railfans' club would request one. Officially, they were issued for educational purposes (locospotting was frowned upon) but, once inside, little attention was paid to the finer points of locomotive design. It was a matter of getting every number down as quickly as possible, especially if this was just one shed among half-a-dozen to be visited that day.

There were occasions when the railtour organiser inexplicably failed to obtain a permit, a fact only relayed as the coachload of 40-or-so arrived at the entrance. Many a railwayman must have had the peace of a Saturday or Sunday in charge of a shed full of quiescent engines shattered by an invasion of the duffle bags. The duffle bag contained the essentials for locospotting: notebook,

pens, 'ABC Loco Shed Book' – a convenient little volume that simply listed numbers and eschewed any pictures or technical information – sandwiches, apples, a bottle of Tizer or similar fizzy cordial and, maybe after one particularly good Christmas or birthday, a camera.

The camera, though, was intended to signify something called 'growing up'. Was this incompatible with collecting locomotive numbers? The question became irrelevant when the steam locomotive was consigned to 'yesterday's' railways. If that was how faithful friends like the Gresley V2s and Stanier 8Fs, the 'Castles', 'King Arthurs' and 'Britannias' were regarded then, perhaps, 'yesterday' was where locospotting belonged, too. But, just in case, you kept your notebooks, your ABCs, and Flight Lieutenant Fuller's guide (even though most of the sheds had been razed to the ground). After all, one day someone might ask you to write a book about it all.

CAPTIONS FOR CHAPTER OPENERS

MONOPOLY TO MERGER **Page 8**: *An official London & North Western Railway photograph, taken on 30 April 1900, of the arrival platforms at Liverpool's Lime Street terminus. Horse-drawn cabs await the passengers off a train that has just arrived behind one of the classic L&NWR 2-4-0 express passenger locomotives.*

A GOLDEN AGE **Page 28**: *This was the scene at King's Cross station, in London, shortly before 10.00am on 4 August 1934. Gresley Pacific No2795 Call Boy, named after the winner of the 1927 Derby, waits to depart with the non-stop 'Flying Scotsman' for Edinburgh. Classmate No2598 Blenheim (the 1930 Derby winner) stands at the head of the 'Junior Scotsman'. To the left, three engines are coupled together awaiting their next duties: Pacific No2746 Fairway (winner of the 1928 St Leger) and two Ivatt Atlantics.*

STATIONS AND SIGNALS **Page 48**: *Straw boaters were clearly in vogue when this photograph was taken of the eastern side of Waterloo Station, London, on 3 May 1912. Dugald Drummond-designed engines of the London & South Western Railway are in charge of all the trains. A suburban service for Teddington is at platform 2, with a train for Bournemouth Central alongside in platform 3. Posters promoting south-coast resorts such as Swanage adorn the kiosk in the foreground.*

RURAL RAILWAYS **Page 64**: *Passengers – including a child clutching a bucket and spade – board their train while parcels are taken to their final destination by horse-drawn cart, all part of a busy scene at a London Midland & Scottish Railway junction station sometime during the pre-war years.*

GETTING AWAY BY TRAIN **Page 80**: *Captured in 1909, passengers at the London & North Western Railway's Holyhead Docks seek out their luggage shortly after disembarking from the SS Cedric and before boarding onward boat trains. Most intriguing of the suitcases and trunks is that belonging to a Miss Wallace, sometime resident of Shanghai, China!*

COMMUTING BY TRAIN **Page 92**: *Engrossed in their newspapers, and with not a word of conversation being exchanged, it could only be a carriage-load of British commuters bound for work on what – to judge from the overcoats and raincoats – was a cold winter's morning. The carriages may have changed but the conditions have not – usually it's still standing room only.*

FAMOUS LOCOMOTIVES **Page 104**: *For many, William Stanier's 'Princess Coronation' class Pacifics were the pinnacle of British express passenger locomotive design. At Carlisle, in the mid-1950s, two members of the class were captured on the prestigious 'Royal Scot' duty between Euston and Glasgow. No46244 King George VI of Camden shed, London (1B) has brought in the northbound train, which will be taken forward by No46231 Duchess of Atholl of Polmadie depot, Glasgow (shedcode 66A).*

DELIVERING THE GOODS **Page 220**: *Heading a rake of vans, with a quintet of 16-ton mineral wagons bringing up the rear (rounded off, of course, by the regulation brake van), a BR Standard Class 4MT 4-6-0 climbs towards Ribblehead, on the Settle and Carlisle line, with a northbound goods on 4 February 1967.*

RAILWAYS AT WAR **Page 238**: *A train crowded with evacuees leaves London shortly before, or after, the outbreak of World War II in September 1939. The children seem happy enough to embark on the adventure, and hoped-for safety away from the city, which it was rightly anticipated would become a target for bombing. The cheerful faces, however, probably conceal a good deal of apprehension, an emotion shared by most of the evacuees' parents.*

THE POST WAR ERA **Page 250**: *The changing motive power scene, circa 1954, is depicted at Leeds Central, with a new Derby-built two-car diesel multiple unit leaving for Castleford. It is coming under the watchful gaze of the driver of Peppercorn A2 Pacific No60535 Hornet's Beauty, of Haymarket shed, Edinburgh (64B). No60535 – itself only six years old – remained at work until June 1965, but the writing was on the wall for the station pilot, Gresley J50/4 class 0-6-0 tank No68988 of 1937. It would soon be replaced by a diesel.*

RAILWAYS FOR FUN **Page 266**: *At Ravenglass shed in 1969, locomotives are prepared for a day's work on the Ravenglass & Eskdale Railway in Cumbria. Opened in 1875, and originally laid to 3-feet gauge, this was the first narrow-gauge railway in England to offer a public passenger service. It closed in 1913 but was bought by a group of enthusiasts, regauged to 15-inches, and reopened over its full 6.25-miles length in 1918. The engines seen here are, from left to right, 2-8-2 River Esk, 0-8-2 River Irt and 2-8-2 River Mite.*

OUT OF STEAM **Page 274**: *Steam on the Southern Region came to an end on 9 July 1967 and, the following day, the yard at Weymouth shed was filled with Bulleid Pacifics and BR Standard locomotives awaiting their fate. Identifiable are 'Merchant Navy' class Pacifics No35003 Royal Mail and No35014 Nederland Line, and BR Class 5MT 4-6-0 No73002. These engines did not number among the ten 'Merchant Navies' or five 5MT 4-6-0s subsequently preserved.*

PICTURE CREDITS

Corbis 38, 53(Bettmann/Corbis), 226, 264. **Daily Herald Archive/NMPFT/Science and Society Picture Library** 46-7(photo: Harold Tomlin), 283. **Greater Manchester County Record Office** 237. **Imperial War Museum** 24(neg no.Q109902), 25(neg no.Q8750), 26(neg no.Q1699), 223(top neg no.D18529), 240, 244, 248(top left corner), 245(neg no.D18910). **Cuneo Fine Arts/National Railway Museum/Science and Society Picture Library** 268(artist: Terence Cuneo). **Getty**: 43, 85, 87, 92-3, 94, 102, 198, 206, 249, 259. **Hulton Getty** 28-9, 48-9, 56-7, 83(top), 107, 131, 238-9. **London's Transport Museum** 96(top, artist: Man Ray), 97, 98(top and bottom, artist: Hans Schleger). **The Museum of Science and Industry in Manchester** 248. **National Railway Museum/Science and Society Picture Library** 8-9, 11(btm), 13, 15, 16, 17 (photo WH Whitworth), 19, 21, 33, 34, 36, 37, 40, 41 (left, artist: CRW Nevinson; top right, artist: Tom Purvis; btm, right, artist: Edmond Vaughan), 42 (artist: Maurice Beck), 43(btm), 45, 51, 55 (photo: John G Glick), 57(right), 61, 64-5(photo: CCB Herbert), 66(photo: RJ Sellick), 68(btm), 70(photo: RJ Sellick), 75, 77(artist: Charles H Baker), 78(btm, artist: John Mace; top photo: Eric Treacy), 80-1, 83(btm, artist: Tom Purvis), 84, 86(artist: Lee-Elliott), 88, 89(artist: P Irwin Brown), 91(top, artist: H Bisis; btm photo: Reverend Arthur C Cawston), 95(btm), 100, 101, 104-5(photo: Eric Treacy), 112(photo: Maurice Earley), 113, 123, 138(photo: Reverend Arthur C Cawston), 152(photo: ER Wethersett), 169, 196, 200(btm), 201, 203(btm, artist: Frank Newbould), 205, 216, 224(btm, artist: Baldwin), 233(top), 234, 236(top, artist: Frank Newbould), 240-1, 242(top and middle, artist: Bert Thomas), 244(top right and btm, artist: Leslie Carr), 246, 250-1(photo: Eric Treacy), 252, 256-7, 261(btm), 263(top), 265(top), 281. **Popperfoto** 247.

INDEX

AUTHOR'S ACKNOWLEDGMENTS

Thanks are due to my colleagues at publishers, David & Charles, for their ever-willing assistance, enthusiasm and fine hospitality, especially Tom McCann, Alison Myer, Jane Trollope and Miranda Spicer. My thanks, too, to Peter Adams for his wise counsel and genial humour. Among the many friends who have given welcome encouragement, I would single out Houda Alaoui and Lyn Brown who, while never quite comprehending my passion for railways, have been generous-hearted enough to come along for the ride.